D1380466

MINCE PIE FOR STARTERS

MINCE PIE FOR STARTERS

by

John Oaksey

Magna Large Print Books
Long Preston, North Yorkshire,
BD23 4ND, England.

British Library Cataloguing in Publication Data.

Oakey, John
Mince Pie for starters.

A catalogue record of this book is
available from the British Library

ISBN 0-7505-2135-X

First published in Great Britain in 2003 by
Headline Book Publishing

Published in Large Print 2004 by arrangement with
Headline Book Publishing Ltd.

Magna Large Print is an imprint of Library Magna Books Ltd.

Printed and bound in Great Britain by
T.J. (International) Ltd., Cornwall, PL28 8RW

Extracts from *The Times, Daily Telegraph, Sunday Telegraph* and *Horse and Hound* are reprinted by permission.

The verse from 'The Borgia Orgy' by John Jowett and Robert Gordon from *Sweet and Low* is reprinted by permission of Samuel French Ltd.

Every effort has been made to fulfil requirements with regard to reproducing copyright material. The author and publisher will be glad to rectify any omissions at the earliest opportunity.

Contents

Acknowledgements

I was first approached about writing my memoirs longer ago than I care to remember. That the book has appeared at all is in no small measure due to the assistance and support of many people, including Elain Mellor, Sue Haine, Brough Scott, Sean Magee, Serafina Clarke, Vicky How, Jeremy Richardson at the Injured Jockeys' Fund, the ever-patient Ian Marshall and Celia Kent at Headline, Marjorie Boulton and Geoffrey Boulton – and most of all my wife Chicky.

To all these – and doubtless to others who have momentarily slipped my mind – I owe an eternal debt of gratitude.

Foreword by Dick Francis

John Oaksey was not only a very successful amateur jockey, his journalistic descriptions of races – especially those in which he took part – were also breathtaking. In particular, his immediate reaction, for the following day's *Sunday Telegraph*, to the 1963 Grand National, in which, when riding Carrickbeg, he was so narrowly beaten into second place, was out of this world.

He has repeated most of these memorable occasions in the pages of this autobiography *Mince Pie for Starters*, and I am happy to add these few words to what I'm sure will be a much sought-after addition to every equestrian lover's bookshelves.

I like to think that it was due to his presentation of the lives of jockeys and trainers – as well as of owners and other racing personalities – that these individuals have now become much more respected sportsmen (and sportswomen) than they were of yesteryear, and I only hope the current 'knights of the pigskin', as well as the everyday racegoer, will realise what a debt we owe John.

After his school and university days, it was

originally intended that he should follow the law life of his renowned father, the much-respected presiding judge at the Nuremberg War Crimes Tribunal. The call of the Turf was too strong, though, and readers of this book will soon realise what great moments the pen of John Oaksey has taken us through, at places like Aintree, Cheltenham, Sandown, Epsom, Newmarket and Royal Ascot. This is a truly memorable work of art.

Prologue

'I know you! – you're the boogger who got tired before yer 'orse!'

He was a grubby shambolic little man, shorter even than me, and he waylaid me as I emerged from the gents at Piccadilly Circus Underground station at about one in the morning after a particularly good dinner in London in the summer of 1978. It was not, to be honest, the ideal time to discuss the matter in detail, so, after replying as politely as I could, I smiled genially and moved on.

But I knew what he was talking about, and I knew where he'd got the idea. Fifteen years earlier I had led over the last fence in the Grand National on Carrickbeg and kept in front almost all the way up that interminable run-in, only to be caught by Ayala three strides before the line. In the following week's *Horse and Hound* I had confessed how 'Even to swing the whip had become an effort and the only thing that kept me going was the unbroken rhythm of Carrickbeg's heroic head, nodding in time with his stride. And suddenly, even that was gone.' In short, I got tired, then he got tired, and we lost the race.

Clearly that dishevelled little man knew what he was saying. But what an epitaph – to be remembered only as 'the boogger who got tired before yer 'orse'.

There must have been more than that...

1

'Would you kindly sign the Visitors' Book?'

If pedigree counts for anything, I was bred for the law. Both my grandfather and my father were judges – my grandfather Lord Chief Justice and my father a Lord Justice who presided over the Nuremberg war crimes trials (my own legal career – twenty years as a magistrate – was a great deal less distinguished).

It was in 1921 that Lloyd George, then Prime Minister, appointed my grandfather A.T. Lawrence, who was himself a High Court judge and seventy-eight years old at the time, Lord Chief Justice. The appointment was strongly opposed by the then Lord Chancellor, Lord Birkenhead, formerly F.E. Smith and famously no respecter of persons. 'A.T. Lawrence,' he wrote, 'is a sound enough lawyer, but suited to the Chancellorship neither by ability nor age.' Lloyd George, who badly wanted the obvious alternative, Gordon Hewart, to stay in the House of Commons, where he was a formidable debater, invaluable to the

Government, stood firm.

So my grandfather became Lord Chief Justice for just eleven months, from April 1921 to March 1922. I do not know to what extent he justified F.E. Smith's foreboding, but have never heard that he disgraced himself. One night, being driven home from Kemble station along a very narrow road, 'Fafa' – a nickname I am proud to have inherited with my own grandchildren – was involved in a head-on collision with another driver. It was, I gather, clearly the fault of my grandfather's chauffeur, and I have always admired the presence of mind shown by the first policeman on the spot. Finding himself in the embarrassing situation of having to report the Lord Chief Justice, he claimed that the cars were *exactly* on the county boundary – one in Wiltshire, the other in Gloucestershire. 'Sorry, my Lord – no jurisdiction,' he said, skilfully avoiding a tricky legal *impasse*.

On account of his unexpected promotion Fafa was also made a peer, and took the title Lord Trevethin – for reasons which are now lost in the mists of time. (Trevethin nowadays is a suburb of Pontypool, and I took my wife Chicky there in 1995 hoping to find an explanation of my grandfather's choice of title. None emerged – even when we asked in the local betting shop, where, I'm ashamed to say, I confidently expected to be recognised. But alas, neither the name John Oaksey nor my handsome 'As Seen On TV' profile meant anything to the lady behind the counter!)

My father Geoffrey Lawrence was born in 1880 and served in the Royal Artillery for the duration of the First World War. A barrister by profession, he became a colonel and was awarded the DSO. His ascent through the legal ranks was rapid, and after the war he was made a judge, rising to sit in the Court of Appeal; then, after another world war and at the age of sixty-five, he was appointed presiding judge when the International Military Tribunal met at Nuremberg to try the most prominent surviving Nazis for war crimes. The eleven months for which he presided over what was then a unique war crimes trial was almost certainly the most difficult and testing period of his whole life – at least in peacetime – and in recognition of his service he was elevated to the peerage in 1947, taking the title Lord Oaksey.

From all that I have heard and read about his conduct of the proceedings, the work of those months was not only the climax of his long legal career but also a valuable contribution to the cause of justice and international law. In 1949 he produced the Oaksey Report on Police Conditions of Service, which recommended significant improvements in the policeman's lot and was widely welcomed by the force. (A Giles cartoon of the time depicted a meek little man whose ramshackle car across the street is being examined with suspicion by a group of policemen. His domineering wife exhorts him: 'Quick! Go over and be nice to them. Tell them you think the Oaksey Report is wonderful.')

But my father's, I'm delighted to say, was by no means a one-track mind, solely pre-occupied with legal niceties. A golfer with a single-figure handicap (Captain of Oxford, he later played with both James Braid and Harry Vardon), he loved riding, hunting and racing and was for several years Counsel to the Jockey Club. He treasured beauty and grace in all their forms – a Guernsey cow, a Thoroughbred racehorse, a picture, a piece of silver, a sculpture or a pretty girl. He decided to marry my mother the first time he saw her – when she was twenty and he was forty-one – and as a matter of fact she was a roadside pick-up.

My father and his brother, my Uncle Trevor, had bought Hill Farm, Oaksey – where I still live – soon after the First World War. At the time they were living in digs near Highworth, from where they hunted with the VWH, the Vale of the White Horse Hunt. (These were the days before it was divided into 'Cricklade' and 'Bathurst' – a process in which my father played a considerable part. When he returned from Nuremberg the two hunts approached him to oversee the division, on the assumption that, after trying twenty-one war criminals, keeping the Cricklade and Bathurst from each other's throats would be comparative child's play!) On Sundays my father and Trevor used to go out in a pony and trap looking for a house, and before long they found Hill Farm. Oaksey is some fifteen miles from Highworth – between Malmesbury and Cirencester – so it must have been a good strong pony.

Once settled in the farm, the two brothers bought a car – and, possibly because they had not yet learned to drive, seem, at least to begin with, to have employed a chauffeur, who almost certainly doubled up as a groom. Whatever his job description, he was driving them back from Cirencester one day when, just past Kemble, they saw two girls on the side of the road – one of whom, a neighbour called Honor Fawcett, my uncle knew quite well. Always keen to help damsels in distress, they stopped, picked up the stranded pair, and carried them to Honor's house. My father, sitting in the front beside the driver, nevertheless seems somehow to have inspected the other passenger, who introduced herself as Marjorie Robinson. He must have liked the look of what he saw, because that evening, getting on a train at Minety (these were very much pre-Beeching days), he said to his brother, 'You know that girl we saw today... I am going to marry her.'

He did not hang about, sending Miss Robinson a telegram next morning which read: 'Will you please have lunch, tea or dinner on Tuesday, Wednesday Thursday or Friday...? Yours, Geoffrey Lawrence.'

My mother understandably played as safe as possible with 'Tea on Friday', but it was a big success. They were engaged within a month and married within a year. Not bad for a short, balding, 41-year-old barrister! Better still, after having my three elder sisters, me and, later, a large crop of grandchildren, they were still married when my Dad died fifty years later. He was, as I've said, a lover of grace and beauty, and it would be abusing the truth to say that he never looked at another girl. But he certainly still loved my mother when he died – and she adored him to the end.

She came from a naval background. Her father, Charles Napier Robinson, was a regular sailor before the First World War, and I believe served (as a midshipman) in the Boxer Rebellion. Later, retiring as a commander, he took up journalism and wrote for many years as naval correspondent of *The Times*. I remember him as a kindly bearded old man who told us exciting stories about his naval life. Like an idiot, I did not write them down.

My mother's mother I always knew as Grannymum, and at the age of ten I was with Grannymum in the dining room at Hill Farm on the morning of Sunday 3 September 1939 as we listened on the radio to Neville Chamberlain's fateful speech declaring that we were at war with Germany. She started crying, and although I had no proper understanding of what was going on, I did have the feeling that nothing might ever be the same again.

I was born in Sussex Gardens, not far from Paddington Station in London, on 21 March 1929 – the day before Gregalach beat *sixty-five* opponents to win the Grand National at 100–1.

I was the youngest of four children – after my three sisters Elizabeth (Libby), Rosamund (Robby) and Jennifer (Jenny) – and most weekends the whole family (or at least most of it) would decamp in our Chrysler to Hill Farm, Oaksey. My mother, who had driven an ambulance in France during the First World War and was a much more enthusiastic and skilful driver than my father, insisted on taking the wheel, and we would set off for the hundred-mile journey west – mother and father, four children, our nanny, Tinger the dog, Algy the cat, and a variable flock of budgerigars (which Algy did his level best to vary).

In 1935, when I was six years old, the family moved permanently to Oaksey, though during the week my father stayed behind in London: by then he was a High Court judge working hard to earn our daily bread. The farm, 160 acres in those days, thirty of them our beloved Bluebell Wood, is about a mile from Oaksey Church, and three miles from Crudwell, birthplace and namesake of the last horse to win fifty races in Britain.

My nanny – and best friend until her death in 1984 – was a lovely lady called Vera Hyatt, a daughter of the GWR station master at nearby Kemble. Her only other job had been as nursery maid to Bill and Pamela Phipps, then living with their son Simon in Dean Farm, Oaksey, the other side of Oaksey Wood. Simon, who won an MC in Italy was later a distinguished clergyman and preacher, and became Bishop of Lincoln.

Nanny had come to the farm as a nursery maid when my sister Jenny was born in 1926, but it was not until 1940 that she married Bill Sherwood, my father's bailiff, head cowman and trusted friend – having, I was always told, refused to accept Bill's proposal until I went to school! She became an insulin diabetic, who had to inject herself twice a day but later presented Bill with a healthy baby son. There is nothing unusual nowadays in an insulin diabetic having a baby but in the 1940s, I understand, it was still regarded as an achievement by mother and doctor alike. Nanny, apparently unafraid throughout, would certainly share the credit for it with her doctor, a surgeon called Lawrence – no relation, but a celebrated pioneer in the treatment of diabetes. The baby my godson, christened William after his father, became a policeman and later worked on the racecourse 'controlling' bookies. He was also a driving instructor in the police – and used to give me kindly advice about speed traps and their likely whereabouts!

Bill Sherwood himself had answered an advertisement for a cowman which my father put in the village shop. Young Bill and his father, who lived between Minety and Oaksey, were walking up to the village hall for band practice when Bill, who had seen the advertisement, persuaded his somewhat reluctant Dad to turn left up our drive so he could apply for the job.

Bill always said that the only serious argument he and my father ever had was over Daddy's refusal to let him join up in 1939. Farm work was a 'reserved' occupation and my Dad understandably wanted a responsible man in charge of the farm while he was busy elsewhere. As a High Court judge, if the expected invasion had materialised he would have been one of those charged with the vital but awesome task of enforcing martial law. It had long been Bill's dearest wish to fly preferably in a Spitfire or Hurricane. I shall always remember his excitement and delight when my sister Robby got engaged to Hugh 'Cocky' Dundas, a pilot who won two DSOs and a DFC: Hughie flew Spitfires (except for one brief, uncomfortable spell in Typhoons) throughout the war, and in the process became the youngest man ever to hold the rank of group captain in the RAF.

After their marriage Nanny and Bill lived in Hill Farm Cottage at the bottom of the drive, which my father had specially rebuilt for them. Bill and one helper milked twenty-five cows (by hand until we got a machine) and for quite a while did the milk round, delivering Guernsey milk, cream and that delicious bright yellow butter – originally by pony and trap, later in a smart little yellow van. At one time butter and cream were sent up to London by the early morning train. Sussex Gardens is just round the corner from Paddington Station, so, with the Cheltenham Flyer or one of its slightly slower Great Western mates from Oaksey Halt or Kemble, my father could have his own butter for breakfast at home or for lunch at his club. Those were the days – and we still have a letter to my father which proves that the Great Western was a whole lot more helpful than British Rail or any of its privatised successors:

Dear Sir
Referring to your call at this Office yesterday we shall be pleased to arrange for a churn of milk, also a small tin of cream, to be forwarded by the 9 a.m. train from Kemble to Paddington daily and for the traffic to be delivered at a Club in St James's Street, Pall Mall, at about noon, and perhaps you will kindly let me know whether it is definitely decided to commence forwarding on Thursday next, the 15th instant.

The charge for the delivery of the cream traffic in the ordinary way is 6d. per cwt., minimum 4d., and a similar charge would also apply for the collection of the empty, but under the circumstances a charge of 6d. for the milk churn and a similar charge for the cream can be raised to cover both delivery and collection of the empties; in other words, 1/- per day.

The empties will be returned by the 3.15 p.m. train from Paddington to Kemble and to avoid any difficulty you will no doubt arrange for the tie-on labels to be affixed to the receptacles both on the outward and return journeys. The label for the return journey should be addressed to Kemble Station.

An account in respect of the carriage and cartage charges will be rendered to you about the 26th of each month.

Perhaps you will kindly let me know whether these arrangements will be satisfactory to you and at the same time give the address of the Club to which the traffic should be forwarded.

Yours faithfully...

My own most grateful memory of Hill Farm butter is of being covered with it from head to toe – having inadvertently fallen into a bed of stinging nettles with no clothes on! The lawn in front of Hill Farm lives up to the name, spreading over a definite downhill slope. Riding a finish against my sister Jenny on our 'Pushy-Horses' with wheels, I overdid it to an idiotic – and extremely painful – extent. Jenny always maintained she didn't push me, and Nanny, the only 'steward' on duty, was probably biased by my screams. But she applied the butter with a will and, after a while, it did the trick.

Bill, who made the butter, was a marvellous all-round country craftsman who could turn his hand to anything. He kept our tractor and farm machinery in such wonderful order that the tractor, thanks entirely to him, was licensed, free, in 1990, as a 'Historic Vehicle'!

Among the many things Bill taught me

was how to shoot – not straight but reasonably safely. Old age tends to make us humans more 'humane', and a rabbit would nowadays need to be doing something seriously anti-social to make me shoot at it. But I still remember fascinating days out ferreting with Bill – the underground drumming of some unfortunate bunny's feet and the thrill when it exploded out of the hole – almost certainly to be missed by me and my four-ten!

I also remember that if you lost a ferret your first move was to send down a 'liner' – another little fellow complete with collar and line. I could show you the tree now, at the bottom of Oaksey Wood, in the roots of which one over-enthusiastic 'liner' got entangled. You could just see the buckle on his collar – and clearly undoing it would solve the problem. But that involved putting your hand through a smallish gap in the roots – and guess who had the smallest hand...

I suppose if it happened again I might be sensible enough to remove the grey mitten which made my hand look so like a rabbit. But you can't think of everything, and how was I to know that a ferret can do a U-turn in much less than its own width? I know now – and I also know, just a little, about how it feels to be eaten alive. Only two fingers, you may say – and admittedly I still have them – but for a moment there I was a convert to vegetarianism.

Bill, though presumably courting Nanny in those days, also had a definite eye for other girls, especially a German land girl called Helena, whose presence at the farm I cannot explain. Physically Helena was on the robust side, so much so that her best friend would almost certainly have advised against the honey-coloured corduroy breeches which were her habitual working kit. Bill didn't appear to mind them – in fact, their effect on him seemed almost magnetic. She filled them well, almost, you could say to bursting. When she sat down to milk, no one in his senses would have laid you better than 6–4 against a break-out!

Although my mother was not at all horsy my father was very enthusiastic about hunting and rode in point-to-points (though he never rode a winner at the Bar fixture, a distinction which I – and my daughter Sara – can claim), and kept several horses at Hill Farm, looked after by a wonderful man named Smith (I'm ashamed to say I can't remember his Christian name). Smith had been with my father in the First World War, and at the end of hostilities had taken charge of the battery's horses on their way back from the front in Palestine. This involved an extraordinarily arduous journey along the

Mediterranean and up through France, but all the horses arrived back in England intact. I can still remember the excitement of the news that old Smith was coming back to Oaksey to help with our ponies and my father's horses. Curiously I never actually saw Smith ride a horse, but he was quite wonderful at looking after them.

My own first pony was Mince Pie. I sat on her when I was barely one, and over the next few years this chubby dark brown little Welsh pony was my constant companion. For a long while my great ambition was to go hunting, and when I was six my wish was granted – albeit under the steadying influence of a leading rein. Mince Pie in her prime was a wonderful gymkhana pony but there was a contrary side to her, and she was perfectly capable of being a stubborn little cow when the mood took her. As you can see from the photograph of me being catapulted over her head, she would have approved wholeheartedly of the slope which, after the 1960 Grand National, the Aintree authorities put on the take-off side of their hitherto right-angled upright fences. In fact, if the Tetbury Hunter Trial organisers had introduced such a thing, she would probably still have considered it grossly inadequate – and reported them to the RSPCA!

That picture, captioned 'OVER –

UNDER THE PONY'S NOSE', appeared on the front page of the *Daily Express* – and inspired a flood of sympathetic messages to my parents, especially from the non-horsy friends of my non-horsy mother. Having never ridden, she regarded the equestrian antics of her children with massive – but heroically concealed – anxiety.

When I began to ride more or less regularly under Rules, she and Nanny became keen and (expensively) faithful punters. Only small stakes, they assured me, 'But it took our minds off things like falls and broken bones.'

Courage, bravery and nerve are fascinating, complicated subjects. Some people are frightened of flying, some won't willingly travel on a train, and I know one otherwise perfectly rational man for whom a five-mile trip on a village bus would be torture – impossible to bear. Several people 'taught me to ride', in many not always closely interconnected lessons and demonstrations. But the man who did most to bolster and reinforce my confidence as a child actually lost his own nerve, for ever, in my presence. There are not many incidents in this book which I remember with such painful clarity.

Bill Harris was his name, and all through what I think of now as my pony period – Mince Pie had later rivals for my affections in the shape of Plum Pudding, Esther and

Titch – Harris was the most important person in my life, and probably at least until they started to take an interest in boys, in the lives of my sisters. He used to take the three of them (two after Libby went away to school) out hunting on Fridays with the VWH. My parents took the view that four children was too many for Harris to handle – so my father and I (and Harris) went on Tuesdays with the Beaufort.

Our arrival at those Tuesday meets was, for me, an agonising business. Through no fault of her own Mince Pie, a portly 25-year-old who could jump twice her own height when she chose (but by this time often didn't), had a deeply embarrassing habit of farting the moment she saw a horse larger than her.

'Mince Pie's collywobbles', the smart Beaufort members called them, and as we wandered along this corridor of posh Blue and Buff side-saddle ladies, she treated them to a tasteful but explosive serenade. All was well once we moved off, and we had one or two sensational days. But they never forgot the collywobbles, and neither did I...

Harris had been a stable lad or groom all his life, and was quite an expert 'maker' of young horses. So when my father bought a five-year-old for us children, everyone accepted that Harris should be the first to ride it.

Hill Farm is, as you might expect, on the

side of a hill. Oaksey Wood and two fields are above it, higher up the hill, and it was in the lower of these that Harris mounted the young horse, who was called Belfast.

To begin with all went well. They trotted, then cantered in a circle. They had reached the top of the hill when something, possibly a pheasant, 'spooked' Belfast. He took off down the slope, and that, I imagine, was the moment Harris realised that this particular field – on a hill, with a stone wall running along the bottom to a right-angled corner with a line of stables – was not the ideal place for riding a young and unknown horse.

If so, it was too late, because by then Belfast had taken full control. As he turned right at the bottom, galloping flat out towards the right-angled corner – in which there was a narrow but open hunting gate – a fatal collision looked the only possible outcome. Harris screamed. It was a sound I had never heard before and one I shall never forget.

What happened next was impossible – so perhaps it was a result of that awful, impossible, inhuman scream. For, somehow, Belfast turned left, through the hunting gate, all of 6 feet wide. Then, with Harris (incredibly) still aboard, he stopped dead, and stood panting and shaking in the stable yard. Harris got off – and never got on another horse as long as he lived.

He became my mother's gardener, a role in which he was so competitive that he was disqualified from the village broad bean class for buying in two matching pods to make up a set of six! He also taught me to bet, and lived to be eighty. But he never got on a horse again.

My sisters were, if anything, keener on riding than I was. Libby passed her Pony Club 'A' test at the age of twelve; I only managed my 'D' with a struggle! Mind you, I was packed off to prep school at the age of eight, while my sisters had a governess until the war and did not leave home.

Our greatest riding excitement in the 1930s was Libby's selection for a combined VWH and Cotswold Pony Club team to do a musical ride in the Horse of the Year Show at Olympia. All dressed up as toy soldiers, they jumped water (from a hose), fire (flames two feet high) and all sorts of other quite fearsome assorted obstacles. Libby riding a pony called Tommy went wonderfully well until the last jump of all on the very last evening performance. They had to gallop round the arena – and out through a castle 'window' in the side. Somehow, we could just see that, although Tommy met it perfectly he pitched on his nose on the landing side – and went base over apex. My mother rushed off, her worst fears apparently justified, and I remember that it seemed to take us hours to get through behind the scenes. But all was well. Libby though furious, was quite unscathed, and Tommy wondered what all the fuss was about. We were back in our seats in time to see the Grand Parade – which featured Brown Jack, my principal horse hero at that time. Nanny had read me Bob Lyle's book on the seven times Royal Ascot winner and, to my delight, Steve Donoghue was there to ride his old friend the night we were at Olympia.

Steve, in the green and yellow colours of Sir Harold Wernher, rode racing length but cantered tight circles and (it seemed to me, anyway) did several 'flying changes'. It is impossible to compare, but the only horse I've heard getting louder, or anyway comparable, applause was Arkle at the Horse of the Year Show after his retirement. That was the night his owner, Anne, Duchess of Westminster, was asked what tune she would like the band to play. She chose, quite rightly 'There'll Never Be Another You'.

My early education came from my nanny and from the governesses who were employed to teach myself and my sisters, but just short of my ninth birthday I was, according to the (uncivilised) custom of the time, dispatched to Horris Hill, a prep school near Newbury presided over by J.L. 'Daddy' Stow, an old prep school friend of my father's. It was my first experience of being away from home for any length of time, and I was very homesick, spending the first few nights blubbing uncontrollably into my pillow. War was looming ever nearer, and for some reason I was convinced that the rest of my family would be bombed – leaving me the sole survivor of the Lawrences.

'Daddy' Stow was not, in fact, much like my father – who never laid a hand on me in anger all his life. Mr Stow, by contrast, was a fierce-looking old slave-driver, kind enough no doubt, but apt to beat boys on their bare bottoms in front of the whole school.

I have never forgotten one such incident. A boy called Barlow had, it seems, smuggled a whole suitcase full of sweets into the school and was caught selling – or bartering – them to other boys. Heaven knows why this should be considered such a mortal sin, but it was. The unfortunate Barlow was hauled before us all, forced to pull down his shorts, bent over – and given five or six painful-looking slaps with a thing like a butter pat.

Having never experienced such a beating (caning at Eton, with your trousers on, was almost certainly more painful), I cannot testify to the effect. But the formal and public ceremony of the Horris Hill method did, unquestionably leave a big (and almost certainly unhealthy) scar on my subconscious. I can still remember the circular marks made on poor Barlow's bottom – and if he was left with sado-masochistic tendencies for the rest of his life, Mr Stow must, in my opinion, take the blame.

That gruesome episode did not help counter my homesickness, and for my first term at Horris Hill I was thoroughly miserable. But moods change quickly at that age, and by the early months of the war I had become a wholehearted belligerent, scouring the newspapers every day full of idiotic hope that hostilities would last long enough for me to take part. Drawing coloured arrows on maps of Europe, I plotted each move minutely – only to be interrupted by an attack of English (at least they were not German!) measles.

Of course, having imported the bug single-handed into Horris Hill (no MMR jabs in those days), I should have been thoroughly ashamed of myself. In fact, swelling up all over and covered with extremely itchy spots I was not supposed to scratch, I was just thoroughly miserable. To make matters worse, the German Blitzkrieg began in France, and, though I don't suppose I realised it at the time, we must have come uncomfortably close to losing the war. Then there was 1940 and the Battle of Britain; and again, spellbound by spectacular dogfights all over the sky we little knew what a close-run thing it must have been.

Not that Hill Farm was spared contact with the war. Early one morning when the Battle of Britain was at its height, my mother – by then Chief Controller in the Auxiliary Territorial Service (ATS) – looked out of her bedroom window and found herself eyeball-to-eyeball with the German pilot of a JU 88, probably on his way to strafe Kemble aerodrome. We were all surprised – and rather disappointed – that the angry gaze of Chief Controller Lawrence was not enough to send the intruder down in flames!

Oaksey village had been taken by surprise in 1938 by an influx of German Communist refugees fleeing from the Hitler regime. About thirty strong, they called themselves the Bruderhof – and took over Oaksey Park, the biggest house in the village. Needless to say all sorts of 'fifth column' suspicions were aroused – but, as time went on and the visitors stayed, minding their own business and doing no harm to anyone, they began to be accepted. Individual members of the Bruderhof were allowed no money of their own but operated a system of barter, exchanging labour for food and other necessities. They invariably gave good value too.

During the Battle of Britain a strict

blackout was enforced in the village, and one night my father, a sergeant in the Local Defence Volunteers (later the Home Guard), was on 'fire watch' duty in the church. An urgent report came through of a light seen flashing from the Park and, with a corporal called Sparrow (all of whose hair fell out one night, leaving his head as shiny as a billiard ball), Sergeant Lawrence set off to investigate.

After walking down the tree-lined avenue which separated the Park from the village, they knocked on the Bruderhof's front door and asked to search the building. High and low they went, but not a sign of light. Finally satisfied and a bit shamefaced, they started back up the avenue – only to hear running feet sounding behind them. My father and Sparrow turned, rifles at the ready as two Bruders ran up. One was clutching a large volume. 'Please,' he said. 'Please. You are our first callers. Would you kindly sign the Visitors' Book?'

The Bruderhof left just before the end of the war to go, we heard, to South America. A few ex-Bruders have come back to visit Oaksey and apparently nowadays they have settled down, happily I hope, in Brazil. They were the first Communists I ever met – and genuine Communists at that, the kind who share everything, with not a Gulag (or Katyn) in sight.

Talking of Germans, our German governess, Olga Sand – 'Sandy' to all of us – went back to Munich in 1938. The timing of her departure seemed, I suppose, marginally suspicious, and when someone asked my father what he would do if she walked up the drive, his quite untypically fierce reply was: 'Shoot her, of course!'

In fact, when he and my mother had to spend nearly a year in Nuremberg for the trials, they ran Sandy to earth in Munich – and found her living in distinctly depressed circumstances. My mother was soon able to get her a job in England with some nice neighbours of ours, the Pitmans. I believe that, thanks to several other 'governess' or 'companion' jobs, she spent most of the rest of her life in England. I just wish she had taught me German.

Back at prep school, all the arrows on my maps had to be hastily revised as Hitler's Blitzkrieg swept through Holland, Belgium and northern France; even to an uninformed eleven-year-old, the radio made England's danger pretty clear. I was lucky enough to hear at least two of Winston Churchill's broadcasts – and can testify to their inspirational effect. Horris Hill had a splendid Scottish matron at that time, who stood up and clapped when the Prime Minister finished. She soon had us all following her example.

Except for one awful episode of which I am thoroughly ashamed, I was never really one of those who felt that a more accurate description of Horris Hill would have been Horrid Hell. If blame for that short-lived nightmare were to be shared out, the first (admittedly infinitesimal) slice would go to Mr Liddell, a lazy and/or over-confident version of Mr Chips who shared the headmastership of Horris Hill with one of the Stow family. Liddell's method of testing yesterday's 'prep' was to set us (his pupils in the second form) questions with one- or two-word answers. Nothing wrong with that, you may well say. But then this scholarly moron read out the answers – leaving correction (and marking) to those who had written them! Well, of course, it saved time and might, in an ideal world, have worked perfectly well. But to anyone who had skimped his prep – or, like me, neglected it altogether – the Liddell system was, simply, a chance too good to miss. Leave a few strategic blanks, and fill them with correct answers as he read them out. Or rather, almost correct, with just a few excusable mistakes; too much perfection might be suspect.

I only did it sometimes – but too much, it soon turned out, for a couple of law-and-order freaks sitting at the desk behind me. I don't think I'll mention their names, but if by any improbable chance they ever happen to read this, I just hope they will be pleased with themselves. Because their little venture into law enforcement certainly caused me a lot more grief than either they or what they called my 'cheating' can possibly have been worth.

At a pompously prearranged meeting, one of them (he is now a doctor and I sincerely hope I never fall into his clutches!) elected himself as spokesman.

'We've seen what you're up to, Lawrence,' he said, 'and we are not going to let it go on. We have told Mr Liddell you are cheating – and no doubt you will be hearing from Mr Stow.'

There are several points to make about that little pronouncement. What, for one thing, has become of the 'Old School Code'? Surely you do not sneak on your mates? Now, sixty years later, I strongly suspect that they had, in fact, done nothing of the sort. But I could hardly know that – and so, for three ghastly months, I lived in a private self-inflicted hell – waiting each day for the dreaded summons to the Headmaster's study – or, even worse, when holidays began, to my father's.

In the early part of the holidays, I remember creeping stealthily downstairs before the rest of the family was up to intercept the post – and opening at least three harmless warnings of 'injections needed' simply because they looked suspicious and carried an ominous Newbury postmark!

I knew that 'cheating' or anything which involved dishonesty would appal my father, and the thought of confronting him on such a charge did, actually wake me more than once in a guilty sweat. But mercifully no doom-laden letter ever appeared, and much the most likely explanation is that my heartless classmates had never, in fact, sneaked.

I still do not remember them in my prayers.

My father's brother, Uncle Trevor, had served in the Royal Horse Artillery as a regular before the First World War, and was a keen hunting man, following packs all over England and Ireland and serving as Master, at one time, of the Teme Valley

In one respect, Uncle Trevor's story is – at least for the rest of the family – a sad one. The fact is that at one stage he had a definite and prolonged walkout with Miss Buchanan, the Black and White whisky heiress. I don't pretend to know exactly what stage things had got to, but attractive, sought-after heiresses were no doubt as hard to handle then as they are now. Anyway before Uncle Trevor could pop the question, off she went to America – and came back engaged to an (English) bachelor called Reggie Macdonald. On account of her fortune and his comparative poverty they had to hyphenate their names when they got married! I have not a shred of evidence to support my theory of broken hearts and an interrupted romance – but even when I knew him, Uncle Trevor was a handsome, dashing old thing. He stayed a bachelor all his life, and it cannot be all my imagination that, whenever we read of yet another success for the (by then) celebrated black and white Macdonald-Buchanan colours, there was a faraway 'might have been' look in his eye...

Uncle Trevor moved to Wales, where he lived in Abernant, my grandfather's house not far from Builth Wells, but the connection with the Macdonald-Buchanans was not severed. After their marriage, the couple bred the wartime (1941) Derby winner Owen Tudor, and later, when his foals began to appear, they set about the search – which some owner-breeders delight in, some dread, and a regrettable minority neglect or ignore altogether – for names connected with the sire or dam, or preferably both. Remembering Owen Tudor's Welsh background, Reggie's wife had a brainwave. 'I know,' she said. 'My old friend Trevor Lawrence lives in Wales. He will give us some Welsh names.' So off she wrote – and, after prolonged head-scratching, my not particularly scholastic uncle sent back a list of Welsh villages, mountains, streams and other features, culled from his AA book and Ordnance Survey maps. High above Abernant, for instance, there is a hill called Alt Mawr. (Nanny Jenny and I walked up it many times – and, on at least one occasion, were pursued down it by what looked to us like murderous mountain cattle.)

When Reggie wrote back to thank my uncle, he said that he and his wife both quite liked the name Alt Mawr – but wondered how the English bookies would pronounce it. In the end, reluctantly (but wisely!) discarding this suggestion, Reggie went on: 'Actually we both agreed that the nicest name on your list was that of your house. So, if you don't mind and the name is free, we would like to call the colt which looks our best Owen Tudor so far, Abernant. He is a real good (grey) racing colour and seems to move well in the paddock.'

How right he was. Abernant was only ever beaten three times: once first time out, through greenness; once, a short head by Nimbus in the last strides of the 1949 Two Thousand Guineas, Abernant narrowly failing to stay the mile; and once, by half a length, in the King's Stand Stakes at Royal Ascot, trying to give the very useful Tangle twenty-three pounds. He won several of the top sprint races two years running – the July Cup at Newmarket, the King George Stakes at Goodwood and the Nunthorpe at York.

Sir Gordon Richards, the twenty-six-times champion jockey called Abernant the best sprinter he had ever ridden, and moreover not only the fastest horse he knew, but also the kindest. According to Gordon, the flying grey was once 'left' several lengths at the start of the five-furlong King George Stakes at Goodwood because he was watching some children playing behind the starting gate! Needless to say he recovered to win comfortably.

So at least, by inadvertently suggesting the name of one of the greatest sprinters of all time, the Lawrence family can claim to have contributed to racing history.

'Aber' means 'at the mouth of' in Welsh, and there is a small stream called the Nant which flowed down into the Wye by my grandfather's house. Good fish have been caught in the Wye near there – or used to be, many of them by Fafa himself. But it was not, in fact, there that my grandfather had the accident in 1935 which killed him when well into his nineties. He was fishing in waders, with his faithful chauffeur-cum-ghillie, Danner, on a stretch of the Usk belonging to a friend. He hooked a salmon and, scrambling across some rocks, slipped and filled both waders. 'It's all right, Danner, I can swim!' were pretty courageous last words from a 93-year-old. But although Fafa lived up to them by reaching the bank, the effort was, not surprisingly, too much for his brave heart.

I did not hear the news of his death until much later that day. Mince Pie and I were competing in a show near Tetbury. No obstacles were involved. In fact, it was a straightforward beauty contest. You can say what you like about the eyesight and impartiality of the judges, but Mincie and I won. (It was, I believe, our solitary showing triumph: we were much better at bending, musical chairs, getting apples out of buckets full of flour, and other competitions in which dignity never mind beauty was not an essential.) I still wish Fafa could have heard about Mince Pie's victory, humble as it was.

As children, we used to go down to stay at Abernant almost every summer – often, I suppose, on our way to the seaside at Tenby or Harlech. (Tenby racecourse was the scene of a famous betting scam in January 1927, when a horse named Oyster Maid won a £44 selling race, leaving the bookmakers so disgruntled that they started to boycott the course. This in turn led to dwindling attendances and tiny fields – in 1935 the same four horses contested both selling hurdles on the same programme! –

and the course eventually gave up the unequal struggle in 1936.) Uncle Trevor, a great storyteller, not only entertained us but encouraged us to ride – he had a pony called Mousie – and one year, when there was building going on at Hill Farm, we took Mince Pie to Abernant for the summer. The hero of Uncle Trevor's stories was usually a dog called Pongo, confused in my memory with Nola, his beloved Kerry Blue who actually lived at Abernant.

In the early years of the war, when an invasion looked a real possibility my mother (who did not fish, and did not, in fact, much like Abernant) laid plans for an 'evacuation' there if the worst came to the worst. We actually buried a trunk full of tinned ham and other goodies in the Nant, halfway up the hill to Alt Mawr. I remember the great excitement when we fished it out in the early 1950s – finding the ham (and everything else) in perfect condition.

Remembering these family summers at Abernant is an appropriate point to say that, as the youngest of four children with three older sisters, I have had the amazing good fortune to have been presented with three brothers-in-law, every single one of whom I have loved and admired. Hughie Dundas, Robby's husband, is sadly dead, and so is my beloved youngest sister Jenny, both victims of cancer. 'Cocky' Dundas – his nickname was not descriptive of his character, only of his reddish hair and admittedly beak-like nose – flew Spitfires in the war, and his book *Flying Start* contains some of the best descriptions of action I ever read. Its last page contains this remarkable passage:

On 29th April Venice was captured.

The next day – the last of that blood-stained month – we were operating at the limit of our range, without bombs. Many vehicles were claimed destroyed by strafing. Four Spitfires were lost, one of their pilots killed, the others baling out or crash-landing. That was the last big day. On 2nd May there were only three missions, involving four aircraft each, and they had instructions simply to report enemy movement, not to attack.

Five days later the Wing Log records: 'We no longer carry out operations from this date. In other words the war in Italy has ceased.'

And I was still alive.

Hughie had made his first flight in a Spitfire on 13 March 1940. It was late in 1949 when he taxied in from his last.

Owing to the loss of his second log book, he did not know exactly how many hours he spent in a Spitfire's cockpit. But what he did know was that in all those desperate years the Spitfire never let him down. 'On the occasions when we got into trouble together,' he wrote, 'the fault was invariably mine.' Lovely to look at, delightful to fly, the Spitfire became the pride and joy of thousands of young men from practically every country in what, then, constituted the free world. Americans raved about her and wanted to have her; Poles were seduced by her; men from the old Dominions crossed the world and oceans to be with her; the Free French wrote love songs about her – and the Germans had to be content with envy of those lucky enough to fly her.

Cocky also has a notable distinction in the racing sphere, as owner of the 1989 Hennessy Gold Cup winner Ghofar. Robby mad keen about racing ever since childhood, asked me to try and find a chaser for them, so I sought the advice of David Elsworth, a trainer whom I've always considered a magically good judge of a horse. When he showed me this really rather weedy chestnut, I suggested that it was hardly the type to make a staying chaser. 'You wait and see,' countered David – and ever since the unforgettable day that my sister's horse beat Brown Windsor and subsequent Grand National winner Mr Frisk to win the great Newbury race, he's never let me forget my reluctance. (When in

November 2002 the *Racing Post* published a ranking of previous Hennessy heroes, Robby was incensed to see Ghofar rated as the worst winner in the history of the race. The paper later retracted this disgraceful slur – in the nick of time, as the perpetrators were about to be skinned by my indignant sister!)

Libby's husband Philip Adams is also dead, but in his time enjoyed an extremely varied and distinguished Foreign Office career, mostly in the Middle East but with one particularly enjoyable and successful spell as Consul in Chicago.

Just before Philip died, his son Geoffrey, then serving as Consul General in Jerusalem, was in London to advise at talks between Tony Blair and Yasser Arafat. The visit gave him time to bid his father a sad but wonderfully appropriate farewell – appropriate because Philip's own first Foreign Office posting had been to Beirut in 1939, to learn Arabic. Somewhat to his surprise, he soon found himself Governor of Tyre! His last posting was as Ambassador to Cairo in 1973. Between those two dates, as one of the Foreign Office's leading Arabists, he was on the spot to experience, at close quarters, every one of the major crises by which the Middle East was so regularly torn apart. (And to get to know many of the eccentric members of the expatriate community.

When Philip waved to a friend on the other side of a street in Khartoum one day Libby asked who it was. 'Oh, that's old "Harpic" Johnston,' Philip replied. 'Been round the bend for years.')

At one vital stage of the Yom Kippur war in 1973, for instance, the Americans, with no representative in Egypt, had to rely on Philip as their sole channel of communication with President Sadat. With Russia re-arming Egypt and America backing Israel, a nuclear confrontation looked as close as at any time since the Cuban Missile Crisis in 1962. On one occasion, when the Americans begged Philip to make urgent contact with Sadat, it was two o'clock in the morning. The President of Egypt had to receive his English friend in his pyjamas. But they trusted each other completely – and a ceasefire was duly achieved.

In charge of Information and Intelligence in the Cairo Embassy at the time of Suez, Philip came to hear the (extremely classified) news of Eden's plan to seize the Suez Canal. Disapproving deeply and horrified at the probable consequences, he flew back to England to protest. But in an extraordinary (or maybe, at that particular stage of our history not so extraordinary) piece of official disinformation, he was, so to speak, patted on the head and told not to worry old man! He flew back, still fearing the worst, and sure enough, it came to pass – with the Anglo-French action disapproved of by very nearly everyone, notably and most importantly the United States.

After those eventful years he and Libby came home to take charge of the Ditchley Foundation in Oxfordshire, a less hazardous post, perhaps, but, since Ditchley hosted regular conferences for international statesmen, one calling for every bit as much delicacy and tact. Philip, who was never short of those qualities, died in 2001 – having, as I've said, seen his son Geoffrey go back to face many if not all, of the same insoluble Middle Eastern problems.

Jenny's husband, Freddy Burnaby-Atkins, a regular officer in the Black Watch, had the misfortune in 1940 to be captured (at the age of nineteen) by the Germans in Normandy. After a hungry and exhausting trek eastwards across Germany Freddy and a number of fellow prisoners decided to escape. Fred and a friend called Fitz Fletcher dug their way out of Oflag 7 at Biberach through what was, at that stage of the war, the longest (and one of the narrowest) tunnels ever attempted by POWs. I understand that the 'Wooden Horse' tunnel, dug later, was a few yards longer, but Fred's was plenty long enough – and, after emerging at the other end, he and Fitz plodded across the Third Reich for eleven days, travelling almost entirely by night, aiming for one particular especially recommended spot on the Swiss border. They hit it precisely and, following the instructions of their escape committee (every camp containing British prisoners had one), waited for the *moment critique* of, supposedly 'lowest vigilance' at 3 am. But then disaster struck. Coming round the corner of a haystack, they found themselves confronted by an aged German with a gun.

Looking back now (Freddy actually took my sister to inspect the spot!), neither he nor Fitz could say exactly why they did not overpower the old fellow. But however old the finger on the trigger, guns do go off if you pull it. Don't forget they'd only eaten a few mouthfuls in the previous ten days.

Not only my mother but all three of my sisters were in the ATS, and Elizabeth (Libby), the eldest, had an extremely active, widely travelled war. She and her commanding officer, Lady Maud Bailey, were two of the first ATS into North Africa, and Libby then followed the Eighth Army up Italy – doing her best not to fall in love with more than one member of that gallant corps at the same time. She has never forgotten one particularly energetic party not long before VE day when a New Zealand VC kept encouraging her from the side of the dance floor with loud, if not especially tactful, cries of 'Go it, Tubby!'

But Libby's heart survived the war more or less intact, only to be captured by a charming, wise and extremely able diplomat. She met Philip Adams in Vienna, where she was working in the embassy for our cousin Sir Harold Caccia. Harold, a distinguished all-round athlete, was, incidentally one of the very few Etonians to get a Blue for rugby football, a game played only by a smallish minority at the Old Coll!

Although we certainly did not realise its significance at the time, I remember clearly the elegant shoulder flash with which my middle sister Robby came home one day to our flat in Melbury Court, just opposite what was then the Kensington Regal cinema. It was the badge of SHAEF, Supreme HQ Allied Expeditionary Force – the huge multinational army which was being assembled in Britain for the invasion of Europe. Robby worked in such close proximity to General Eisenhower that she knew in advance the proposed date of the D-Day landings – and was horrified on the expected day to turn on her radio and hear precisely nothing about any military activity. What she did not then know was that the weather had intervened and caused D-Day to be postponed.

But by then I saw my sisters only on rare occasions. I was incarcerated at Eton.

2

'That greatest of posts, Mr Lawrence'

Although both my grandfather and my father had attended Haileybury it was decided that I should break with family tradition, and in September 1942 I was deposited at Eton College, an institution very different from Horris Hill.

For one thing, I had a room of my own – small and rudimentary but true luxury after the dormitory at prep school. For another, Eton had its own language – for example, a term there is a 'half', even though there are three of them a year (Winter, Easter, Summer) and they last approximately as long as terms at other schools. Still, getting used to the jargon was simple compared with adjusting to the other traditions and customs of Eton.

There was, for example, the outfit. Although I didn't have to wear tails when I was first there as I was below the minimum height, the mandatory stiff white collar was desperately uncomfortable and undignified, and the short Eton jacket left you numb with cold in the winter. Often it lived up uncomfortably closely to its nickname 'bum-freezer', and you sometimes almost longed for the call of 'Boy!' – the signal for a stampede of lower boys, which at least had the merit of warming you up. The last one to report to the library member or prefect who had shouted the summons had to perform a chore. This was the system of fagging, whereby junior boys undertook various menial services for older boys. (The words 'fag', 'fagging' or 'fagmaster' cause quite a bit of confusion outside the world of Eton and Etonians – especially in the United States, where the first and principal meaning of 'fag' is a male homosexual!)

For my first two halves I fagged for a splendid man called Teddy Hall, who was to become one of my best friends. (He later married a beautiful South African girl called Jeffie de la Harpe, and I have to confess that I was more than half in love with her myself. When she was working as a model in London for Hardy Amies – yes, she was *that* beautiful – I used to walk up and down the route which she always took to the Underground, in the hope that I might 'accidentally' bump into her. Alas, I succeeded only once in waylaying Jeffie, and not surprisingly Teddy Hall won the prize!)

'Fagging' covered a multitude of tasks, from making tea for the senior boy to sitting on the lavatory seat to warm it up for him, but my first job as a fag was to polish Teddy's Sam Browne belt, a cherished relic of his father's military service. Like many such belts it bore the polish of ages but, I regret to say it was with me the work of only a few minutes to reduce its sacred shine to a battlefield full of shell holes. Teddy would have been well within his rights to beat me or do some even more extreme violence to my person, but in fact when the disaster was reported to him he blamed the senior fag Bob Dolbey, a boy who also later became a friend of mine.

Another great friendship which began at Eton was with Peter Gatacre, whose mother Alice de Steuss was from Gelderland in Holland. She had been living near the German border towards the close of the First World War, when at a tea party at the American Embassy to welcome exchanged prisoners of war she met a young British officer named Gatacre, who had been captured by the Germans. They soon fell in love, but the snag was that he was already married to a lady in Dublin. That marriage was eventually annulled, and Gatacre moved to join Alice de Steuss in her castle near the German border – where he designed an addition to the main house and built new stables and a coach house, as well as establishing his own pack of harriers. The new Mrs Gatacre endeared herself to her son – and to Peter's fellow Etonians – with regular supplies of strawberries and eggs.

But the most lasting of the friendships I forged at Eton began with the arrival in January 1944 of Gay Kindersley. Gay was already something of a celebrity when he first entered the college, as his name had been splashed all over the papers. During the early years of the war his father Philip, who had been captured by the Germans in France, had fought a legal battle (from his prisoner-of-war camp) to ensure that Gay came to Eton, 'instead of being brought up and misinformed in Ireland' as his divorced wife Oonagh (*née* Guinness) wished. 'I don't want her brainwashing the boy into Sinn Fein or the bloody IRA,' he declared, and surprisingly enough an Irish court found in his favour. Gay remembers being dragged by his grandfather through a crowd of screaming Irish mothers – 'Sure, and how can you take the poor little spalpeen back to England to be bombed and killed?' – and deposited on the ship to Liverpool. As you might expect, the strain began to tell on him, and when he was taken up on to the bridge – a great honour; but then, his grandfather owned the boat! – he 'parked a custard' (Gay's colourful phrase for being sick) all over the Captain's trousers.

Gay has been a great friend of mine ever since Eton days, and, as you'll see, played a huge part in my racing and riding life.

No Etonian in his senses would claim that homosexual relations are unknown at the school, though I suspect they are not nearly as common nowadays, when, after all, the average fifteen-year-old boy has a good deal more contact with the opposite sex than his comparatively monastic counterpart in the 1940s. In those days it was quite common – and perfectly understandable – that large, mature sixteen- or seventeen-year-olds should 'fall in love' with attractive curly-headed little boys who looked – and in some cases behaved – more like girls than red-blooded heterosexual males.

I speak only from partial, and thankfully remote, experience. But I did get two of what I suspect the authors intended as 'love letters', which went on at some length about my 'beauty' – and, before you do yourself an injury laughing, I may say, Non Swanks, that until it began falling out at about the time I came of age, my hair was plentiful and curly. No one, in those days, actually ran their fingers through it – but I wouldn't have been all that surprised.

The thousand-plus boys at Eton were divided into 'houses', each of which took the name of its housemaster and was generally known by his initials. Mine was HKM, presided over by a man called H.K.

Marsden, more generally known as 'Bloody Bill'. He owed the nickname partly to his appearance and partly to his attitude to discipline. Never happier than when tracking down a 'criminal' – his word for anyone breaking the school rules – he was also one of the very few housemasters who used the cane himself. Beating (with a cane) was normally left to the Captain of the House – or, if the offence had to do with games, the Captain of Games. It was, or could be, extremely painful, and as luck would have it one of my three encounters with the cane featured a Bothamesque figure called Henry Hely Hutchinson (who, curiously has a connection with the greatest horse I ever saw: he was a distant cousin of Mark Hely Hutchinson, who has the unique distinction of having ridden Arkle in a race but never won on him). Blessed – or from my angle cursed – with wrists of steel and an eye like a hawk, he hit me six times on what felt like exactly the same spot. Bill himself beat me on only one occasion – just three strokes and much less painful.

But an evening (after Prayers) knock on your door was still a nasty moment. 'You are wanted in the Library,' the messenger said – and, unless you had a cast-iron alibi, the game was probably up.

It was certainly up for one of my best friends, Colin Fyfe-Jamieson, one day in the school gymnasium. He was climbing, upside down, up a rope suspended from the gym ceiling and was just about to reach the summit, when from out of his pocket plopped a condom. (History does not relate whether it was in a used or pristine state.) Helpless to retrieve it from his lofty position (still upside down), he could only watch impotently as the gym master strode across and picked up the offending object – then waited until the climber had regained *terra firma*.

'Fyfe-Jamieson – *WHAT* is this?'

'Why Sir – don't you know?'

Whether for possession of the condom or for the cheek shown to the gym master, there was only one, inevitable fate in store – an encounter with Henry Hely Hutchinson's cane. *Fifteen times* he was struck, and at the end of the session, which must have caused him unimaginable pain – the six that I suffered I can still feel today – walked to the door of the Library turned round and took his leave of his assailant with the words, 'Thank you very much.'

Bill Marsden's propensity for detective work was well known. No one in his senses would, for instance, smoke in his room, and although some bold characters did drink alcohol of various types, they either kept it well hidden or drank it outside the house. Bill presented a terrifying aspect as he crept around the passages, and sometimes we put sugar down on the floor so that the crackling would alert us to his proximity.

Betting was strictly forbidden in Eton as a whole and in HKM in particular, and although there were well-known school bookies in other houses, I had never, at that stage, patronised them. In fact, to tell the truth, without the expert advice of Bill Harris I would not have had the faintest idea how to set about it.

In 1943, for instance, I did not even know that Saturday 19 June was Derby Day. During the war the race was run at Newmarket instead of Epsom, but I did not know that either. So imagine my surprise when Bill Marsden came storming into my room, waving a telegram form and demanding an explanation. 'What's this, Lawrence, what's this?' he growled, holding out the paper, which read:

> Have drawn Straight Deal for you.
> [signed] Beauchamp

Well, that meant less than nothing to me. I had never heard of Straight Deal, nor of Beauchamp, the ham-fisted idiot who by spelling my name wrong as 'Larrence' gave Bill an excuse to open and read the wire, thereby dropping me deep in the mulligatawny. Betting was a 'sackable' offence –

that is, you could be expelled – in those days; but Bill Marsden (quite rightly) made it a point of honour never to have a boy sacked. A beating – to within an inch of your life – was his preferred alternative and that, for the rest of that day was the dark shadow which hung over me.

When it comes to physical (or mental) pain, I am, undoubtedly a coward – and now the only (admittedly pitiful) move I could think of was to ring my mother. It may seem a pretty craven course, but how right I was. When I read the telegram over to her she snorted like a warhorse. 'Beauchamp!' she said. 'It's that idiot Beauchamp.'

It turned out that an old friend of my father's named Beauchamp Seymour was doing a spell as his 'marshal' – a kind of ADC to a circuit judge. It is an essential role, because a judge on circuit is representing, and taking the place of, the monarch. Thus the judge has to be met – in person – by the High Sheriff or his representative at the front door of the judge's lodgings at each place he visits, just as if he were the Queen. In those days marshalling was a surprisingly well-paid job (£2 a day and all found), much sought after by struggling law students. I had the great pleasure of marshalling for a time for Toby Pilcher – the only High Court judge, I believe, to ride a winner of the Pegasus Club

(Bar) point-to-point while actually on the bench. (Two comparable sporting feats are those of Edward Cazalet, the only High Court judge to have ridden a winner at the Cheltenham National Hunt Meeting – Lochroe in the 1958 Kim Muir, with Mr J. Lawrence second on Taxidermist – and, in a different field, Ian Balding, who played full back at rugger for Cambridge and rode a winner over fences at Huntingdon on the same day.)

A potentially sticky situation was resolved in the course of a conversation between Bill Marsden and my mother. Bloody Bill did not normally talk much (if at all) to mothers, but throughout my career at Eton my own got on with him surprisingly well: Bill may have been impressed by the fact that she was a controller in the ATS, which made her the equivalent of a brigadier, and her appearance in uniform, complete with red tabs, would certainly have made a mark on him. Her explanation about Beauchamp and Straight Deal seems to have convinced Bill and saved me from the cane – and I doubt whether he noticed that Beauchamp's selection actually won the Derby beating Umiddad by a head with the enigmatic Nasrullah having one of his off days and finishing only third.

Never excessively devoted to my studies, I had a particular antipathy for maths – I nearly failed to get into Eton at all on account of my lamentable arithmetic – and a particular liking for history for which I was 'up to' (Eton parlance for taught by) a teacher named G.B. Smith, whose nick-name 'Egg' reflected his being – allegedly – completely bald all over. Egg was a true scholar and an exceptionally good teacher: indeed, he was the first person who ever attempted to teach me to write 'proper English and give some thought to how to structure a sentence.

The Straight Deal incident apart, I paid little attention to racing while I was at Eton. For one thing, the programme was severely restricted on account of the hostilities; for another, sneaking off to see live action at Windsor (Ascot was closed during the war) was strictly forbidden, punishable by expulsion. As a confirmed goody-goody I was never likely to transgress.

Nor did the war itself have a great effect on school life. We followed the progress of our troops in the papers, and every now and again had to make our way down into the school air-raid shelters when nearby Slough was threatened with bombardment. For us, there was a positive side to the bombing: if we were still down in the shelters after a certain time in the evening we were exempted from early school the following day.

For me, the best aspect of Eton was undoubtedly the sport, which the school provided in almost infinite variety: soccer, rugger, fives, squash or racquets, boxing, judo, karate, athletics, cricket in the summer – and those games peculiar to Eton, the Wall Game, held against the long red-brick wall on the Datchet Road and played principally by Scholars, and the Field Game. Of the two, the Wall Game has rules which have proved quite impenetrable to most outsiders (and, indeed, plenty of insiders!). Traditionally the College Wall plays the Oppidan Wall on St Andrew's Day – and the Oppidan team is made up of more or less athletic non-Scholars (Oppidans) from the other forty-odd houses. I never played the Wall Game, being fully occupied in the Winter Half with the Field Game, a far better mixture (in my prejudiced opinion) of rugger and soccer, played with a round ball. The Field Game is played only at Eton, and one of the great pleasures for Old Etonians has long been returning to those famous playing fields to take part in a scratch team against the School XI. I still have a cutting which describes one such game from 1953, which is worth quoting to give the flavour of this unusual sport:

The Scratch was a good one, though not quite as good as the list of distinguished names [which included my great friend Colin Ingleby-Mackenzie, later a notable cricketer and Captain of Hampshire] might at first suggest, but it was never allowed to settle down. The School bully under their ferocious leader, started off at a tremendous pace and kept it up, unrelentingly for the full hour of play. It is difficult to describe their combined fury: there is a purposeful surge and thunder as they sweep in towards the defenders, and though one player or another may suddenly dart out like a hornet, the rest are immediately with him, and one has the impression that they are all there, all the time. The School pressed at once and Pinckney nearly scored. Lockhart, who did a great deal of valuable and constructive hard work, came even nearer to doing so, but it was James who got the first rouge. The Scratch managed to clear, but James was soon back with a fine run and scored again. In neither of the rams was the ball forced, thanks to that greatest of posts, Mr Lawrence. Even this School bully can learn a thing or two from him. Yet the badly shaken Scratch could not get the ball away. Another rouge looked imminent, when Orwin darted inwards and shot a goal which left the defence no chance, though one of them did try to get a hand to it.

'That greatest of posts, Mr Lawrence.' Any

subsequent plaudit which I may have received pales before that!

Bill Marsden, although a terrifying figure in some ways, was very proud of HKM's sporting achievements, and for my first four years at Eton I was never on the losing side in any of the various Field Game competitions. Then there was a change of housemaster. Bill retired and was replaced by E.P. Hedley and eventually our team was beaten. After that terrible defeat I was walking home towards the house, tears streaming down my face, when I was joined by a long, lean figure walking in the same direction. It was Bill, and he was crying too...

The best player of the Field Game during my time at Eton was a great friend of mine named Alisdair Hilleary. A large, handsome Scotsman, incredibly powerful and one of the fastest runners I have ever known, Alisdair was 'Fly' for the Field – that is, the First XI – and, needless to say for our house side as well. But he was also somewhat oversexed, and fell passionately in love with a beautiful blue-eyed boy named Desmond Guinness. The details of a story involving a school-wide prostitution racket are too murky to relate here, but the upshot was that Alisdair's passion for Desmond was discovered – as was the manner in which it was expressed. Bill Marsden's usual reaction to this sort of disruption in his house was to avoid at all costs any of his charges being sacked: beat the guilty parties to a frazzle by all means, but avoid the scandal becoming widely known. But this was a problem that affected the whole school, and exposure could not be avoided; so poor Alisdair was 'asked to leave'. This verdict was eventually commuted and he was allowed to stay on after all, though he was excluded from the position of Keeper of the Field – captain of the school team. After leaving Eton at the proper time he went into the army and had both legs blown off in Jerusalem. Never ask me to sympathise with Jewish terrorists.

I played the Field Game to a much lower standard than Alisdair, but my real sporting passion in those days – apart from horses, of course, but all equestrian activity was confined to the holidays – was boxing.

I do not know if my father did much boxing in his youth but he was, quite rightly keen that I should learn the art of self-defence, and had sent me at the age of seven, before I went to Horris Hill, to be coached at Oakley Hall, a now defunct prep school in Cirencester run by a family called Letts. Being small for my age, I boxed in the lightest weight divisions and found that the blows did not hurt much – unless you got hit squarely on the nose. The Oakley Hall instructor, an ex-petty officer called Chief, had been a good featherweight in the navy and was very keen to teach us how to avoid being hit, saying that you needed 'springs in your heels and rubber in your hips and neck'. The only aggressive move I can remember him teaching was 'a feint to the balls and left hook to the jaw', a manoeuvre which I did manage once or twice in the ring – but not with any sensational success. (I came close to trying this move much later in life when attempting to quell a little local difficulty in the beer tent at the Oaksey Knockout – our village fête. When a disturbance broke out among a few lads who had imbibed not wisely but too well, I was dispatched to sort things out – only to find that the main offender was (a) at well over 6 feet, far too big for me, and (b) a former boyfriend of one of my sisters. I decided promptly that discretion was the better part of valour. Indeed, I can honestly say that I have never in my life hit anyone in anger.) Chief could stand a yard in front of you and, however hard you tried, with both hands, you could not lay a glove on him.

My earliest boxing hero was Tommy Farr. There was, of course, no television in those days, so I could only follow Tommy's deeds in the papers and – on just one occasion, a great thrill, I remember – at a trip to the movies, seeing him fight on the Gaumont

British News. I don't know whether my nanny approved of boxing, but until I learned to read she cheerfully recited newspaper accounts of the great man's fights. Even in those days Henry Longhurst, who occasionally covered boxing as well as golf, was my favourite sports correspondent. I shall never forget the piece in which, having been told that he must give up drinking whisky Longhurst extolled to his sympathetic readers the alternative qualities of Carlsberg Special Brew. 'It has very nearly the same effect,' he said, 'and, after all, is only beer.' He is, or was, quite right – and although he died soon afterwards, I have no reason to believe that Special Brew played any part in his demise.

Jack Petersen was another heavyweight whose name stayed in my memory. The Lonsdale Library book on boxing was a constant companion, and I had been thrilled to find on my arrival at Eton that Lord Knebworth, one of the Lonsdale contributors, had won his weight several times in the school boxing. I think I remember him writing – or perhaps being quoted as saying – that a straight right counter, properly timed and placed, was an almost guaranteed knockout. Those were the days – although I never personally succeeded in putting his Lordship's theory into practice!

Isn't it strange, by the way how completely

karate, judo and other forms of 'unarmed combat' have taken the place of boxing as the preferred method of self-defence among fictional heroes? My own heroes used to be Bulldog Drummond, Jonah Mansel in the Dornford Yates books and/or Leslie Charteris' The Saint. Come to think of it, the last of these – a.k.a. Simon Templar – usually had a somewhat un-English throwing knife strapped to his forearm. But Drummond was strictly a straight left and right hook man – even if his views on trade unions might be regarded as politically incorrect by Mr Blair!

Anyway boxing was up there competing hotly with football as my favourite sport, and one year at Eton I was even Captain of Boxing. I chose the worst possible moment, too – because the Thames burst its banks that Easter and most of the school laughed their way home, leaving me to collect a team from far and wide for our most important fixture. Called The Quadrangle, it involved four schools, much the strongest of which was Bedford. Haileybury, Dulwich and Eton were strictly supporting cast. I am ashamed to say that in my year Eton did not win one of the eight weights, but I did earn a few brownie points for collecting eight boxers – albeit a motley crew.

We had really fancied our chance in the heavyweight division that year, owing to the presence of a massive boy called Talbot Rice. Quite apart from his size, weight and boxing expertise, he had a black belt in judo, and to say that he could take care of himself was an understatement. So imagine our dismay when we heard not only that Talbot Rice had decamped to America, but also that the only feasible substitute was on holiday in Scotland. It didn't help, either, that our heavyweight was drawn against Bedford. The list of suitable and/or willing substitutes, short to begin with, got even shorter when the draw was known. I was searching in vain for inspiration when someone said, 'Why not try James? – he's big enough.'

Well, there was some truth in that. James Morrison, later Lord Margadale, was very big indeed; but – well, he was not exactly fast. Worse still, he seemed to have a cast-iron alibi. His parents had a house on the Isle of Skye, and when my telegram arrived James was out on the hill sneaking up on some unfortunate stag. All things considered, it was a truly heroic act of self-sacrifice to get on a boat, as he did next morning, change on to a sleeper that night, and appear, all thirteen stone ten pounds of him, in the Eton gym on Saturday afternoon.

If there was any justice in the world, this tale would have a happy ending, and perhaps in a way it did. For if the only punch James threw – in the first twenty seconds of the bout – had landed six inches lower, it might well have given the Quadrangle its first verdict by decapitation. Instead, his Bedford opponent was lucky enough to take it squarely on the forehead – and must have had rubber or ivory between his ears.

God knows how the poor fellow felt afterwards – but by that time he had belaboured poor James so effectively that the verdict (on points) was a foregone conclusion. You never saw a braver or more honourable loser, and the whole Eton team, comprehensively beaten in the overall match, could at least look back on the heavyweight bout as one we could be proud of.

My undistinguished career as Captain of Boxing – which looks and sounds so much better than it was in real life – led, I suppose, to an even more undeserved and misleading appointment, as president of the English Amateur Boxing Association. Heaven knows what persuaded me to accept that invitation when I had already (in 1964) become a founding trustee of the Injured Jockeys' Fund. The story of that genuinely worthwhile charity (one of the few things in this book of which I am unreservedly proud) is told in chapter 12.

'Unreservedly' is an ugly word, hard to spell and even harder in many cases to justify. But I have such a bee in my bonnet about head injuries and the need for the best possible protection that some years ago, when the Queen and Ronald Reagan rode together in Windsor Great Park, she in a headscarf and he in a cloth cap, I actually penned a letter to *The Times*. At least arguably, I wrote, these are two of the most valuable skulls and brains in the whole world. How can we allow them to be risked in this unforgivably casual way? And never mind the President – you can, after all, elect another one. How on earth can the Queen, an enthusiastic rider all her life, set such a disgraceful example to her people, and, most of all, to the thousands of riding-mad children who, by doing as she does, may so easily end up damaging their brains – the one part of our body which cannot be healed or regenerated?

As I realised too late, there is surely a definite conflict between encouraging young men (and now, God help us, women) to hit each other about the head for sport, and raising money to look after other young men and women who have injured their heads (or brains) by falling from horses in pursuit of another sport.

Fully aware that the respective merits of the sports involved are very much a matter of opinion, I have taken the view – both prejudiced and personal – that racing has more to recommend it than boxing. We could argue the rights and wrongs of that all night, so let's just take it as read.

Amateur boxing, strictly controlled to prevent avoidable injuries, seems to me to do a measurable and admirable amount of badly needed good in modern Britain – releasing aggression, increasing self-control and encouraging sportsmanship. Compare the standard of behaviour in an amateur ring with that on an amateur or, come to that professional, soccer pitch. I know which spectacle is more likely to make me proud to be British, and it would not be the soccer.

I do not admire the wheeling and dealing which appears to go on behind the scenes in professional boxing. No doubt some of those fat cigar-smoking 'managers' are good at their job and have the interests of 'their' fighters at heart. I just prefer to keep out of their world and enjoy preferably on television, the courage, skill and just occasionally expertise of the men on whose blood and sweat they live.

Thanks to the *Daily Telegraph* (hoodwinked, I'm afraid, by my 'amateur' pretensions!), I have twice been employed to cover a serious professional fight. Both occasions involved the great Muhammad Ali (in his Cassius Clay era), and in both I was merely a stumbling, inept interpreter for another of my heroes, the French former light-heavyweight champion of the world Georges Carpentier.

In the second and by far the less interesting fight, at Earl's Court, Cassius Clay took apart a lumbering, clumsy Brian London in less than three rounds. He stylishly disposed of the rumour that he lacked a knockout punch – but the most memorable sight of the evening was the ringside kiss the young, still handsome, unmarked champion bestowed on Mrs Brian London. 'He did his best,' said Cassius Clay – and that was just about all there was to say.

Carpentier, who thought that Jack Dempsey 'might have made Clay think – but probably not for long', was much more interested by our other venture together, the night at Highbury Stadium when Henry Cooper landed probably the most memorable left hook of his illustrious career.

The tragedy from my point of view was that, with London in its most Arctic mood, Georges Carpentier turned up nearly an hour early dressed for the Riviera. The elegant grey silk suit he wore made you shiver just to look at it, and although he coped heroically with our freezing open-air seats, his teeth were chattering long before Cooper and Clay appeared.

My job was supposedly to ask the great

man questions and 'get him talking' about the fight. But even when 'Enery's 'ammer sent Clay sprawling, a few frozen monosyllabic grunts were all I could get. As for the 'excuse' which delayed the start of the next round, that one of Clay's gloves had come unstitched – well, either my French wasn't good enough or, much more likely Carpentier's professional reaction included some Gallic boxing slang which the author of my phrase book had never dreamed of. Whatever the rights and wrongs, it wasn't Clay's finest hour – and it certainly was, as Henry said afterwards, 'one of the sweetest hooks I ever threw'.

VE day in May 1945 was used as an excuse for all sorts of wild behaviour at Eton. Buses may not actually have been overturned in the High Street, but some were definitely brought to a standstill. Several members of Pop (the Etonian equivalent of prefects) were sent out by their housemasters to restore order – and one of these, a curly-headed little fellow named Brunner, with ideas well above his station, made himself thoroughly objectionable.

That, anyway was the majority opinion of the unruly mob which gathered that evening down by the river on an expanse of grass called Fellows' Eyot. It was my first experience of 'mob violence', and the extraordinary way a crowd can be moved, influenced and led by one or two people. In this case the cry went up 'Let's throw Brunner into the river!' A sort of lynch mob quickly formed and Brunner was rescued only by the intervention of some fellow members of Pop, who, being older and bigger, were able to form a fairly effective bodyguard.

It may be selective amnesia but I do not believe I took any active part on either side. I certainly hope I did not in the next 'pursuit' that night, because this time the only distinguishing mark of the quarry, a Scholar called Vos, was that he looked extremely Jewish. There was always a certain amount of prejudice against Scholars – or 'Tugs' as they were called – simply because they were 'clever', and at least thought to 'swot' or work harder than the rest of us. It may be imagination distorted by old age, but the fact is that I remember sensing that night a definite element of anti-semitism in the cries of 'Let's get Vos!'

They did not get him – for the excellent reason that he was not there. Safe in College, Vos may not even have known until afterwards that there was a 'mob' baying, if not for his blood, at least for his forcible immersion in the River Thames. I only know that my impression, however mistaken, of this not easily forgettable scene was of about a hundred upper-middle-class Etonian youths pursuing an exceptionally Jewish-looking boy with a Jewish-sounding name. It was, to say the least, a peculiar way of celebrating the victory of the free democratic world over the most wicked, unscrupulous and anti-semitic dictatorship that there has ever been.

That episode, regrettable as it was, cannot be considered typical of my time at Eton, and the greatest gift which the college inculcated in me was a true sense of *esprit de corps*, an appreciation of the value and lasting benefit of teamwork. Be it Bloody Bill's dogged insistence to have no one from his house sacked, or his equally dogged determination that his teams should never lose at the Field Game, the knowledge that pulling together serves the best interests of all was the best lesson that Eton taught me.

But I was also learning lessons about the horrors of the world outside Eton.

3

'They wanted a Lord'

Very early in my fourth year at Eton, on 25 September 1945, my father received a letter from 10 Downing Street. It was signed by the Prime Minister, Clement Attlee, and it told of an agreement, reached in London on 8 August, between America, France, Russia and the United Kingdom, 'concerning the trial of the major war criminals of the European Axis'. Mr Attlee went on to say that each of the four signatory nations was to appoint a member of the International Military Tribunal (IMT) set up for this purpose – and asked whether my father would accept the appointment as Britain's representative. He added that Mr Justice Birkett had already agreed to act as his 'alternate'.

There had, in fact, been a surprising confusion over appointments to the tribunal. Birkett was at first under the impression that he had been invited by both the Prime Minister (Attlee) and the Lord Chancellor (Jowett) to be Britain's representative, but the Foreign Office intervened – 'out of snobbery', according to Birkett's diary as 'they wanted a Lord' – and Lord Justice Du Parcq was approached. On the verge of retirement, Du Parcq understandably declined – so my father was invited, with Birkett as his alternate.

When the letter arrived my parents had just got home from the wedding of Jane Pleydell-Bouverie, a great wartime (ATS) friend of my sister Robby It had been a longish drive, and my father went straight to bed without bothering to open his mail. First thing next morning a telephone call came through from the Prime Minister's office: 'Had Lord Justice Lawrence received the letter from Downing Street and what was his reply to the Prime Minister's invitation?'

He opened the letter pretty promptly then – and never told me how long it took him to make up his mind! I do not believe that the thought of refusing ever seriously entered his head. Still, from the first it was all too clear that this would be a task incalculably more complex and testing than anything he had ever attempted – at least in peacetime. No one had ever done anything quite like it before and no one, literally no one, could foresee the outcome. From a personal point of view, the possibilities of failure were pretty horrific – and it was not all that easy to see what might be regarded as a 'success'.

Quite apart from the language problems – which were, in the event, solved with surprising success – there were important differences in the legal systems and procedures of the four prosecuting nations. For instance, of the four who signed the London Charter to set up the IMT, only the United States and Great Britain recognised 'conspiracy' as a criminal offence. It simply did not appear in the legal codes of France and the USSR. In fact, the leading American judge Francis Biddle tended, at first, to support the French view, and at one stage, well before the trial began, there was real danger of a deadlock – with Britain and Russia (who saw that, without a charge of conspiracy some defendants might escape altogether) on one side and France, with a reluctant America, on the other.

Eventually a compromise was reached in which it was agreed that a 'conspiracy' had definitely existed from 5 November 1937, when Hitler, Goering, Von Neurath and the four service chiefs (Keitel, Jodl, Doenitz and Raeder) had made plans for the invasion of Europe – detailed and emphatically aggressive plans in the case of Austria and Czechoslovakia. Like much of the indictment and final judgement, these difficult passages were put into words by Norman Birkett.

Although not close friends, my father and

Birkett got on pretty well and my father greatly admired his alternate's command of the English language. The tribunal made constant use throughout the trial of Birkett's literary flair and exceptional ability as a legal draughtsman. Birkett himself was one of those deeply dissatisfied with the (understandably) primitive version of the English language to which some of the interpreters were reduced. He also got very impatient with the long and often repetitive proceedings. Writing in his diary he criticised, at least by implication, the freedom my father allowed the defending lawyers – going so far, in one passage, as to declare that 'the Trial is now completely out of hand'.

I am not sure how much my father knew or took notice of these criticisms. Presumably as his alternate, Birkett made them known to him in the private sessions, which all four alternates attended and at which they were encouraged to express their views.

I can only say that, after eleven weary months, my father did not look back on Nuremberg with either pleasure or satisfaction. He did not enjoy conducting the trials and, understandably found the need for prolonged concentration (through headsets!) a considerable strain.

But I think I know what his answer to Birkett's criticism would have been. Surely it was better, he would have felt, to give the defence free rein to make all, or nearly all, the points they wanted, rather than be accused of unfair prejudice against one or more defendants. As I often heard my father say a defendant who chooses to represent himself in a British court is always treated as a special case, and given extra latitude over the presentation of his case and the evidence and examination of witnesses.

The defendants at Nuremberg were, of course, professionally represented, by defence counsel of their own choice. But my father felt that the need to ensure a scrupulously fair trial – with justice both done and seen to be done for all time by the rest of the world – made them, in a different but parallel sense, very definite 'special cases'. 'I have always been convinced,' he wrote afterwards, 'that the length of the trial, if not forgotten, may be forgiven, but that any unfairness would never be forgotten or forgiven.'

The indictments (in German translation) were served on the twenty defendants already in Nuremberg gaol by Major Airey Neave on 19 October 1945. Major (later Lieutenant-Colonel) Neave, a distinguished and much decorated officer, fluent in German, had been captured at Dunkirk in 1940 and, after several daring attempts at escape, imprisoned in Colditz. He was one of the few to escape from that almost impregnable prison, and fought with the French Resistance for the rest of the war. A prominent member of the Conservative Party he was later, to the fury and disgust of his many friends and admirers, murdered in Westminster by a cowardly assassin of the IRA.

Airey Neave had been seconded to the tribunal's secretariat with the special assignment of dealing with the defendants and their lawyers, and found it no easy task. Goering, for instance, wanted nothing to do with lawyers: 'They will be no use in this trial.' In fact, he eventually accepted Dr Otto Stahmer, a judge from Kiel – and later (before committing suicide) expressed his satisfaction with the fairness with which the tribunal was conducted. As was pointed out by Robert H. Jackson, who had stepped down from the US Supreme Court to lead the American prosecution, Goering's treatment was infinitely more scrupulous than anything his opponents in Nazi Germany could have expected.

As for Julius Streicher, after reading Neave's list of lawyers he said: 'They all sound like Jews to me. I want an anti-semitic lawyer.' In fact, like seven of the other defendants, he was, in the end, represented by a former member of the Nazi Party! Streicher and Kaltenbrunner were two defendants about whom – partly I suspect, on account of their repulsive and villainous appearance you never heard a word of justification or excuse.

The quickest – and probably the wisest – choice of counsel was made by Doenitz. 'I want Otto Kranzbuehrle,' he said at once, naming a naval judge advocate with the rank of captain. Kranzbuehrle turned out to be one of the stars of the defence team, and his representation of Doenitz led to an even more successful postwar career at the German Bar.

As Birkett recorded in his diary the cross-examination of Goering was eagerly awaited throughout the first half of the trial. Hitler's second-in-command, who had been taken off both drink and drugs since his arrest, had visibly lost several stone in weight – but none of his courage or shrewdness. Goering had an agile mind and, almost always, a wide mastery of the facts about which he was being questioned.

At 12.15 in the afternoon of 18 March, Mr Justice Jackson, who had opened the trial with an eloquent, comprehensive and widely admired survey of the US section of the prosecution case, rose to begin his long-awaited cross-examination. General confidence was felt now in his ability to 'win' the most crucial examination of the whole trial. Alas, as Birkett wrote in his diary, 'The cross-examination had not proceeded more than ten minutes before it was seen that he [Goering] was the complete master of Mr Justice Jackson.'

Suave, shrewd, adroit and resourceful, Goering quickly saw the elements of any situation and, as his confidence grew, his mastery became more apparent. Jackson, as Birkett wrote, 'had never learnt the first principles of a successful cross-examination as it is understood in British Courts'. In my slightly prejudiced opinion, however, Birkett did himself no credit when he went on to write: 'The Trial from now on is really outside the control of the Tribunal, and in the long months ahead its prestige will steadily diminish.' It was, in the fullest sense, absurd to suggest that the 'prestige' of Nuremberg would stand or fall by Jackson's success or failure as a cross-examiner.

The trials took place in the American zone of Germany and it was inevitable that the organisation should have an American flavour. It was partly for this reason that Biddle voluntarily – though not, I think, willingly – stepped back when the question of who would be the president of the tribunal was being decided. With him, Jackson and Birkett all suffering some degree of jealousy or at least offended pride, I suspect that my father had to tread a narrow and delicate path around the sensibilities and disappointment of his colleagues. According to (admittedly unreliable) backstage gossip, Jackson had definite ambitions to run for President of the United States. If so, they probably never recovered from his comparative failure with Goering.

When the leader of the British prosecution, David Maxwell-Fyfe – later, as Lord Chancellor, Lord Kilmuir – took over from Jackson, the improvement in technique was noticeable. Maxwell-Fyfe chose to concentrate, first, on the shooting of RAF officers who had escaped from Stalag Luft 111. He did not, in fact, succeed in proving Goering's actual involvement in the killings, but he did catch him out in several falsehoods and/or exaggerations. An attempt by the defence to establish that Goering had, at the time of the escape, been on leave 'in the Nuremberg area' was, for instance, neutralised when it was shown that he had been in easy and constant telephone contact with his own office and adjutants.

From this time on it seems that Maxwell-Fyfe rather than Jackson was accepted and generally regarded as the leading figure of the prosecution, and Jackson's inadequate performance with Goering was a blow from which the American only gradually recovered. (Goering himself, I suspect, looked back with some satisfaction at his clash with Jackson and, although Maxwell-Fyfe made far better use of the overwhelming case against him, Hitler's second-in-command, who flew a fighter in Richthofen's famous First World War squadron, probably looked back on Nuremberg with more 'pride' than any of his fellow prisoners.)

I was (quite) reliably informed that in the Anglo-American press compound the British prosecution team – all barristers used to steady and varied courtroom appearances at home – were from then on generally rated superior to their US counterparts.

Maxwell-Fyfe's success, even if only partial, was followed by the turn of the Russian prosecutor Rudenko, and he too succeeded, at least in establishing Goering's responsibility as head of the four-year plan, for parts of the forced labour programme. These admissions were strong evidence of his guilt under counts three and four (war crimes and crimes against humanity).

The trial of Goering took twelve days – raising the grave danger that the examination of the remaining defendants might, if allowed the same scope, take another ten months. However, an announcement was made on 22 March 1946 to the effect that no other defendant would be allowed to cover the same ground a second time. In fact, the remaining twenty required an average of about four days each – a total of seventy-eight days, which had to be followed, of course, by the trial of the 'organisations' and the final speeches. This meant, as it turned out, that proceedings lasted to the autumn of 1946.

I was lucky enough to be able to spend two weeks of my summer holidays in Nuremberg in 1946, and saw enough to appreciate the strain under which my father and his colleagues on the bench – indeed, all those regularly employed in the courtroom – had to work.

The complicated system of simultaneous interpretation into four separate languages must have put great strain on the interpreters, but they – or most of them – achieved an amazingly high standard. Of course, the need to wear headphones throughout – everyone had a numbered dial, with which to select the language you needed – greatly increased the danger of falling asleep. Headphones are notoriously soporific and my mother, who went over soon after the beginning of the trial and stayed until the end, enlisted the aid of a cooperative Snowdrop (member of the US Military Police, so called on account of their snow-white helmets) to keep an eye on my father in case he should drop off! I do not know what she meant the gallant sergeant to do if he did – but there is no record of his assistance being needed.

Anyone attending court over a period became used to the different interpreters – who came in all shapes, sizes, styles and levels of ability Perhaps the best known while I was there was a statuesque and splendidly eloquent German-into-English brunette known, on account of her various *coiffures*, as 'The Passionate Haystack'.

One junior member of the British prosecution team started an ante-post 'book' on her choice of hairstyle. 'Haystack' was generally a 3–1 favourite, despite the fact that it must have taken at least ten minutes to construct, with 'Veronica Lake' a 4–1 shot. Ingrid Bergman (in her bubblecut *For Whom the Bell Tolls* style) was a 20–1 outsider – but only because to imitate the great Swedish star (my own long-worshipped favourite) the lady would have needed to cut all the rest of her hair off!

The Americans were responsible for security at the trial and all arrangements regarding logistics and supplies. This, to a sixteen-year-old Briton with four years of rationing behind him, meant the unheard-of luxury of American PX rations. Just the weekly chocolate allowance – two enormous Hershey Bars – was a real joy and 200 cigarettes, though no use to me personally, would have been worth a small fortune on the black market. Unfortunately by the time

I got there my father had been appointed president of the tribunal, and it was pointed out to me in no uncertain fashion that the president's son must, in every respect, keep his nose not so much clean as spotless.

Not all the delegations maintained quite that high standard of behaviour. One high-spirited American general was so captivated by the curve of my mother's bottom that, possibly under the influence of vodka, bourbon or both, he gave it a large but friendly pinch. Not quite the sort of treatment expected by a controller in the ATS – but, in the interests of diplomatic relations, my mother ignored the gesture. On another occasion, at a party given by the Russian prosecution team, there were no fewer than twenty-five toasts, and my mother's *sang froid* was put through an even more searching test.

The guest of honour that night was Alexei Vyshinsky, then the Soviet Deputy Foreign Minister and delegate to the United Nations. To most of us, of course, he was first and foremost an ominous figure with blood up to his armpits – a reputation earned as chief prosecutor in the infamous purge trials of 1936–8, which had resulted in the execution of literally thousands of military and political officials who had, in one way or another, earned the dislike or mistrust of Stalin.

One of the toasts, proposed by Vyshinsky, was: 'To the defendants. May their paths lead straight from the courthouse to the grave.' Vyshinsky drained his glass before the translation was completed, as did almost everyone in the room – including, to his horror, the American alternate Judge Parker. When he learned the toast which he had drunk, this kind and conscientious Southerner was understandably dismayed. Until calmed down and restrained by Francis Biddle, he was on the point of upbraiding Vyshinsky in no uncertain manner.

Nor was Vyshinsky finished. As the coffee (and still more vodka) went round, he stood up, drained his glass yet again – and proposed, through an interpreter, of course, my mother's health. She, poor thing, had to sit through an avalanche of flowery (interpreted) compliments – including, I remember, one in which the cornflowers of the Ukraine were compared unfavourably with the blue of her eyes! Luckily she learned only later of her 'admirer's' sanguinary past.

The trial had opened on 20 November 1945 in the main courtroom of the Bavarian Central Courts of Justice – the same courtroom where, just over a year before, the leading conspirators in an unsuccessful bomb plot on Hitler's life had been tried.

The presiding judge then, we were told, had been a ranting tyrant who would doubtless have scorned the courtesies which were to mark the proceedings of both bench and counsel in the International Military Tribunal.

Wives were not encouraged to attend in the early stages, but the French contingent soon overcame that, and by the time of my visit my mother had taken charge of the British 'Judge's Lodgings' – a neat red-brick house on the outskirts of Nuremberg. Much of the town had been comprehensively bombed, but part of the old town was left comparatively intact – including an area around the courthouse.

Transport was a hazardous affair in postwar Bavaria, with a motley collection of huge American lorries surrounded by a swarm of jeeps – not all of them driven with excessive care and attention. For one short but exhilarating spell, my father was lent a magnificent six-wheeled Mercedes. Said to have been used by the late Heinrich Himmler, it had bullet-proof windows, armour-plated coachwork and an enormously powerful engine designed to pull its huge weight at high speed.

Among its other accoutrements, the car was equipped with a strident ear-piercing siren, which, if you switched it on a mile or so before entering a village, guaranteed a pedestrian-free passage at whatever m.p.h. you chose. I'm ashamed to say that I did persuade our (English) Military Police driver to use it once or twice. He did so – reluctantly – and, sure enough, there was not a soul to be seen as we drove through.

One scorching September day we set off – in two cars, I think – for Berchtesgaden, intent on visiting the Eagle's Nest, Hitler's famous mountain hideaway. Sandy Sanderson, one of my father's ADCs who had been a prisoner of war, and I were in a jeep, following my parents in the Mercedes. Some way from the top of the mountain, we had been told, Goering had built himself a house, and equipped it with a swimming pool. To us, hot and sweaty by the time we found it, it was an irresistible temptation – crystal blue in the blazing sun. Without a second thought, we stripped off what little clothes we had, and plunged in. If Goering had been watching it would have warmed his heart – and that would have been the only warm thing in the vicinity! We were, it turned out, several thousand feet up – and altitude means cold as opposed to warmth. Goering's swimming pool – unheated owing, no doubt, to its owner's absence – was a couple of degrees above freezing. Luckily neither Sandy nor I had (at that time anyway) a weak heart. Otherwise, Hitler's second in command – who in any case cheated the hangman at Nuremberg – might have carved a couple more notches on his already overcrowded totem pole.

The overriding issue about the Nuremberg trial, of course, is how far it provided a lesson which we should be learning today about the trying of war criminals. In 1947, in his presidential address to the Holdsworth Club, the legal society of the University of Birmingham, my father declared:

The fundamental purpose of the trial at Nuremberg was not only the punishment of those who were guilty but the establishment of the supremacy of International Law over National Law, and the proof of the actual facts in order to bring home to the German people and to the peoples of the world, the depths of infamy to which the pursuit of total warfare had brought Germany.

And later in the speech he posed the big question:

Unless in some way war can be prevented and International Law takes its place, what future is there for the world? The most important question of International Law raised by the Nuremberg trial was whether it was an international crime to plan and make an aggressive war...

I much regret to say that were he able to observe the current state of international justice, he could not feel that the lesson of Nuremberg had been truly learned. There is no international court strong enough to pose a deterrent against aggressive war, and the only country capable of bringing such a court about is the USA, which has apparently set its mind against the idea.

The Nuremberg trials continue to reverberate in my life.

My mother compiled, with wondrous care and dedication, beautifully bound albums – 'scrapbooks' is far too inadequate a word – of my father's time in Nuremberg: newspaper cuttings and other documents, photographs, and my father's weekly letters home, in which he detailed all that had been going on, small events as well as large.

These albums – four in number – are perhaps my most treasured possessions, and in 2000 they were featured in the BBC television programme *Antiques Roadshow*. They proved a highly popular item in the programme, and were voted among the items the viewers most wanted to see again – so I duly obliged. I do hope my mother was looking down, proud of her splendid industry and imagination.

After these two broadcasts it was quite

extraordinary how many listeners wrote in to say how much they had enjoyed them. It just shows what lasting interest there is in Nuremberg, the International Military Tribunal and the trials.

4

'Read something else while at Oxford'

After five years at Eton (or any comparably upmarket academy) you are very apt to consider yourself the answer to every mother's prayer – or, more to the point, every daughter's. But the abrupt transformation from top hat and tails on a sunlit Fourth of June to itchy new battledress on a windswept Catterick parade ground is definitely a character-forming experience. A public school, you suddenly discover, is not, after all, the be-all and end-all of your education.

Catterick was the second stop of my round of National Service, upon which I embarked after leaving Eton in 1947. First stop had been the Royal Sussex Regiment, based at Chichester in Sussex, where I signed up along with my Eton friend Jeremy Smith. Carrying our little suitcases, we turned up at the main gate of the barracks, where we were greeted by a huge and fearsome sergeant major.

'WHAAAAAAAAAAAAAAT'S YOUR NIME?' he bellowed at me.

'Lawrence!' I cheerily replied.

'LAWRENCE WHAT?'

'Lawrence, Sergeant!'

'LAWRENCE – THREE QUARTERS OF YOU TRICKLED DOWN YOUR MOTHER'S LEG!' – which to this day remains the rudest thing ever said to me.

After two or three weeks of (very) basic training I was sent up to Yorkshire to join the Royal Armoured Corps at Catterick, a seriously bloody place where for the first time in my life I was to find out what hard work really was.

You can say what you like about conscription, and no doubt the spin doctors are right and it *would* now be electoral suicide to put National Service in your election manifesto, yet the fact remains that two years in khaki did me far more good than harm – even if it could be a painful experience at the time.

The culture shock for a young toff like me of being thrown into the social melting pot of a barrack full of young soldiers from all backgrounds was considerable – though I'm relieved to report that I narrowly managed to avert the humiliation visited upon a fellow recruit who was fresh out of Harrow. On the first night in the long barrack room – twenty beds on each side – I was about to unpack the beautiful silk pyjamas which my mother had bought me when my neighbour, a tough-as-teak Scot who, it later turned out, was the son of a Glasgow bookmaker, hissed at me under his breath: 'Hide them – or at least make out they're old rags for polishing!' I took the first option and rammed them back into my kitbag, but my Harrovian comrade blithely carried on unpacking his own silken night attire, provoking hoots of derision from the rest of the barrack and lumbering himself with the name 'Pyjama Percy' for the rest of his time at the camp.

I learned a great deal at Catterick – such as blancoing a webbing-belt, polishing buckles, getting that real deep, 'bullshit' shine on the toecaps of your boots, and making your bed with blanket and sheets precisely and geometrically arranged. I also learned almost all I know about taking care of myself. To a captain of the Eton boxing team, you might, I suppose, think that the noble art of self-defence would come as second nature – but in fact that was far from the case, and I have to thank my Glaswegian neighbour Jock for enlarging my education. The corps bully (whose name I have mercifully erased from my memory) spent our first few days at Catterick systematically working his way down the barrack room, terrorising the raw recruits by threatening to beat them up unless they gave in to his demands that they clean his kit – and promptly delivering on that threat should any be foolhardy or reckless enough to offer resistance.

I had not put my Glaswegian friend down as a wimp, and when this monster hurled his kit on to Jock's bed and demanded 'Blanco that, you little f**ker!' I was amazed by the reaction. Jock gave a highly lifelike imitation of a man petrified with fear, seeming to shrink as he edged closer towards the bully. 'What do you want me to do, eh? How do I do that?' he whined and cringed, and in a few moments was standing pathetically right under the bully's nose – then suddenly delivered the most effective piece of violence I have ever seen, standing up straight and 'nutting' his tormentor, spreading his nose across his face like jam.

The terror of the barrack room crumpled like a rag doll and was soon carted off to hospital, where he spent the next two weeks coming to terms with his new look – and, I hope, reflecting on how he came to get his comeuppance. I was not able to discover whether the experience left him a man changed in the mind as well as the visage, as we never saw him again.

Jock was not disciplined for his admirable part in administering this lesson, as – you won't be surprised to hear – there were no witnesses to what happened.

After three months at Catterick came a

spell at OCTU – the Mons Officer Cadet Training Unit – at Aldershot, before being given a commission as second lieutenant with the 9th Queen's Royal Lancers at Glencorse Camp, near Edinburgh.

The 9th Lancers holds a proud place of honour in Grand National history: David Campbell won the great race in 1896 on The Soarer, and shortly before the Second World War two former Lancers landed the Aintree race in consecutive years on Reynoldstown – Frank Furlong in 1935 and his brother officer Fulke Walwyn in 1936.

Shortly after I joined, it was decreed that any officer so minded could spend a fortnight at Colonel Joe Dudgeon's legendary riding academy in Dublin. I leaped at the chance, thereby subjecting myself to formal riding tuition for the first and only time in my life. We were made to ride round and round the ring (and over jumps) without stirrups, all the time having inculcated into us the correct position of the hands and feet. Nor did all this tuition come from human experts. I remember one old horse who did everything you asked him, so long as you asked him properly; give the wrong signals, however, and the horse simply ignored you and carried straight on. In his younger days this wonderful animal had been ridden by Joe Dudgeon himself in a regimental trick ride: without saddle or bridle, and controlled only by his rider's legs, the horse jumped a sword planted blade upwards in the ground.

Back in Scotland, it was not only horses who captured my attention. Jean Busher, daughter of the colonel at the neighbouring Royal Scots barracks, was an exceptionally attractive young lady given to taking her dog for a walk at certain times of the day, and if forewarned I would arrange to be somewhere in the vicinity at the appropriate time so that I could accidentally encounter her. I came to an arrangement with the sergeant major in our guardroom that he would (for a suitable consideration) alert me when she and her dog emerged for their walk; but unbeknown to me I had a rival who overheard me making this arrangement and who got the run up the rails by bribing the sergeant major more handsomely!

In October 1949 I went up to New College, Oxford – my father's old college – to read PPE (Philosophy, Politics and Economics). It was still expected – if not very often discussed – that I would follow the family tradition and enter the legal profession, and my father suggested to me, 'If you are going to do law all your life, it is slightly less boring if you read something else while at Oxford.' Little did he (or indeed I) know...

While I can claim to have shown very little

academic distinction at England's oldest university, I enjoyed my time there enormously, and made many lasting friendships. Several fellow undergraduates I knew already from Eton – Gay Kindersley, Jeremy Smith, Paul Fletcher, Patrick Lindsay, John Julius Cooper and Teddy Hall among them.

John Julius, with whom I shared a house at 96 Holywell Street under the watchful eye of our landlady Mrs Hall, has remained a lifelong friend. One term he suddenly announced that we should spend a few days in Paris. His father Duff Cooper – Viscount Norwich – had been Ambassador there, and the French government had made available to him a cottage deep in the woods near the great racing town of Chantilly. We travelled across to stay with his parents in the cottage (though that word does scant justice to the scale of the place) and I spent a memorable morning at Les Aigles, watching the horses – Arab-like in their quality with long flowing manes and tails and coats like marble – at their morning exercise.

The evening was hardly less memorable, with John Julius's mother, the legendary beauty Lady Diana Cooper, treating us after dinner to a spirited rendition of Rudyard Kipling's 'Ballad of *The Mary Gloucester*'.

(It was on a different Paris trip, I think, that an evening in a night club of dubious propriety led to an extraordinarily uncomfortable sexual experience with a tart. I was well aware of the likely consequence of such an ill-judged liaison, and the expectation, for days afterwards, that every pee would hurt made the whole episode even more uncomfortable. Curiously that expected after-effect never took place.)

Diana Cooper once lent me her huge and magnificent Chrysler to drive to Liverpool for the Grand National, and somewhere in Cheshire I picked up a rather scruffy-looking hitch-hiker. He clearly did not feel comfortable with the speed at which I was driving around the winding roads (this was decades before the M6), and eventually made some pretext to be let out of the car. I slowed to a halt, and as he walked away noticed to my dismay that the back of his trousers was soaked in what only could be urine – then discovered to my considerably greater dismay that there was a similar dark patch on the passenger seat of Lady Diana's splendid Chrysler...

That car came to an unfortunate end, rolling into the harbour at Cannes after its owner had inadvertently left the handbrake off.

Teddy Hall's house at 149 Banbury Road was the scene of many memorable parties, including one to which he invited the whole female cast of *Annie Get Your Gun*, that wonderful musical which had captivated him completely. We also had a club called the Boojums, which originally was confined to members of New College but was later opened to outsiders after – on my instigation – we invited Prince Nicholas of Yugoslavia, an extraordinary storyteller whose particular *tour de force* 'Rotten for Daphne' has found its way into many an Oaksey after-dinner speech. In the unlikely event that you haven't heard it, here's a potted version, told in the person of a diplomat:

Towards the end of the war – and soon after I had married Daphne – the Diplomatic Service posted me to the South Seas. It was a terribly long voyage, and our ship was torpedoed.

Rotten for Daphne! – and rotten for me as well.

We had to take to the lifeboats, and after two days cast adrift ran out of water.

Rotten for Daphne! – and rotten for me too, actually.

Then we were cast up on to a desert island. While we were stretched out exhausted on the beach a horde of fuzzy-wuzzies suddenly appeared out of the jungle and came charging down upon us, grabbed us and tied us, faces inward, to two trees.

Rotten for Daphne! – and rotten for me too, actually.

I hardly dare to tell you this, but the fact

of the matter is that then this massive high priest – head-dress, bone through his nose, flowing robes, the lot! – came clattering down out of the jungle and buggered us both.

Rotten for Daphne! – but not so bad for me, as I'm an Old Etonian.

The first night we invited Prince Nicholas he was scrambling around under the table and put his hand on a broken glass. Out gushed blood – sadly red, though it should of course have been blue – so we bundled him into Teddy's huge Humber Hawk and scorched off to the Radcliffe Infirmary with the prince's hand dangling out of the window and spurting blood all over the road. On arrival at the hospital we rushed into Casualty, where the tiny Sister asked Prince Nicholas his name.

'Nicholas.'

'No, your surname.'

'Yugoslavia.'

He was put on a trolley and wheeled off.

Oxford saw a rapid increase in my experience of driving.

When with the 9th Lancers I had been in control of the scout car troop, which involved driving all over the country – including many memorable trips in these lightly armoured vehicles into the Highlands, and an even more memorable one when we drove six of them through the Mersey Tunnel, or rather, drove six scout cars *into* the Mersey Tunnel, then used five of them to push out one which had chosen that inconvenient spot to break down.

At Oxford, my first regular early morning route was the road to Bicester, ten miles long and more or less dead straight. At night, or in the very early morning, in a healthy car with no speed cops about, you could, if necessary, break ten minutes. In Gay's geriatric Wolsey Hornet or John Julius's 1922 Bean, the journey took at least three-quarters of an hour – often, in case of punctures and/or start-up failures, a very great deal longer.

I mention these two venerable conveyances because, unable to afford a car of my own at the time, they were the ones I was most often allowed to borrow. I once left the Bean's engine running in Cirencester Market Place while I went off to shop, an incident so earth-shattering in what must have been a very quiet week for news that it found its way into the local paper:

'OLD CROCK' BAFFLED THE CONSTABLE
Driver fined at Cirencester

The car – you could just about call it that –

stood in the market square at Cirencester, a proud, vintage example of British engineering as it used to be. It was made in 1922.

It was a cold day just before Christmas, yet the car's engine was ticking over quite firmly and smoothly despite its years.

But that was just the trouble. It shouldn't have been ticking over so demurely. There was no one in it.

PC Johnson eyed it speculatively and approached it with a certain amount of apprehension. How did one stop the engine? He looked and studied hard, but it was no use. He was unable to turn it off.

Shortly afterwards the owner arrived. 'How about switching the engine off?', said PC Johnson. 'It's an offence to leave it unattended.'

The owner looked slightly abashed. 'I can't switch the engine off. I shall never get it started again,' he said.

The facts were reported, and so it was that the owner, John Lawrence, of Hill Farm, Oaksey was summoned for leaving the engine running.

Mr W.J. Croome, chairman of the Cirencester Magistrates' Court, smiled when he heard PC Johnson's evidence. 'The position was that you could not stop it and he could not start it, I take it?' he queried.

'Yes, Sir,' said PC Johnson.

In a letter to the court, Lawrence said he

did not realise it was an offence to leave the engine running, and added, 'I won't do it again.'

Lawrence was fined £2. 'It is not for the Justices to say when a car is thirty years old, whether or not it should be on the road,' said Mr Croome. 'But if they are on the road and the law is broken we must do something about it.'

In Gay's Wolsey we had many draughty drives to Cecil Bonner's stables in Bicester – or if late (we often were) straight on, post haste to the 'gallops' round Bicester Aerodrome. For while at Oxford I had for the first time started to indulge my ambition to ride in races. My first ride came in April 1950 on my sister's hunter Paula at the VWH point-to-point at Siddington, not far from Cirencester. We pulled up after six fences. Later that month Paula and I came third (of eight runners) in the lightweight race at the Bar point-to-point.

Riding out regularly at Bicester for Cecil Bonner – a wonderfully wise, slow-speaking countryman who never gave us novice race-riders a rocket unless it was absolutely necessary! – was an important part of keeping in trim for these occasional forays in the point-to-point field. We schooled horses over jumps near Cecil's yard, and if we needed a longer gallop the aerodrome was not much used by the RAF.

Like another of my riding mentors Bob Turnell, Cecil – though by then well advanced in age – taught by example and never went in much for talking. But his horses always looked bursting with health, and if he said one was fit that was all you needed to know.

The Bonner family reigned supreme over the hunting, pointing and horsy worlds of the Bicester area. Harry Cecil's slightly upmarket brother, bought many of Lord Bicester's famous chasers – giants like Roimond, Finnure and Silver Fame. But for riding-mad undergraduates like Gay and myself, Cecil's yard in the middle of the town, presided over by an uncommunicative head lad called Reg, was an equestrian Mecca, infinitely more attractive – and informative – than the unintelligible lectures on PPE for which our indulgent parents were forking out with such ill-advised generosity.

Except for some round-the-field tuition from my mother – who had driven an ambulance in France in 1917–18 and did not believe in driving schools – my motoring education began in the army. Certainly the only 'test' I ever took was in a Daimler scout car – in the middle of a field with nothing coming the other way. There were no traffic signals either – which, come to think of it, was not much of a qualification for the twenty years I was to spend as a Justice of the Peace on the Malmesbury Bench, dispensing wisdom (and penalties) to erring motorists. Speed kills and, without much doubt, I was lucky to live long enough even to have a driving licence, let alone to tell other people how to drive.

My friend Jeremy Smith had the great good fortune to be given his own car – a gleaming, infinitely enviable, cream-coloured open MG – and I shall never forget collecting it from one of those amazingly grand automobile emporia in Berkeley Square (Jack Barclay's, I think). Jeremy's father – who narrowly missed and, by the sound of the citation, should certainly have won a VC in the First World War – had been a 9th Lancer and, as a couple of adolescent conscripts, we followed nervously in his footsteps. Eric Smith was also on the boards of Rolls-Royce, the National Provincial Bank and several other far from impoverished City companies. So Jeremy's credit rating was pretty unimpeachable. As we soon learnt, however, that did not release him from the laws of gravity friction – and speed.

I have a fairly precise idea of how fast we were travelling when disaster struck that night in 1952 on the road between Burford and Bibury – because this, I regret to say was a race: between Jeremy's brand new pride and joy and Paul Fletcher's equally vaunted and beloved HRG. We had been invited to a party near Bibury given by the Henriques family – Robert, now dead, wrote successful novels and one of his sons, Michael, is a member of the Jockey Club and director of Cheltenham Racecourse – and *en route* had dined at the Bay Tree, a slightly deceptive restaurant in Burford. I say 'deceptive' because the Bay Tree was staffed in those days by ex-debs who, though at first glance not shy of flaunting their undoubted attractions, seemed – unless you were Gary Cooper – to be equipped with such efficient mental chastity belts that even the briefest eye contact meant instant rejection. (Hell, you probably notice, hath no fury like an undersized, prematurely balding 23-year-old undergraduate scorned not once but several times.)

Be that as it may leaving the Bay Tree that night we knew, from past experience, that the HRG's top speed was eighty miles per hour. So when Jeremy – who, thank God, was driving on this occasion – began to overtake on the slightly downhill bends before Aldsworth, our MG must have been approaching eighty-five.

It may not seem much nowadays – but have you tried it backwards? For that was what came next. Like the memory of most racing falls, it is all a bit jumbled – but my clear impression is that our right front wheel touched an unfriendly bit of the right-hand verge. So unfriendly that it turned us round – and that is why I claim to know how it feels to go down a road backwards at eighty-five miles per hour.

It didn't last long – and as for what happened when the poor little maltreated car finally hit the other verge and turned over, here my memory becomes even more jumbled. Very much like a racing fall – except that you seemed to stay rather longer in mid-air. Perhaps we did: the road is quite wide at that point (I cross my fingers every time I pass it now), and both Jeremy and I negotiated it airborne. We cleared several yards of tarmac to land in providentially long grass on the other side.

The car (my memory is also suspect here) seems to me to have rolled down the road like a football – and for me, still believing Jeremy was in it, that was not the best moment of the night. I honestly cannot remember at all what I said when, seconds later, he picked himself out of some more grass three yards away. 'Mr Smith, I presume?' would have been what my children call 'cool' – but I'm afraid a few carefully chosen obscenities are probably nearer the truth.

A sore ankle was Jeremy's only 'injury', and mine was a two-inch tear in the back of my dinner jacket. 'Luck' often seems one of the most inadequate words in the language – but whatever you choose to call it, we had more than our fair share that night.

For Paul Fletcher and his companion, it must have been (though not in any way their fault) a fairly hair-raising spectacle. (I once drove on a rally with Paul in that same HRG – and we were going really well when, after twenty-four hours more or less non-stop, we got stuck in a sand dune above Llandudno! I *was* driving that time – but he took it wonderfully well.)

My only other memory of that dreadful evening comes from the lavatory – of which, not altogether surprisingly I found myself in urgent need on arrival at the Henriques house. All thought of my churning insides was banished by a newspaper cutting from the *Daily Mirror*, framed and hung on the opposite wall. I have never forgotten its contents:

Private Entwhistle of the REME was admitted to Aldershot Military Hospital on Friday evening, having inadvertently become entangled with the zip fastener of his battledress trousers. After a minor operation Private Entwhistle was disentangled and released. His condition is described as 'comfortable' and he hopes to be discharged next week.

Although delighted for the private's sake, I took this as a timely reminder that there are worse things in life than falling out of cars...

The incident in Jeremy's MG was much my most violent accident – so far, that is. (I am incurably superstitious, so touch all available wood when making rash statements like that. I not only say 'Good morning' to every magpie I see, but also, to singletons, add politely: 'How's your wife?' One magpie, you'll remember, is for sorrow, and two for joy – hence the wife. I do not personally bother to carry on beyond 'three for a girl and four for a boy'. But I don't walk under ladders if I can help it, and any thirteenth arrival at our table is politely asked to sit elsewhere.) But I had a slower and much less violent – if even more idiotic – driving disaster earlier that very same year, this time (which made it even more traumatic) in my mother's faithful and much-loved Hillman Minx, which I had borrowed. For an eighteen-month spell in the 1940s, during her time as a controller in the ATS, she had to drive herself weekly quite often twice weekly back and forth across Salisbury Plain, often in the blackout. Not at all surprisingly she loved that little car.

On a week's leave from my spell as a conscript in the 9th Lancers, I was invited to a party at Tetbury and for some reason (almost certainly to impress a girl I was pursuing without success) decided to pull out all the sartorial stops. 'Blues', the regiment's formal evening dress uniform, comprised a bum-freezer jacket, tight trousers with a yellow stripe down either leg and, if you really wanted to push the boat out, ornamental spurs!

It was drizzling when we arrived for dinner but well before we started dancing it had (unknown to me) begun to freeze. The result, by the time of the last dance around 2 a.m., was that the house was surrounded by an oversized skating rink. But we did not take much notice of that. Who cared? The stars were bright, the moon was out and although nothing like what I would in those days have called 'drunk', I very much doubt if I would have passed a breathalyser test. We just did not think about such things in 1952.

The car park was in a field, and somehow I got out of that all right. There seemed to be no snow visible on the road – so, forgetting that you cannot see black ice, I set off gaily down a gradual hill towards the first slight bend. What I did not realise was that, on ice, 'gradual' and 'slight' are irrelevant features. Whether I applied the brakes or turned the steering wheel, it made not the slightest difference. The Hillman's reaction was the same. It simply went straight on. A (luckily) insignificant stone wall made not much difference either – but the ploughed field it guarded was better than a set of disc brakes. No wonder, because recently thawed and frozen plough is not exactly the Rowley Mile. After two steps I was glad I hadn't worn the spurs; after four I was up to my knees; and from there to the road I was really struggling. Nothing could be worse than this, I thought – and was speedily proved wrong. I should have remembered the skating rink. No doubt it would have been possible to walk the two hundred yards of frozen tarmac back to the house – but it was easier, I found, to crawl along the frozen verge. Not too good for the overalls. Then again, I never much liked those yellow stripes. It was not much consolation, as I crawled, to see three ditched cars which had not even got as far as I did.

Was this, I wonder, the first time a so-called officer wearing the formal evening garb of the 9th Queen's Royal Lancers has beaten such an ignominious retreat? Probably not. I just hope my predecessors, if any were not quite as muddy bedraggled and sorry for themselves as I was.

Having begged a shamefaced lift home, I

still faced the prospect of waking my mother next morning with the news that her beloved Hillman Minx was up to its axles in a ploughed field two miles west of Tetbury She took it like a heroine. No wonder my sisters say I am spoilt rotten.

Driving offences, of course, occupy a good deal of the average magistrate's time and attention, but being a magistrate does not, as far as my experience (many years after Oxford) goes, get you any special treatment from the police. It just makes it more embarrassing when you are caught. Feeling that a drink-driving conviction would mean immediate and automatic resignation from the bench, I tried to be correspondingly careful – and still had one desperately narrow escape.

I was speaking at a dinner the night before a team chase held on behalf of the Injured Jockeys' Fund, and had the bad luck to come last of four speakers. None of the others exactly set Becher's Brook on fire – and they also banged on a bit too long. So I did not altogether blame my neighbour when, pouring a nearly full tumbler of port, he pushed it across with the cheering words, 'For God's sake get this down. It might make you a bit less boring than that lot...'

It had been a long night – and I came desperately close to taking his advice. What harm, after all, could it do? My first wife,

Tory deserves all, or very nearly all, the credit. 'Don't expect me to drive,' she said firmly: 'I'd have no chance of passing any test. You promised to drive us home – and anyway what about the team event?' That did it. For in the big event the next day Tory and her wonderful little mare Blue Bonito were, in every sense, the leaders of our team, The Tory Party. Tuscan Prince and I were strictly backers-up and so were Ernie Fenwick and Edward Cazalet.

The reason I only give Tory a 'share' of credit for stiffening my resistance to that drink is that when the next day came, in fact, she and Bonito made one of their rare mistakes. At about halfway there was one of those zig-zag fences. You had to jump it four times – turning right, and left, and then the same again. Tory jumped the first all right – but then stormed on, missing the next two fences. You've never heard the noise that Ernie, Edward and I made. Talk about waking the dead: graveyards for miles around must have been exploding. 'What on earth did you think all the shouting was?' we asked Tory afterwards. Her answer was brief and rather magnificent. 'Applause,' she said, 'I thought it was just applause.'

A bit later the previous night, I *had* been applauding her – and thanking my lucky stars. Because, as we drove out of Stow-on-the-Wold, a blue light flashed ominously behind us. I had never been breathalysed before, but I know the procedure now.

'Have you been drinking, sir?'

'Yes, just a bit.'

'Would you please blow into this?'

Long pause – which would have been a whole lot longer if I had drunk that port...

Oxford also introduced me to the great thrill of flying. I had always wanted to learn to fly and was lucky enough to do so (after a fashion) with a marvellous organisation named the University Air Squadron. By that time, having done my National Service, I was already a second lieutenant – if not, on account of age, an actual lieutenant – in the 9th Lancers. Now, believe it or not, I was suddenly a pilot officer, getting *paid* to do something I would otherwise have been quite willing to pay through the nose for.

I first got off the ground at Kidlington, not far from Oxford, in a Tiger Moth, a pre-war biplane which looked a bit Heath Robinson to me but was, according to its admirers, 'as safe as a house'. The only reason I felt even as safe as a semi-detached was the presence of an experienced instructor in the back seat. The seriously exciting moment comes, of course, when after about fourteen dual hours he gets out and you are on your own. Sadly I never flew enough to get a licence – which in any case I could never have afforded to keep up. But even my pathetic total of about 120 hours' flying showed me just a little of what proper pilots must go through.

Of course, no one ever shot at me. The nearest I ever got to a battle was as reluctant playmate to my old friend Patrick Lindsay – a serious hazard if you had the bad luck to be airborne at the same time and in the same square mile as him. Patrick's 'hobby' was driving veteran racing cars, the sort which went at least as fast as they did forty years earlier, but lacked all the improvements to tyres, brakes, suspension and track without which no modern Grand Prix driver would leave the pits. Patrick was, until his luckless death from cancer, one of the few men I've known who either had no fear or simply refused to recognise the meaning of the word.

In the cockpit of a Tiger Moth – or the De Havilland Chipmunks with which we were soon equipped – he was immediately infected with an over-developed Biggles complex. One moment, you would see another aircraft at least a mile away. The next, if it happened to contain the Hon. P. Lindsay it would be breathing down your neck.

Patrick could never resist the temptation of 'buzzing' any Oxford colleague – which meant diving on to or past your tail as close as possible. I need hardly say that Patrick's idea of 'close' was a great deal too close for the comfort of whatever unfortunate mug he happened to be buzzing!

Sir Neil Foxley-Norris, the extremely distinguished officer who commanded the Air Squadron when I joined in the early 1950s, became a marshal of the Royal Air Force before he retired. I'm not sure he ever had full control over Patrick – but no doubt he consoled himself with the reflection that quite a few of the brave men with whom he flew in the Battle of Britain were notable more for their daring than their regard for discipline or convention.

I am proud to say incidentally that Sir Neil was the first person ever to ask me to make an after-dinner speech, at the Air Squadron Dinner on 29 November 1951 – the start, you could say of a slippery downhill slope!

I left Oxford in June 1952 with a third-class degree (the same level, incidentally that my father had achieved). Rather than move straight on to study for the Bar, I applied for a Henry Fellowship, a scholarship which annually supported two students from Oxford and two from Cambridge to spend time studying in the USA. The wonderful aspect of the scheme (at least for me) was that being accepted depended on your success at interview rather than your academic brilliance – 'The ambassadorial function should be of prime importance,' according to the application criteria – so my third was no insuperable barrier.

But during the crucial interview itself a possible barrier did emerge – when I said that, if successful, I would like to study at the Harvard Business School, which had a tremendous reputation and seemed just the place to get a qualification which would stand me in good stead later. Eyebrows were raised: why go to Harvard Business School if the idea was to study law? Time for a quick rethink: no, no, I assured them, on second thoughts Yale Law School would do me fine. Somehow I managed to convince them that I would perform the 'ambassadorial function' well enough.

I have to admit that the idea of serving as an ambassador for British legal studies was not top of my list of concerns as I prepared for the trip. Much more important was the news that several of my friends were crossing the Atlantic at the same time – among them my beloved Tizzy Chancellor. Tall and lovely – too tall for me, I'm sorry to say – Tizzy was being posted across the Atlantic by her parents in a bid to extricate her from the clutches of another Eton friend Peter Gatacre. As their bad luck would have it, she found herself crossing the ocean on the same boat as Peter's old friend Lawrence! My luck was certainly in, as her destination in New York was the Fifth Avenue apartment of her parents' friends the Starrs. Cornelius Starr, a multi-millionaire who had made his packet by among other things, selling life insurance to the Chinese, had just fallen in love with skiing, at the age of sixty. His response to this new infatuation was to buy a whole mountain in Vermont – Mount Stowe, which he promptly proceeded to turn into one of New England's best ski resorts.

So, on our arrival in New York we were welcomed with open arms by Mr Starr and promptly invited up to Stowe – where began my lifelong love of skiing, under the tutelage, as it happened, of some of the best skiers in the world, including several who had won medals in the previous Winter Olympics and whom Starr had brought over to Vermont. Although I duly made an appearance at Yale, I found myself in the wonderful position of having no exams. My year in America taught me a great more about skiing than about law.

As soon as the formal period of my Henry Fellowship was completed in the spring of 1953 I decided the time had come for a good look at the USA, and a group of us – including Raymond Bonham-Carter, Mike Faber and Hugo Kindersley (Gay's cousin) – clubbed together to buy three gas-guzzling cars, in which we set off across the continent. We foregathered in Washington DC, then, on the day after the Coronation back in England, set off down Skyline Drive in blazing hot sun with the roofs of the cars down (Mike Faber got seriously sunburned) and made for Charlottesville, Virginia, where we stayed with Judge John Parker, who had served as second American judge at Nuremberg. An absolutely charming, old-fashioned Southern gentleman, he took our unpunctuality with unflurried calm and entertained us royally for several days.

A proper retelling of all my adventures on that trip across the USA would require a book of its own, but one incident is worth recalling here.

Very late one night we came upon a motel in the middle of the desert showing a welcome *VACANCIES* board but without any obvious sign of life. Desperate for somewhere to stay we piled into two of the (unlocked) rooms and went to sleep – only to be awakened early the following morning by an extremely irate landlord. We protested our innocence – and that, more than just innocent, we were innocent Brits – but it was already too late: the cops had been summoned, and we had better wait around and face the consequences. The local police arrived in the form of a man closer in looks to Gary Cooper than anyone I had ever seen (including Gary Cooper) – tall and handsome, with a drawl to match. Having heard the circumstances of our supposed trespass, and having further listened to the landlord's complaint that we were refusing to pay the amount he (but not we) thought we should be paying, the Gary Cooper-lookalike pronounced: 'This is a most regrettable situation, but I think we owe it to our relations with the British people to smooth it over.' Another triumph for the Special Relationship. And although the landlord fulminated against this display of *détente*, we were soon on our way. Twenty miles down the road we stopped to take stock – and discovered that in all the arguing and pleading our case we had forgotten to pay *any* bill! Perhaps that landlord had a point after all...

We drove coast to coast, down via New Orleans and Baton Rouge into Texas and then across to California, where I had an illustration of the sheer scale of that state. On arrival in Los Angeles we phoned the friends we were due to meet there and announced, 'We're just the other side of town' – and were told that we were actually *eighty miles* short of the part of LA to which we were heading! We then moved on to Lake Tahoe, Nevada, from where I took a Greyhound Bus back across to New York City and booked my return passage to England on the *Queen Mary*. I arrived back late in 1953, twenty-four years old, the beneficiary of an expensive and, geographically wide-ranging education. But beyond the vague notion that I would now be expected to turn my mind to qualifying for the legal profession, without any clear aim in life – except, of course, a burning ambition to develop my career in one particular pursuit far removed from the law.

5

'He's left it a bit late, if you ask me'

I had learned at a very tender age that being around horses opened up a multitude of exciting activities – not least of which was betting. I must have been about six when I struck my first wager: sixpence on the nose of a horse named Nettlebed at the Pegasus Club – that is, the Bar – point-to-point. My principal recollection of Nettlebed is the colour of his jockey's hair – flaming red, as was revealed when his hat fell off (no chinstraps in those days) at the first fence. Nettlebed looked destined for the runner-up spot until the leader conveniently fell at the last, leaving me five bob richer – and hooked on horse racing.

Formed in the nineteenth century the Pegasus Club catered for lawyers, barristers, judges and any other variety of legal luminary provided that he liked riding horses, did not consider fox or stag hunting an indictable offence, and was at least prepared to contemplate risking his legal neck out hunting or in a point-to-point.

The Pegasus meeting was held once a year,

with 'confined' races for lightweight (runners to carry twelve stone) and heavyweight (thirteen stone seven pounds) legal eagles of one sort or another. My grandfather had laid out one of the early courses at Hoppingwood Hill, and my father was such a faithful Pegasus supporter that in 1947, when entries were short after the war, he persuaded Jenny to enter Libby's twenty-year-old chestnut hunter Lohengrin for the lightweight race at Kimble, near Princes Risborough. (Libby was still away in the ATS.) Since I was considered by my sister too young and certainly too incompetent to take the ride, a law student called Gerald Ponsonby (later Lord de Mauley) was engaged.

Gerald frankly admitted that, owing to imminent Bar exams, his fitness left something to be desired. But my father's object was only to make up the numbers, and no one was surprised when, by halfway Lohengrin was left a field or two behind his seven opponents.

Kimble was rare among pointing courses in that it boasted a water jump. The first judge – or other legal eagle – who arrived at this unexpected obstacle was hurled into the water by what turned out to be a determinedly *non nat* steed,* and the splash

**Non nat*: 'He does not swim.' At Eton the phrase applied to a boy who was to be excused swimming.

and general watery confusion which followed his horse's refusal so upset the other runners that they either stopped too or at least paused to consider the situation. There followed a distressing scene in which some of the language was of a type more often heard in the cells of the Old Bailey than on the bench.

Through this chaotic free-for-all Lohengrin picked his disdainful way with the raised eyebrow and curled lip of a disapproving dowager outside a pub at closing time. He had heard of 'refusing' – something they do at Pony Clubs – but the thought of it never entered his mind. Over he sailed, and as he approached the second last fence only one blaspheming judge had negotiated the water.

But that judge was closing fast, and now the clammy fingers of fatigue were creeping up Gerald's legs. At the second last fence Lohengrin, though weary too, did nothing seriously wrong except that he did not remain between Gerald and the ground.

'UR' – Unseated Rider – they call it in the form book, and to avoid those dreaded letters following my name I have (twice – what a confession!) intentionally tripped up a horse on to whose blameless ears I had just been flung. If you have not done it yourself you may not believe me, but I promise that, in the record of two 'fallen' rides of mine, there *should* be either 'UR', or just possibly 'BDBR' (Brought Down By Rider).

This certainly did not apply to Gerald Ponsonby He was simply too exhausted to stay on board – but luckily before the pursuing judge could catch up, willing hands had hoisted him back into the plate.

But sadly those clammy fingers had tightened their grip, and poor Gerald fell off again at the last fence; gallantly however, he allowed himself to be hauled back into the plate once more. Off he set for the line, with the one surviving judge coming ever closer. There may have been more exciting finishes – Special Cargo's Whitbread, perhaps, or Red Rum catching Crisp – but for me the last ten yards of the Bar Lightweight point-to-point in 1947 will do. There was no photo-finish, but when the judge (different sort) gave Lohengrin the verdict by a short head, nobody argued.

Having put my godfather John Barstow's pound on at 20-1 I am, of course, talking through my pocket. But Lohengrin and Gerald richly deserved their moment of glory and, touching all available wood, the Pegasus Club point-to-point is still going – thanks to the hospitality of various hunts.

My own early riding owed an awful lot to 'confined' races. I mentioned in the previous chapter my first attempt on the nursery slopes of race riding on Paula, but I soon realised that it was not point-to-pointing itself which captivated me. It was *winning* – and that indescribable feeling of riding in a race when everything goes right: when your horse sees every stride in the just the same way that you do, when he comes up and lands far out on the other side and is back in his stride immediately stretching out towards the next, and then the next, and then on to the winning post.

My very first intake of this highly addictive drug was on a mare named Next Of Kin. The occasion was the Bar lightweight race at Kimble in 1951, and, truth to tell, our expedition did not start auspiciously: Next Of Kin tried to live up to her somewhat pessimistic name and came over backwards twice in the paddock. But a few minutes later she confirmed my inclination to go for a racing rather than a legal career by giving me the experience of my life to date. By the time she sailed over the last fence, the well-meaning judges and barristers who had dreamed up the Pegasus Club had, however unwittingly deprived their learned profession of my services.

Just as well, probably I have always liked an argument, and from that point of view the Bar might have suited me fine. But it could never have given me anything like as much excitement, exhilaration and pleasure as twenty years' riding over fences and hurdles. In any case, my daughter Sara won a Pegasus point-to-point – like me, she was eligible as a law student – and, although he has not yet learned to ride, my son Patrick is a barrister, so he at least has carried on the legal side of the family tradition!

Sara, in fact, was just getting going in points and hunter-chases when, in two separate falls, she damaged her head so badly that the Jockey Club Medical Adviser (Michael Allen at that time) refused (quite rightly I'm afraid) to let her go on riding. She had, poor darling, also inherited an asthmatic tendency from me, and is now so susceptible to throat infections that she is compelled to live with a more or less permanent tracheotomy. Married to Mark Bradstock, who trains in Tim Forster's old yard at Letcombe Bassett, Sara still rides out regularly and would, in my obviously prejudiced opinion, have made a first-rate amateur rider. Now her hopes – and mine – are centred on her and Mark's children Alfie and Lily. As I write this they are only nine and seven, but watch this space...

After winning at Kimble I was hooked – and the next thing to do was to get some badly needed racing experience. My own, at that time, was strictly limited to a very few rides in point-to-points – unless you count having Bob Lyle's wonderful book *Brown*

Jack read to me by my nanny patting that great stayer's neck when he appeared at Olympia for the Horse of the Year Show, and backing a few sixpence-each-way winners with my Turf adviser and first riding instructor, Bill Harris.

Over the next couple of years I managed the occasional ride in point-to-points, while living in London and paying a form of lip service to studying for the Bar at the Inner Temple. Part I of the Bar exams consisted of six separate papers, each interminable, including things like Roman Law – in which, believe it or not, I got a First and passed out top! Unfortunately that convinced me that the exams were a piece of cake, and I failed to notice that Part I was mainly a memory test. Disgracefully I never took the finals, which were far more complicated and needed actual knowledge: I just sat through part of the period without writing anything down, handed in some blank sheets and left feeling thoroughly ashamed.

Later that day I had a photographic appointment to earn money with my hands – not working, but holding the foot of a bad-tempered model for a fashion photographer friend of Bob McCreery's called Michel Molinare.

Michel had asked Bob to find some hands that 'looked like a workman's', and my suitably grubby pair were just rough enough for the part. So I spent an uncomfortable two hours lying on my back in danger of being stabbed with a stiletto heel. According to Michel, the pictures were just what he wanted; according to the model, it was an unacceptable waste of her time; according to me, the great thing was the money. I can't remember the figure, but it paid the rent.

I did, I think, eat the required number of dinners at the Inner Temple, which were presumably organised so that the Benchers (senior members of the Temple) could see that the students and would-be barristers used their knives and forks in the right manner.

On one memorable night I found myself at dinner sitting next to a startlingly pretty Pakistani lady with whom I seemed to get on remarkably well. She did mention that her father was the High Commissioner, but that did not stop me suggesting that we went to have a drink and a dance at The Carousel. Sadly as we emerged from the dining hall I found two large and dusky chauffeur/bodyguards standing by the shiny Daimler (complete with national flag) which awaited my hoped-for date. They made it painfully clear that I was not expected to board, and since I could not understand her explanation to them, I still don't really know how hard she tried on my behalf. She apologised charmingly enough, but I never saw her again. Off she glided while I, her frustrated suitor, was left standing on the pavement.

At the time my parents had a perfectly good flat at Melbury Court, opposite the Regal cinema in Kensington High Street, but rightly or wrongly I wanted to set up on my own. My first 'share' was a top-floor flat in Ennismore Gardens with Tony Lloyd, a friend from Eton and these days an incredibly grand former Lord of Appeal. We were burgled once, and Tony has always claimed that the thieves took only my suits, expensively tailored by Lesley and Roberts, and not his, which came from Moss Bros. That's Tony's story anyway. It is also possible, of course, that they were very small burglars.

My next share was in Queen's Gate Mews with Bob McCreery who had a light blue Austin Healy in which we drove to the races. (I was still carless.) Bob's girlfriend at the time was a beautiful angel called Margaret Gilder, and when their romance came to an end she married, perhaps partly on the rebound, an American called Alan Bridges and tragically died giving birth to twins. She was one of the most admirable and lovable girls I ever met.

Bob and I then moved to Bloomfield Terrace in Chelsea, where we were joined by

Martin Jacomb: he was already rocketing towards the top as a barrister and businessman and seemed the natural candidate for the largest room. Bob came next in the pecking order, and I was relegated to the box-room. Martin's arrival left us short of beds, so I went off to buy a new one at a large store, where an elegant limp-wristed gentleman with floppy blond hair quickly approached me. 'Single, double or *occasional* double, Sir?' he lisped, and with only slight misgivings I went for an occasional – mainly I may say because I had been fobbed off with the smallest room.

Martin has reminded me that our rent at Bloomfield Terrace was five pounds a month each, for an unmodernised and uncleaned flat which had an original hob in the kitchen and a totally untended garden. I am sorry to say my desk was piled with unopened bills and letters, just as it is now. The other problem was heating, particularly because Bob insisted on operating the gas poker (meant for lighting fires) and regularly burnt out at least one a week.

Romance was very much in the air at this time and Bloomfield Terrace was the scene of some surprisingly happy parties, considering how often love blew in and out. I am glad to say that almost all the friendships are still intact, even if the combinations have changed. Bob soon got engaged to Jeanette

Wright, and Martin to Evelyn Heathcoat-Amory.

Bob himself was to prove instrumental in pushing my fledgling riding career to a higher level, and for this I owe him an unpayable debt of gratitude.

My first memory of him at Eton was of a fifteen-year-old with a lot of butter-coloured hair (which he still has, blast him!), bowling deceptively hittable-looking lobs on Agar's Plough – one of the playing fields on which the Duke of Wellington almost certainly did *not* suggest that the battle of Waterloo was won. Bob went on to become a highly accomplished amateur rider, sharing the championship with Danny Moralee in 1955–6 and winning it outright in 1956–7. Some time in 1955 – after we were no longer living in London – I met him at Cheltenham races and he invited me to dinner at Shannon Cottage, the cosy Lambourn nest he was sharing with the great jockey Dave Dick. It was just across the road from Saxon House, the Lambourn yard in which Fulke Walwyn had for years been preparing winners of all the worthwhile steeplechases in Britain.

Thanks to his beautiful wife Jeanette, Bob's cuisine and menu have, thank heaven, improved since those bachelor days. That first evening at Shannon Cottage they consisted of an (unopened) tin of steak and kidney pie, and I was just wielding the opener when, with a crash, the room was suddenly full of D.V. Dick himself – then quite easily the most overpowering and, if you liked that kind of thing, impressive figure in the National Hunt weighing room. Dave was wasting to do seven stone four pounds when he rode Gloaming to win the 1941 Lincolnshire Handicap, and was still wasting (even harder) to do eleven stone three pounds when he and ESB were handed the 1956 Grand National after the sensational collapse on the run-in of the Queen Mother's chaser Devon Loch. No other jockey so far as I know, has attempted, let alone completed, the Spring Double of Lincoln and Grand National.

That night in Lambourn, pink-coated and muddy from a day's hunting with the Pytchley, Dave was bursting to regale us with stories of the fences he'd jumped, the foxes they'd killed, the ladies he'd chased – and how delighted they'd all been when he caught them. As I learned gradually over the years, you could make up your own mind how many pinches of salt to use with Dave's lavishly embroidered stories – though a surprising number of them did contain a definite element of truth!

Could Bob really be sharing a cottage with this amazing character? This has to be the life, I thought. Law and the Inner Temple suddenly seemed even less attractive.

In March 1956 Bob inflicted another mortal wound on my moribund legal ambitions by getting me a ride in the Foxhill Cup at Newbury – my first ride ever in a 'proper' steeplechase under National Hunt Rules, as opposed to a point-to-point. Bob, booked to ride a well-fancied runner named Green Branch, introduced me to John and Mary Sellar, whose mare Fire Alarm had produced two lovely agile daughters, of which Pyrene was the younger by five years. As Bob was not available they offered me the ride, and Pyrene carried me round Newbury in a delicious mixture of terror and exhilaration. She finished fourth, God bless her. (The opening race of the Newbury programme that afternoon was a four-year-old hurdle, which provided a first victory for the odds-on favourite Taxidermist, a horse of whom you will be hearing a great deal more.) Two weeks later at Sandown Park, Pyrene gave me my first winner under Rules in the Past and Present Hunters' Chase: 'rapid headway from 20th', reads the form book, 'quickened to lead close home'. If my first point-to-point victory on Next Of Kin had been thrilling, the experience of winning round the finest steeplechase circuit in the land – Sandown has ever since been my favourite racecourse – was ten times more so. You can see what I mean about the debt I owe Bob McCreery!

The other great formative influence on my early riding was without doubt the trainer Bob Turnell, who heads the list of the kind souls who have put up with my incompetence. In my early years as a 'bumper' I was often able to observe one of the racing world's most attractive phenomena – that if a beginner, however green and inept, is seen or believed to be doing his or her best, mistakes and/or failures are treated with amazing tolerance and sympathy. It will not last for ever, of course, but, at least to begin with, the greater the knowledge and longer the experience of your mentor, the more sympathetic he is likely to be. Bob Turnell epitomised that attitude.

I met Bob through my mother's friend Lady Apsley, mother of my great friend George Bathurst and his brother Henry, and – despite being confined to a wheelchair by a back broken out hunting – joint master of our local hunt, the Vale of the White Horse. She had a horse or two in training with Bob at Ogbourne, near Marlborough, and told my mother that he was just the man for me. We were introduced at Cheltenham races and, as Bob's wife Betty told me later, he came home that night saying, rather gloomily: 'Bloke here for breakfast tomorrow. Says he wants to be an amateur rider. He's left it a bit late, if you ask me.' I was twenty-six years old and almost as bald as I am now, and of course Bob was absolutely right.

He was a fine one to talk about age, mind you – having held a professional jockey's licence for thirty-one years from 1926 to 1957! In fact, he had ridden his first winner as a fifteen-year-old apprentice on the Flat the year I was born – 1929 – and was still claiming a jockey's weight allowance when he came out of the army in 1946. But the seventeen-year gap had not been wasted. Much of it was spent in his beloved hunting field, mostly pursuing the Duke of Beaufort's hounds around Gloucestershire, Wiltshire and Somerset, and often riding young, green horses over the stone walls and infinitely varied obstacles of that still sporting country. One of these horses was Pas De Quatre, dam of the 1960 Gold Cup winner Pas Seul – and even in his heyday after winning the Gold Cup, Pas Seul himself was quite often seen out hunting, ridden by his trainer.

Winning the 1946 Grand Sefton Chase at Aintree on Mr John Rogerson's War Risk, Bob must have opened a lot of eyes to the fact that this was no ordinary 'middle-aged claimer'. He always swore he should have won the 1950 Grand National on Cloncarrig, who was still just in front of the winner Freebooter when he fell at the second last.

Years of rough riding for his father and others had undoubtedly produced an all-round horseman of extraordinary versatility. I never saw Bob bucked off or run away with, and if any newcomer to the yard showed signs of giving trouble, his reaction was always the same. He simply got on and, however explosive the antics, that, in a very short space of time, was that.

When Bob took out a trainer's licence in 1954, still often riding his own horses, Mr and Mrs Rogerson were among his first owners. In her youth Mrs Rogerson had ridden the winner of the Newmarket Town Plate, and Bob was to win her the 1966 Champion Hurdle with Salmon Spray. Many of his best winners carried the famous black, red cap of her uncle H.J. (Jim) Joel – and it was, of course, for Mr Joel that Bob's son Andy trained Maori Venture to win the 1987 Grand National, five years after Bob's death. Maori Venture was ridden by Steve Knight, yet another first-rate jockey whose early education and experience was in the Turnell academy.

The great yard at Rockley, long deserted now, was a sad sight in June 2001 when I looked over the gate on my way to Betty Turnell's memorial service. Forty-six years earlier, when I first rode out there, it was a thriving, bustling scene full of old soldiers like fourteen-year-old Greenogue (luckless second to Silver Fame in the 1951 Gold Cup) and stars of the future such as Pas Seul and Salmon Spray, as well as budding jockeys like Johnny Haine and Jeff King. Bob had already chosen Bill Rees to succeed him as stable jockey, and it was a real blow to him when Bill accepted an invitation to ride for Peter Cazalet. Involving as it did regular rides in the royal colours, that was obviously an offer difficult, if not impossible, to refuse; but sadly just as Bill was proving himself at Fairlawne, his luck ran out when Dunkirk was killed and Bill broke his thigh as they were trying to stretch Arkle in the 1965 King George VI Chase at Kempton Park.

Bob had spotted Johnny Haine out hunting with the Beaufort. Jeff King, a stable lad up the road with Sir Gordon Richards, was already getting too big for the 'easy' life of a Flat jockey and one of Bob's twin sons Andy, born in August 1948, was itching for his first ride in public.

So it was into a yard already bristling with riding talent that I walked that morning in 1955.

Not surprisingly given his first 'left it a bit late' impression at Cheltenham, Bob chose my first steed with care, and came up with Arctic Slave, later a pretty successful stallion but in those days, as the trainer knew well, a horse who took far too much care of his elegant self to do anything uncivilised like whipping round, bucking or running away. Even I was able to keep him under reasonable control – and as we sailed up the canter I wondered, in my ignorance, what on earth all the fuss was about. Needless to say, I soon found out.

Harry Frank, who owned Pas De Quatre and was therefore, however unwittingly the breeder of Pas Seul, had a daughter and a son, Judy and Andy, both of whom loved hunting. Andy, who shared my ambition to ride as an amateur, owned or part-owned with his father a big, dark brown gelding called China Clipper, which he planned to qualify and ride in hunter-chases.

Bob Turnell must, I suppose, have decided that China Clipper was a docile 'married man's' ride, suitable for an ageing would-be amateur; for, arriving for my second morning at the yard I was directed to his box. The saddle into which I was hoisted felt an awful long way up – but its large, long-legged owner seemed to accept my presence willingly enough.

A dense fog had descended around the fifteen of us who walked out towards the Rockley gallop, an oval circuit, mostly used left-handed and about a mile round, just off the road from Marlborough to Wootton Bassett. Bob himself led the string on David

Gibson's game little chaser Cottage Lace, and my orders on China Clipper were simple – stay at the back. Even the little I had learned from the book *Steeplechasing* (the gospel according to John Hislop) had taught me that back meant back. The cardinal sin, to be avoided at any cost, was to overtake any of your galloping companions.

Sadly, no one had told China Clipper that. It took him about two hundred yards to work out who was in control and then, as my soft, unfit arms and back grew weaker, I fatally changed my hands to take a fresh and shorter hold of his head. They say that fear travels down the reins, and so, emphatically does weakness. The one signal changing your hands does *not* give is, 'Slow down, old thing. All's well.' It is far more likely to be (mis)interpreted as a 'pick up', the signal a jockey gives to balance and poise his mount for a challenge at or near the finish of a race. China Clipper had not, I think, run in many races at that stage – but he knew all about weak, amateurish riders.

There were fourteen horses in front of us when we started our uncontrolled advance – and the reactions of their riders varied widely. The first, as China Clipper and I loomed upsides, was anger – because our appearance beside them was making their horses pull harder than before. The second was partly frivolous encouragement – 'Go on: you'll catch him yet!' – and the third was a mixture of the two, with quite a bit of straightforward pity built in, because at the rate we were going one certainty was that, any moment now, we would overtake the Guv'nor!

Well, of course, we did just that; and right then, for the first time that awful morning, something happened which was not entirely my fault. Before the last turn in the Rockley gallop, we had just drawn level with Bob Turnell and Cottage Lace when, hitherto hidden by the bend and the fog, a flock of sheep appeared across our bows.

If, which may well be the case, you have never seen a string of fifteen galloping Thoroughbreds confronted in mid-career by a flock of frightened sheep, I can tell you that it is a chaotic spectacle – and, if you feel even partly responsible for it, a terrifying one, calculated to live for a long time in your nightmares.

For me, what's more, it was not over yet – not by a longish chalk. For one thing, I had still not got China Clipper under even minimal control. In the end, after aiming up the steepest hills available, exhaustion came to my rescue – his as well as mine. He simply got tired, or maybe bored, with running away. Some of the others took a while to settle down, but eventually a string of sorts regrouped to walk back along the

Marlborough Road.

Speaking for myself, it was one of the gloomiest mornings of my life. Twenty-six years old, after two years in the army how could I possibly have made such a comprehensive idiot of myself? I found tears of shame and mortification streaming – well, anyway trickling – down my face. Every muscle in my body seemed totally starved of energy and, scarcely able to walk, I led China Clipper into the yard – never more certain in my life of getting the rocket I so richly deserved.

It was, in fact, five minutes before I found Bob Turnell, and when I did so what he said were three of the kindest, most welcome words I ever heard: 'Be here tomorrow.'

6

'They seemed to be giving a cup to somebody'

Perceptive readers will have noticed that I had reached my late twenties without stirring myself to any excessive degree towards finding what might be called a 'proper job'. What with pursuing a hectic social calendar in London (and elsewhere) with Bob McCreery and continuing to ride in races whenever I could persuade anyone to put me up, I was busy enough not to think of such matters. But the time eventually came when I knew that I had to turn an honest penny.

I had known for some time that an ex-sailor named Bill Curling was courting an extremely pretty girl called Libby, daughter of Lady Bonham, who lived in Crudwell House, two and a half miles from Hill Farm. What I did not know was that Bill wrote as racing correspondent under the name Hotspur in the *Daily Telegraph*, and that he had a plan to make my friend Bob McCreery the *Telegraph*'s answer to John Hislop, whose combination of riding and journalistic skills was then making him one of the key attractions of the *Observer*. Luckily for me, Bob did not much like the job, and not surprisingly his somewhat reluctant efforts did not hold the *Telegraph* sports room spellbound.

By this time Bob and I were sharing a London flat and, rather daunted but also galvanised by his example, I wrote to Frank Coles, sports editor of the *Telegraph*, asking for an interview.

As it happened, I had no sooner posted the letter than, riding out at Ogbourne one morning, I fell off a horse called Alpine Eagle. There was nothing unusual about that – but this time I fell on my shoulder and it hurt. Not counting various minor bruises from low-level tumbles off Mince Pie in Pony Club gymkhanas it was, I think, my first 'riding injury'. My collarbone turned out to be broken – and the only significant thing about this otherwise unimportant incident is that when I turned up for my interview with Frank Coles my arm was in a sling.

Frank, who must have been well over sixty by then, was an indomitable Fleet Street veteran. Not allowed to join up for medical reasons, he had, by all accounts, sub-edited (and quite often written) most of the *Telegraph* sports pages throughout the war. By the time I knew him, the editing process was quite often rounded off in the bar of the King and Keys, the pub next door – but it got done just the same. I told Frank the reason for the sling, and I honestly think it may have helped get me the job. As he told me later: 'Well, I thought anyone who could get close enough to a horse to fall off it must know *something*.'

The *Telegraph* (not yet expanded to include its sister Sunday paper) was still in those days next door to the *Daily Express* in Fleet Street – and the interior was just about as unlike its modern Canary Wharf equivalent as you could imagine. The sports room, covering *all* sports from rowing to tiddlywinks, was just that: a single over-crowded room with the sports editor in one corner. Racing thought itself lucky to have three chairs, complete with typewriters. (Can you believe, incidentally that my expensive Eton education had not included even basic typing?)

At first I was only allowed to watch, but after my first six (fairly chaotic) weeks in the sports room – including an attempt at sub-editing: a *major* disaster – it was decreed by the powers that be (presumably Frank Coles, Bill Curling and, quite possibly the chief sub-editor Bob Glendinning, who suffered most from my dyslexic scribbling) that I should be dispatched into the outside world; specifically to go to as many of

Britain's racecourses as possible and 'cover' a day's racing at each of them. It took me quite a while to visit them all – but this was more than fifty years ago and I managed a clean sweep by 1990!

There were quite a few more when I started, mind you – jumping 'gaff' tracks like Buckfastleigh and Woore are no longer with us, and nor are more urban courses like Birmingham, Manchester and Hurst Park – and some of them took quite a bit of finding. But the racing press as a whole were even more hospitable then than they are now. For instance, I remember Jimmy Snow, northern correspondent for *The Times*, actually accosting me in the press room at Redcar, because, in his words, 'You looked in need of someone able to show you round.' That first day at Redcar – when Jimmy introduced me to the great trainer Captain Charles Elsey which at the time was like meeting God – was, I'm glad to say the start of a long friendship which ended only with Jimmy's death in 1987. If I close my eyes I can still see him and Clive Graham – Peter O'Sullevan's fabled partner on the racing pages of the *Daily Express* – sitting at the far end of the press room at York, deeply absorbed in the form book and in a bottle of gin, which by the end of the afternoon would be empty

That same week ended with a visit to the

now defunct racecourse at Manchester, where, walking across one end of the parade ring, I saw a big grey filly galloping, loose and unattended, down towards me. She had come across the infield from the racecourse stables – through a regular obstacle course of spiky wrought iron fences, motor cars and other man-made hazards. I never even looked like catching her, but someone else did – and he (or she) deserves the gratitude of the British racing world. Because the runaway was Prince Aly Khan's Petite Etoile, making a first – and what could so easily have been a last – appearance on a racecourse. Even with only one opponent, the budding Northern sprinter Chris, Petite Etoile did not win that day but at least she went home more or less in one piece. The curtain was safely up on one of the most dramatic and spectacular Flat careers in my memory

It was about that time that my own somewhat less glamorous career as a racing journalist came unpleasantly – in more than one sense of that word – close to an abrupt and undignified termination. One day at Newmarket, Bill Curling, looking as if some much-loved relative had walked in front of a bus, pulled me into a corner of the press room.

'Did you really have to write this?' he asked, brandishing a copy of the previous Friday's paper. It contained what seemed to me a fairly harmless account of the afternoon's doings at Ayr – in which, as I now recalled, a couple of odds-on favourites had been beaten. I remembered one of them particularly well – a beautifully bred filly of Lord Rosebery's who, when asked to go and win her race, said, almost as clearly as if she had hoisted a signal, 'Not today thanks. I would much prefer a quiet game of croquet...'

'What on earth did you mean by that?' my old friend asked. 'Just look at this.'

'This' was a letter written on paper so rich and thick that you would be ill advised to use it in a lavatory. It was addressed not to anyone as humble as a sports editor, but to the editor himself:

Your correspondent at Ayr last Thursday knows nothing about racing and should not be employed by a newspaper like the *Daily Telegraph*.

Yours
Rosebery

I explained to Bill that the filly had not tried a yard at Ayr, that Lord Rosebery had not been present, and that his Lordship was clearly relying on someone else. What I did not then realise and therefore did not say – was that the December Sales were not far ahead.

Before them, as it happened, the filly was due to run again at Newmarket, and Bill Curling, who had so far bravely stood by me in the face of the editor's consternation, had invited Roger Mortimer – *doyen* of the press room – to watch her with us.

Well, if she had been a puppet with me pulling the strings, I could not have asked for more. The famous primrose and rose hoops were always prominent, and when Eph Smith asked her to go the filly still looked full of running. But then – Glory Hallelujah!, what a superbly negative display! The ears went back, the head came up – and when Eph was unwise enough to use his whip, the tail came up too. She finished a sulky third and I'm glad to say that Roger's verdict was unequivocal. 'I don't think she would even have won a croquet match today,' he said – and Bill very kindly reported my 'acquittal' to the editor.

I never met Lord Rosebery and if I had I would probably not have been brave enough to bring the subject up. He was, I believe, a clever man, a bold rider and a first-class cricketer. But he was also a powerful figure who abused his power to serve his own selfish interests. That gets the thumbs down from me.

One day not long after this incident Frank Coles suddenly said: 'You must have a *nom de plume*. All our sports correspondents have a *nom de plume*.' Except that it seemed quite a hopeful omen for keeping the job, I thought no more about it – until a few days later Frank said, 'I know. We'll call you "Marlborough". You're always reversing the charges from there.' Well, of course, I had several objections. The Duke wouldn't like it. I was never at the school – and I didn't even live there.

Nothing more was said until, out of the blue, one evening when I rang Bob Glendinning to check my Sandown copy he ended our conversation with 'Good night, Marlborough.' And in the next morning's paper, there it was...

You could say that abandoning the study of law to become a *Daily Telegraph* racing correspondent – with the basic aim of riding as an amateur – was a fairly drastic step to take. Having spent a good deal of time and money on my (intended) education as a lawyer, my father was seventy-six years old when I told him my change of plan. He was fully entitled to bore an infuriated hole in the ceiling, and I shall never forget his reaction. 'If you can find someone prepared to pay you to do something you really enjoy don't, for Heaven's sake, let them out of your sight.' Those were his words – some of the wisest and kindest I was ever lucky enough to hear.

Clearly no one in their senses was going to

pay me to ride in a race, and in those days the rules about 'amateur status' were very much stricter. Professional jockeys were certainly not allowed to write for newspapers (compare today!) and the idea of a journalist-amateur was almost unheard of.

Almost – but not quite. John Hislop was, I suspect, already writing for the *Observer* when he rode Kami to finish third in Caughoo's 1947 Grand National. If he wrote an account of his ride for the Sunday paper I never read it – but deadlines and newspaper production methods were so different in those days that I may well be wrong. John certainly wrote about that and many other races later – and was, at his best, the most literate and informed racing journalist of my time. His wonderful book *Steeplechasing*, superbly illustrated by that great sculptor, artist and raconteur John Skeaping, was the Bible of my early attempts at race-riding.

Riding styles and methods have changed, of course, but I would still recommend Hislop's great book to any amateur – or, for that matter, conditional professional – who intends to ride over fences or hurdles. Hislop's advice on nearly everything is still excellent, but the sage who said that a picture is worth a thousand words must have been looking at Skeaping's drawings.

At this time my own race-riding was still

confined to hunter-chases and other races restricted to amateur jockeys, but my experience had gradually been broadening, not least with my first ride over the Grand National course – the only time I jumped the Aintree fences in their old, upright, pre-slope form. My first walk round before the 1956 Foxhunters' Chase was not a happy experience, but as luck would have it, I had chanced on a perfect 'safety first' conveyance. John Sellar's Minimax, twelve years old at the time, was an absolutely genuine hunter, not fast but agile, and determined to take no chances whatsoever. Self-preservation came high among her priorities.

Although certainly much too frightened and green to think it at the time, I have reckoned ever since that a Foxhunters', on good ground, riding a bold but careful jumper in a single-figure field, must be just about *the* ideal way to inspect the greatest, most famous steeplechase fences in the world.

Among eight runners on 22 March 1956 (the day after my twenty-seventh birthday), Minimax and I were, as *Chaseform* accurately recorded 'a. wl bhd.' – always well behind. What the form book did not record – and maybe just as well – was the language used by that formidable amateur Danny Moralee when his mount, the favourite Happymint, fell at the fourteenth fence. With only two others still standing – and only three fences between us and the winning post – Danny set off in vociferous and eventually successful pursuit of Happymint. One of the two survivors fell, but the gallant Minimax survived. Quite undeterred by Danny's obscenities, she plodded home, having given me a guided tour of Aintree worthy of Thomas Cook. They have an electronic 'virtual reality' joyride nowadays, I believe – and no doubt it feels a bit more hectic than our eight-runner Foxhunters'. But if only Minimax could package and market the 'feel' she gave me that day I would be a rich man.

The couple to whom that fortune should rightfully belong are, or were, John and Mary Sellar, owner-breeders of Pyrene and Minimax – the two mares, both out of Fire Alarm, without whose skilled and sympathetic assistance I would probably have lived my working life as a down-at-heel barrister.

In March 1957 I had my first ride in another of the highlights of the amateur rider's year, the Kim Muir Memorial Chase on the opening day of the National Hunt Meeting at Cheltenham, the three greatest and most competitive days of jump racing in the world. The Kim Muir, named after a much-loved amateur rider killed in the war, used to be confined to amateurs who had served in the armed forces. Just old enough to have been a conscript soldier, that suited me fine – and in 1957 I rode in the Kim Muir on a horse named Mr Chippendale, trained by the great Fulke Walwyn.

I was courting my first wife Tory Dennistoun at the time, and it was her father 'Ginger' who introduced me to Fulke. The two shared many colourful military and sporting memories, which used to get more colourful – but less printable – as the night wore on. Fulke always claimed, for instance, to have saved Ginger's life – by stopping him going to France with the British Expeditionary Force in 1940. Fulke, the story goes, had just moved into Saxon House – his yard in Upper Lambourn – and invited Ginger and his wife Nancy to have dinner and stay the night. Nancy was shown their bedroom and, having retired for the night, closed the door behind her. But it then transpired that the previous owner of the house had, for some uncharitable reason, removed all the locks to the upstairs rooms. You could get in all right while the doors were open; but, once shut, they were locked.

Well, Ginger wasn't having that. Some time, and just conceivably a few more drinks, after Nancy had gone to bed, he clambered out on to a narrow ledge which, he thought, went past her bedroom window.

Maybe it did – but Ginger didn't. The ledge was only one floor up but his injuries, though not fatal, were quite bad enough to stop him going to France. He always claimed that Dunkirk would never have happened if he'd got there – but Fulke was probably right...

'What was he like?' Ginger asked his old friend anxiously after my first ride out at Saxon House – a 'school' on Mr Chippendale in which, appropriately enough, Mr Chips was the schoolmaster. 'A fine example of the Old English Lavatory Seat,' was Fulke's reply – and although I rode a few quite good winners for the greatest trainer of steeplechasers there has ever been, I never had any illusions about his opinion of my riding.

My orders for Mr Chippendale in the Kim Muir were clear. 'He goes fast asleep, so after you've gone round once you must really wake him up. Not just a tap, mind you. A real wake-up call!' Well, I had never properly hit a horse before, but after passing the stands I walloped the poor old thing with all my strength. It did not seem to do much good, but we finished a fairly respectable third.

It was as we walked into the unsaddling enclosure that I heard two senior jockeys describing my handiwork. 'Jesus, will you look at that!' one of them said: 'He didn't miss him, did he?' I looked round at Mr Chippendale's quarters and saw, to my horror and shame, a ghastly weal. The last time I saw a comparable mark was on my own bottom after being beaten at school by Henry Hely Hutchinson.

Of course, I know that a horse in the hot blood of a finish is different from a stationary small boy – and, on the latter, of course, the whip is *meant* to hurt. No doubt there are horses who 'go' for the whip and a few who will not go without it. But for a large majority I suspect, the whip used excessively hard is merely a painful distraction. Doubtless my somewhat extreme and sometimes controversial attitude to the whip and its misuse has partly been coloured by that memory of the quite unnecessary beating I gave poor Mr Chippendale at Cheltenham.

The following month came another episode which I recount with some shame.

At the start of the 1956–7 season I had bought – for £600 advanced by a kindly and indulgent bank manager – a six-year-old mare named Cautious, with whom I had fallen madly in love on Bob Turnell's gallops. Bob was well aware that his training fees would materialise when Cautious not only reproduced her home form on the racecourse, but also – even less likely – managed to stay between her owner and the ground. The rent of the flat which Bob McCreery and I were sharing in London at the time was equally dependent on her efforts.

So things looked black – or, in the bank's eyes, red – when, with our money down at fancy prices, Cautious ran like a hairy sheep at Wincanton and Warwick. By April 1957 we were in despair, and despair of such profundity that one of the Bobs – McCreery – went so far as to suggest a change of jockey.

I managed to deflect that blow to my pride, but the picture changed when the ground dried up and Cautious, by now in disgrace and completely unbacked by us, ran in a novice hurdle at Wincanton. Before the race was half over it became clear even to me that this was an entirely different Cautious – the one on whom we had staked our all the previous autumn in heavy going and waited for so expensively in vain.

What to do? Not a penny on, the mare pulling double and jumping like a stag inspired – and her rider with even less idea about how to stop a horse winning than he had how to get one home in front!

A veil had better be drawn over the next few seconds, but Cautious somehow finished fourth, with *Chaseform* dismissing her as 'never placed to challenge'.

Scurrying shamefacedly towards the

weighing room and praying that no one had noticed this blatant exhibition of 'non-trying' – rightly considered a riding crime of extreme gravity – I met my mother, a mad keen but not particularly expert race-reader.

'How wonderful to finish fourth!' she cried. 'The silly thing is, I forgot my race glasses, but luckily I was standing with General McCreery [Bob's father], so I asked him to watch you for me.' The snag was that the general was senior steward at Wincanton that day... But he was also one of the nicest, most understanding men I have ever known, quite apart from being among the Second World War's greatest and best-loved commanders in the field.

'Ran well, John,' was all he said – and when, three weeks later, Cautious came home at 6–1 in a novice hurdle at Chepstow, retrieving all our bacon, the General wrote me a letter of congratulation which will always be one of my most treasured possessions.

Cautious herself played a very minor supporting role in one of the less pleasant occurrences in Bob Turnell's yard at about this time.

Bob trained a big grey horse named Seringapatam, a very useful hurdler and chaser whose main flaw was a streak of strong-minded wilfulness. Never far from the surface, this waywardness suddenly reappeared one morning when, without any warning and for no obvious reason, he ran out at a simple schooling fence – leaving Bill Rees uncomfortably stranded on the wing!

Hard as we tried, Seringapatam would not go near that or any other obstacle that day and next morning the answer was, stubbornly the same. R.E. 'Taffy' Jenkins, one of the toughest, most fearless and, as a sad result of his own courage, most frequently injured jockeys of my time, happened to be riding out for Bob that morning. 'Looks like a case for my electric spurs,' he said as we rode back – and, cross-examined by Bob at breakfast, he admitted to possessing this unusual and, needless to say utterly illegal piece of equipment. 'It's not much of a shock it gives them,' Taffy assured us. 'Just something different, that they've never felt before...'

That evening Bob demanded a demonstration, and Taffy produced his device, which consisted of a belt containing a battery from which two insulated wires ran down each leg to connect, through the heel of your boot, with a small, blunt spur. Bob tried it himself, on both his own hands, and pronounced its effect 'no worse than an electric fence'.

Personally loathing electric shocks of any kind, I did not offer my services as a guinea pig. But the trainer was interested, and before first lot next morning Seringapatam – a suitably equipped R.E. Jenkins up – set out with two companions for the schooling fences. It was a typical grey old Marlborough morning, and Taffy was instructed by Bob to try out the spurs on the flat before attempting a fence. The result was – if you like that kind of thing – sensational.

Bob, if I remember right, was riding an old favourite of his called Rosenkavalier, and I was on Cautious. As we set off, Cautious and I were on Bob's left, with Taffy and Seringapatam between us. Taffy's instructions were not to 'switch on' before halfway up Bob's straight six-furlong gallop. But when he did so the result, predictably I suppose, was electric. If Seringapatam had been a cherry pip and our two horses the fingers of a giant, the grey could not have shot from between them with more explosive alacrity One touch from Taffy's spurs was all it needed. No one ever mistook Seringapatam for a sprinter, but in the next two hundred yards this rapidly vanishing bundle of grey-coated muscle could easily have doubled for The Tetrarch. When Taffy finally pulled him up and we walked across to look at the first schooling fence, I asked the little Welshman how he was feeling.

'How do you ****ing well think?' was Taffy's not surprising answer. 'I only hope this bugger keeps his eyes open – because mine will be tight shut!'

No doubt they were, too, because as they set off towards the first in Bob's oval circuit of schooling fences, it started to pour with rain. And I mean pour – adding in several ways to Taffy's already fearsome problems. Rain, for some reason, tends to make a horse pull harder. It also makes the reins slip through your fingers. All things considered, Taffy would probably have been wiser not to use the spurs. I'm not even sure he meant to!

As I've said, the spurs and their battery were connected by an insulated cable. It was supposed to be insulated, anyway – though I very much doubt if the electrician responsible had been told to cater for a short-legged jockey galloping through a thunderstorm on an over-excited Thoroughbred. Electricity and water are notoriously dangerous workmates, and in the circumstances I don't believe that electrician can be blamed for the slight – though admittedly from Taffy's standpoint, significant – failure of his insulation system which with every stride sent eye-watering electric shocks through his most private regions.

Taffy sadly is dead, and so, for all I know, is the electrician. I could not, in any case, pass on the messages Taffy sent him that damp but unforgettable morning. They were, I think, in Welsh, but when I attempted to repeat them to my beloved nanny (who spoke a bit of Welsh), either I got the pronunciation wrong or she was too shocked to translate...

Of course, you could say it was all Taffy's fault, and no doubt self-satisfied members of the RSPCA will be rubbing their hands and saying that it serves the cruel little so-and-so right. I can only plead for the defence that Seringapatam never refused or ran out at a fence again and won several more steeplechases. As for Taffy he rode on for several seasons before becoming a trainer, and was kind enough to give me the second-best ride I ever had in the Grand National – on Norther, brought down in the notorious pileup at the twenty-third fence in Foinavon's year. Taffy was certainly not a cruel man – and neither was Bob Turnell.

Throughout the 1956–7 season I was getting more rides against professional jockeys. Cautious at Chepstow gave me my first win in professional company and in November 1957 I scored for the first time against pros in a steeplechase when I won a novice chase at Plumpton on Foolish Man, trained by Ginger Dennistoun – my first opportunity to commandeer a press-room phone as soon as the mud had been wiped from my face and report a personal victory in the following morning's *Daily Telegraph*:

Novice chases at Plumpton are often hazardous affairs, but I had the extreme good fortune to watch today's contest from the back of Mr A. Norman's Foolish Man, a beautiful jumper who learnt his trade first over banks in Ireland and then in the hands of Tim Molony who has ridden him twice this year.

Carried wide by a loose horse turning into the straight for the first time, Foolish Man made ground doggedly up the hill and was third behind The Gnat and Devil's Luck, the favourite, as we jumped the water.

Skilfully interpreting his rider's somewhat frenzied efforts at encouragement, he sailed past them as they tired two fences out and stayed on gallantly to beat Devil's Luck, who had made some desperate mistakes, by five lengths.

My efforts on Foolish Man, however frenzied, clearly caught the eye of other trainers at Plumpton that day as I was soon being given rides by the likes of Ken Cundell, Jack O'Donoghue and Frank Pullen – and, stranger still, the opportunity to ride in 'proper' races.

In those days the Imperial Cup at Sandown Park was not only the top handicap hurdle of the year but one of the most prestigious races of the whole National

Hunt season, and in March 1958 I seemed to have a real chance of a first big-race victory on Flaming East, trained by Colonel Ricky Vallance. I had ridden Flaming East in his previous two races, most recently finishing a highly encouraging fifth in the County Hurdle at Cheltenham, but still went to Sandown more hopeful than confident, as the following Monday's *Daily Telegraph* confirmed:

Mrs R.D. Vallance's Flaming East won the Imperial Cup at Sandown on Saturday carrying on his gallant back a flabbergasted amateur rider who is still, 24 hours later, hardly able to believe that the race was real and not a dream.

There is an abnormal air of tension and excitement about the start of the Imperial Cup. Everyone knows that the race will be run at a tremendous pace and to the traditional jockey's question 'Who's going on?' the answer is simply that the devil will take the hindmost.

To win at all needs luck – to come from behind and win needs all the luck in the world and the skill of a Houdini besides.

So I heaved a sigh of relief when Flaming East shot out of the gate and into his stride like an arrow from a bow, so that we jumped the first and second hurdles in line with the leaders.

Down the hill only the grey Beau Chevalet, Camugliano, Mariner's Dance and perhaps one other were in front of us, and all along the Railway straight I tracked Arthur Freeman on Mariner's Dance while Camugliano made the running as he had the year before.

Now, above all, the Fates were smiling on Flaming East and me, for a clear path seemed to open miraculously before us and at every hurdle save one he stood back and flew, gaining now a yard and now a priceless length.

Camugliano was clear as we tore round the long bend for home, but once again the dice rolled our way for as Mariner's Dance tired he hung to the left and Flaming East was able to gallop past him and meet the final hill with only one to beat.

Rene Emery was working now, and between the last two flights Flaming East sailed up to him and Camugliano, beat them, and galloped on, brushing aside the last hurdle as if it were tissue paper to win a race that I, at least, will never forget.

Five weeks later Sandown Park was the venue for an even more memorable experience.

That same March, Fulke Walwyn had offered me a ride in the Kim Muir Chase at Cheltenham on a six-year-old called

Taxidermist – the horse I had seen winning the four-year-old hurdle at Newbury two years earlier on the day I rode Pyrene. Bred by Evan Williams and owned in partnership by Fulke's wife Cath and Mrs Priscilla Hastings, 'Taxi', as he was nearly always called, had won over fences as a four-year-old and was five when I first met him and popped him over three hurdles on the Mandown schooling ground high above Lambourn. He was a medium-sized bay gelding, and nothing particularly remarkable to look at, but his great attribute was that he was beautifully balanced.

At Cheltenham he was giving me a marvellous ride when, going down the back on the final circuit, he – or I – somehow managed to get the headpiece of the bridle pushed over his ears, so that the bridle was held tenuously in place only by the bit in his mouth. But we managed to keep going, and soon he was demonstrating his extraordinary ability to stage a finish: once over the last fence (though of course he had no obvious way of *knowing* it was the last!) he caught fire and started making up ground hand over fist. The leaders were too far ahead to be caught by the time he shifted into overdrive, but he ran on stoutly to finish second, twenty lengths behind the odds-on favourite Lochroe (ridden by my great friend Edward Cazalet, son of the royal trainer Peter).

Our effort had satisfied Fulke enough for me to be offered the ride in the Whitbread Gold Cup at Sandown Park at the end of April.

This was only the second running of the Whitbread. Before the first running in 1957, racing in England had never staged any commercially sponsored event, and the steeplechasing scene was dominated by the Grand National. Mrs Leonard Carver won £8,695 when her horse ESB was driven by the indefatigable Dave Dick past the stricken Devon Loch to win the 1956 Grand National in such sensational style; the same year's Cheltenham Gold Cup had been worth £3,750 to the winning owner. With a very few exceptions, a decent staying chaser was trained with the National in mind, and after Liverpool the season dwindled to a somnolent end.

Colonel Bill Whitbread, who had got round in two Grand Nationals (1925 and 1926), proposed to the National Hunt Committee that his family firm should put up the money for a three-mile-five-furlong handicap at Sandown Park three weeks after the Grand National, and with the inaugural running in 1957 (from which the winning owner netted £4,842) the shape of the season was immediately transformed – and to Colonel Whitbread the sport owes a lasting debt of gratitude.

Much Obliged, winner of the inaugural Whitbread, was in the field again in 1958, and started second favourite in the betting behind Mandarin, who was ridden by Fulke's stable jockey Gerry Madden. Mandarin, then a seven-year-old and winner of his last two races, carried top weight of twelve stone. (There were in fact three past or future Cheltenham Gold Cup winners in the Whitbread field of thirty-one runners, with twelve-year-old Gay Donald, Gold Cup winner in 1955, joining Kerstin, who had won at Cheltenham the previous month, and Mandarin, who would win the Gold Cup in 1962.)

I hope you'll forgive me if I relive one of the greatest days of my riding life through the words I filed for Monday's *Telegraph*:

As Taxidermist and Mandarin jumped the last fence side by side in the Whitbread Gold Cup on Saturday two men among the thousands at Sandown Park were as happy as they have ever been in their lives.

I was one – but the other, Fulke Walwyn, had far greater cause for pride and joy. For in saddling two horses to finish first and second in a race such as this he had surely achieved one of the greatest triumphs of training in the history of National Hunt racing.

Taxidermist had run (and won) seven months ago, and Mandarin won the Hennessy Gold Cup last November. Altogether this season the pair have run between them 16 times and except for Mandarin's first race and one fall apiece neither has finished out of the first two.

To keep two horses at the peak of condition for six or seven months and then produce them fit to run for their lives in a race as severe as any – save perhaps the Grand National – represents to my mind the absolute summit of success in one of the most difficult and complicated of all professions.

I suppose that no reporter has ever had his mind further from his job than I did as the 31 runners squeezed and jostled up to the tapes on Saturday. But here for what they are worth are my tangled kaleidoscopic impressions of eight unforgettable and dreamlike minutes.

I lined up beside Fred Winter on Roughan. Taxidermist (bless him) hurtled out of the gate so that we landed over the second fence in front and mercifully free of the interference which every rider dreads in such a field.

Up the hill and round the bend Colonel Bagwash, Mandarin and perhaps seven others went past us. Down the back straight the pace was so terrific that a single blunder must mean the loss of several priceless lengths – well nigh impossible to recover.

All this time Taxidermist was going as fast as he was able, but it was his jumping – bold, carefree and accurate as a slide-rule – that kept us in the hunt.

Passing the stands a gap opened on the rails in front, but, reluctant to accelerate so far from home, I let it close and felt a cold spasm of terror as what looked like an impenetrable barrier of horses formed ahead as we galloped breakneck down the hill.

Along the railway I tracked Gay Donald, who was going strong and well until he was badly struck into from behind.

At the water I could see Mandarin not far ahead, and now for the first time the blood-warming thought of victory entered my fuddled head.

Mandarin led round the last long turn, and at the Pond he, Much Obliged, Kerstin and Taxidermist were the only four still in the race.

Much Obliged fell back first, beaten by his 7lb penalty. Kerstin faltered soon after. Two from home, Taxidermist made his one mistake, but was hard on the heels of his heroic stable companion.

As the last fence loomed up, Gerry Madden and I rode knee to knee. 'Sit tight,' I thought. 'Now above all, sit tight.' But there was no need, for Taxidermist met it in his stride. He took off, soared, and landed safe, to sprint up the hill as if he could go on for ever.

Poor gallant Mandarin! What bitter feelings may he have had as his crushing burden bore him down and his friend and brother in arms galloped past him.

What a fine race Mandarin had run. To keep so light-framed a horse out of trouble Madden had no choice but to lay up from the start, and it was cruel bad luck that he was left in front so far from home.

Without robbing Taxidermist of his hard-earned glory he must surely share it with Mandarin, beaten only by the handicapper and established once and for all as the best and bravest chaser in the land.

Kerstin, too, and Much Obliged ran to their form within a pound, and all in all, this wonderful race, for which every racing man in England owes an enormous debt of gratitude to Colonel Whitbread, ended as satisfactorily as a handicap ever can.

What of the winner? Well, as Taxidermist stood eating unconcernedly last night (both he and Mandarin are none the worse), he may well have reflected that he has come a long way since Mrs Hastings and Mrs Walwyn paid £400 for him as a three-year-old.

Soon after that Fulke Walwyn paid 150

guineas to buy him back after winning a selling hurdle, acting against the advice of a senior trainer who considered the price considerably too high!

Now, at the age of six, the name of Taxidermist is known up and down the country. He might one day win a Grand National. But whatever his fate, I hope he will accept the heartfelt thanks of his lucky rider.

His courage, speed and superb fencing have given me a day to remember for ever.

Not for the first – and certainly not for the last – time, my report contained a signal inaccuracy. For when, a couple of days after the race, I suggested to Fulke Walwyn what a thrill the finish of the Whitbread must have been for him, he exploded. 'Thrill?' he snorted. '*Thrill?* I wasn't ****ing thrilled at all. I'd done my boots on Mandarin!'

I could see his point of view, for in a racecourse gallop at Sandown not long before the race Taxi, hating the heavy ground, had finished miles behind Mandarin, and must, to his trainer, have looked an unlikely winner.

But for me Taxidermist's Whitbread remains the nearest thing to pure joy I ever experienced on a racecourse, and I have on my wall as I write this a permanent reminder of that great day in the shape of six elegant John Skeaping drawings. Skeaping has long been one of my heroes – I mentioned earlier his wonderful illustrations to John Hislop's great book *Steeplechasing* – and a Skeaping bronze of two long-dogs in full flight is one of my dearest possessions. I owe the presence of the six drawings to the kindness of Peter O'Sullevan, then one of the most avidly followed racing journalists in Fleet Street and already a legendary commentator for the BBC.

The prize for the 1958 Whitbread Gold Cup included 'a trophy value £500 to the winning rider' – which as an amateur I was not eligible to receive; generous as Taxi's owners always were, there was no question of ready money passing hands. Talking to Peter O'Sullevan about this one day not long after the race, I was not greatly surprised when, with a broad grin, the Voice of Racing said: 'Just leave it to me.'

Peter told me to meet him in a Charlotte Street restaurant (not, as it happened, my father's old favourite L'Etoile but one two doors away which has vanished long since). Knowing Peter's opinion of my punctuality I made a special point of being on the dot – and was surprised to find him, immaculate as usual, deep in conversation with a small, rather untidy gypsy.

That, I soon learned, was what the great artist often looked like – and Skeaping had, as it turned out, just got off a boat from Ireland. But if you are ever lucky enough to get hold of his autobiography *Drawn From Life* you will see that no one ever had a better excuse for looking a trifle scruffy. Once, late at night and full of wine, I had the delight of hearing John retell all, or nearly all, the stories in his book – plus a whole lot more, which, even if you buried them in spadefuls of salt, could have earned (and lost) him several fortunes. Earned in books and pictures, that is – but sadly I'm afraid, an odds-on certainty to be forfeited in libel damages!

After that Charlotte Street lunch we went back to the great man's studio in Knightsbridge, where from a drawer he produced an armful of wondrous sketches and asked me to take whatever I liked. Gratefully, I chose those six – and they remain proudly on my wall to remind me of Taxi's triumph.

Taxi's Whitbread was one of eighteen winners I rode in the 1957–8 season, enough to make me amateur champion.

Any amateur rash enough, these days, to call himself a 'gentleman rider' in this country would probably get the well-deserved rejoinder: 'nothing like a gentleman and not much of a rider'. But the expression has always been taken rather more seriously in the rest of Europe. In fact, the International Federation of Gentlemen Riders – Fegentri – is an honoured, respected and prosperous body with its own hotly contested flat race, hurdling and steeplechase championships.

Until 1957, except for occasional forays as invited guests, the British took little or no part in Fegentri, with the Jockey Club and National Hunt Committee (still separate in those days) both looking down their collective noses at all these foreign goings-on. 'Why they even pay travelling expenses – and still call themselves amateurs! Can you believe it?' But in the 1950s and 1960s two men – both blessed with courage, enthusiasm and a certain amount of disposable income, set about altering that regrettable state of affairs. Besides the desirable qualities listed above, both Gay Kindersley and Beltran, Duke of Alburquerque, shared an orthopaedic lexicon of broken bones, acquired in their favourite sport of riding across country.

It was the Duke, a splendidly determined Spanish sportsman, who set the Anglo-Spanish ball rolling in 1958 by inviting horses and their owners, trainers and riders from all over Europe to what he boldly entitled the Championship of the World (Campeonato del Mundo) for Gentlemen Riders. He persuaded the Hippodromo di Madrid to put on two races, one flat and one over brush hurdles, round its small but attractive garden of a racecourse in the outskirts of the Spanish capital.

No one knows to this day how much of the Duke's own fortune was involved, and there may well have been some undercover commercial sponsorship. But however it was done, *all* expenses were paid – not only for horses, riders and trainers, but for owners plus spouses as well. The presence of amateurs from Germany, France, Switzerland and Italy lent a cosmopolitan air to the proceedings – and with Madrid *en fête* for the great Spring Festival of San Isidro, Saturday night was a whirl of gaiety curbed only for visiting riders, by the need to stay reasonably sober.

On one of our party, Gay Kindersley, this requirement was enforced with special strictness. Gay had recently bought, for a sum beyond most of our wildest dreams, a French four-year-old called Gama IV, whose form in Paris seemed to make the Hippodromo's mile-and-a-quarter flat race a straightforward matter of going down and coming back. The entire British contingent had, accordingly plonked all available pesetas on Gama's nose and Gay – not, at that time, famous for his sobriety – had been given strict orders not to mess about.

With nineteen runners, the first attempt at a start (no stalls in those days) was chaotic – a sort of equestrian Spanish omelette flavoured with a Tower of Babel selection of multilingual bad language. But eventually we got away in a line of sorts, and Gama was close enough to the leaders to satisfy his fan club. On our reading of the European form book, the only conceivable danger thereafter seemed to be of Gay falling off – and, as I've said, his consumption of wine the night before had been rigidly controlled. So, as he and Gama turned for home in front, the British contingent breathed a collective sigh of relief. It was then that things started to go wrong.

My own steed was a selling hurdler called Duet Leader, trained by Doug Marks – the remarkable man who, as a stable lad in 1940, turned out to be the only rider a brilliant but temperamental filly called Godiva would tolerate on her back. The then King's trainer William Jarvis had lost his stable jockey Jack Crouch in a flying accident the year before and, with some senior jockeys called up, he searched in vain for a suitable substitute. Godiva however, would do anything for Marks, the eighteen-year-old apprentice who looked after her. None of the established jockeys could even stay on the filly's back, let alone make her gallop, so Doug Marks got the ride – and proceeded to win the two fillies' Classics in 1940 for Esmond Harmsworth, later Lord Rothermere. Both the One Thousand Guineas and Oaks were run at Newmarket because of the war – but that made no difference to Godiva. They were home games for her.

Sadly Doug Marks was unable to make immediate use of his sudden spell in the limelight. Following a bad fall at exercise he spent no less than four years in hospital – his condition being aggravated by tuberculosis. Not surprisingly his weight became too high for the flat – so he cheerfully took to jumping.

Cheerfulness, in fact, has always been a characteristic of this extraordinary man. Doug rode jumpers successfully from 1946 to 1951 and, taking out a licence to train in 1949, has done that successfully ever since. Always full of life and enthusiasm, he had considerable success with horses like Golden Fire, Welsh Bede and Shiny Tenth. Fireside Chat, whom he trained for the well-known theatrical manager Colin Berlin, is a name familiar to admirers of Mill Reef, for whose first race at Salisbury Fireside Chat started a 9–2 *on* favourite. He was, in fact, the only horse ever to have the rather doubtful honour of starting favourite for a race in which Mill Reef took part.

Before our Spanish venture Doug sold the Uplands stables at Lambourn to Fred Winter – who, of course, became champion National Hunt trainer no fewer than eight times from that celebrated yard.

But back to Spain where, despite all his trainer's skill, hard work and wisecrack-laden enthusiasm, Duet Leader should, on all known form, have had about as much chance of finishing in front of Gama and some of the others as a small snowball in the hottest part of Hell.

Nobody however, had told him that. Heaven knows what brand of insect stung Duet Leader half a mile from home – but I suddenly found him trying to pull my arms out. Gama and Gay were still in front, but it would have needed the biggest display of non-trying in the history of the Hippodromo to keep them there. When I incautiously let out half an inch of rein, Duet Leader made Gama look like a milestone. We came back to what I can only call a deathly hush – at least in the British part of the stand. One or two locals may have clapped, but I never remember riding a much less warmly welcomed winner.

Happily patriotic punters got it all back on Gold Wire, the wonderful little globetrotting marvel which Bob McCreery owned in partnership with Chesney Allen of the Crazy Gang. Spain was the fifth country in which Gold Wire had won, and he turned the steeplechase into a procession. Durable, versatile and tough as old boots, Gold Wire and his owner-rider richly deserved, for this day at least, the title of 'world champion'.

The following week, Bob and I had the pleasure and privilege of conveying Gold

Wire's large silver (well, it looked like silver) World Championship Cup to Chesney Allen at the Victoria Palace Theatre. Bob had given advance notice of our mission, and the corks were already popping in Chesney's dressing room when we arrived. The Crazy Gang were in their usual explosive form, and God knows what the rest of the audience thought about all the superlatives lavished on World Champion McCreery Gold Wire and the rest of the team. We were seated in the 'gag box' – which turned out to mean that when any member of the Gang came in the back you were well advised to duck, because he would at once be engaged in an artillery duel with other members on stage – throwing anything from eggs to water bombs, custard pies and other assorted missiles. 'Crazy' is the word when they got going, and you could not imagine a greater contrast than the Crazy Gang and the ducal castello outside Madrid.

I would, incidentally bracket Bob McCreery with Alan Lillingston as the two best amateurs of my time. Alan, who won the Champion Hurdle on the one-eyed Winning Fair, was – and though I have not seen him in action lately may well still be – one of the best men to hounds across the formidable country of Limerick and Tipperary. It may not be politically correct to say so, but the twenty days (I thought them well worth counting) I have spent from time to time trying to follow the Limerick, Tipperary and Scarteen (Black and Tan) hounds in southern Ireland were not only the best, most exciting hunting I have ever enjoyed, but were also as good a test of all-round cross-country riding as I ever saw. And that comes not from a triumphant graduate – more a respectful failure.

That night after the racing, when Beltran entertained us at his magnificent castle, we understood the full, hypnotic meaning of Spanish hospitality – feasting on wine, delicious meat and seafood, more wine, Flamenco music to warm the blood and girls to kindle it with castanets, black gleaming hair and swaying hips. There were certainly moments that night when, however slight your claim, you *felt* like a champion of the world.

San Isidro is partly a festival of bullfighting and, having given myself repeated injections of Hemingway, I was already halfway to addiction before I ever entered my first Plaza de Toros.

Your heart, sensibility, feelings – whatever you call them – seem to get softer, maybe more scrupulous, with age. Now, forty years after my first bullfight, I find the whole thing – especially the inevitable, unavoidable plight of the bull – very much harder to accept. The equally inevitable fate of the picadors' horses was always difficult to bear – close to impossible, in fact, for anyone whose life and livelihood have depended as much on the horse as mine.

So now I shall never go to another bullfight – not even a display of *rejoneador* expertise as elegant as the one I saw a few years ago. The art of the *rejoneador* – a bullfighter mounted on a horse – requires horsemanship of a high order and, unless things go very badly wrong, the horse is comparatively safe. I have never seen one seriously hurt – and now I never will. Because even at its highest, most artistic level, the fact remains that the bull will first be made a fool of, then badly hurt – quite badly even (my old excuse) in the hottest of hot blood – and then, inevitably killed. And however much I admire the courage and grace a good, truly brave bullfighter must have I can no longer get pleasure from that as a spectacle.

Taxidermist opened his 1958–9 campaign at Hurst Park, coming third behind Lochroe in the Grand Sefton Trial Handicap Chase. (The Grand Sefton Chase was in those days the highlight of the autumn meeting at Liverpool.) He was then aimed at the Hennessy Gold Cup at Cheltenham, where, as in the Whitbread, his opponents included Kerstin and Mandarin (who had won the first running of the race a year earlier –

highly appropriately as he was owned by Madame Kilian Hennessy). Mandarin – again top weight – started odds-on favourite, while Taxi drifted in the market to 10–1, on account of the ever-softening going. For most of the race even that price seemed pretty skinny – but let Marlborough tell the story of the race as he saw it:

Twenty miles from Cheltenham the rain was falling steadily on Saturday morning. It seemed to me to be drowning what slender hopes remained for Taxidermist. It seemed unlikely that he would run at all – let alone that six hours and a few hectic seconds later I should hear those final wonderful words that announced him the winner of the second Hennessy Gold Cup.

As we cantered to the post the horses' hooves were cutting deep into the soggy turf. I remember with a sinking heart how in a gallop at Sandown last spring poor Taxidermist had floundered hopelessly through the mud to finish tired and miserable more than a furlong behind his stable companion, Mandarin.

El Griego, Haytedder and Valiant Spark set off in front; and in the first mile things began to look brighter. Taxidermist was able to keep his place and as always no jockey could ask for a more perfect ride.

Steadily and sensibly he measures each

fence long before it is reached. Five strides away his ears cock forward and often when a lesser horse would be in trouble up he sails outside the wing to land as thistledown and gallop on with the smooth economy of effort that makes the champion chaser.

As we came down the hill for the first time Mandarin just in front of us was badly baulked. Only an equine acrobat could have stayed upright and only Gerry Madden, used as he is to this kind of antic, could have kept his seat.

The weight and the going seemed to beat Mandarin in the end but he had no luck in running and I for one shall expect him soon to prove that this was not his real form.

Passing the stands I could feel the going have its first effects on Taxidermist. The pace was quickening and he began to change his legs. He was not tired and his jumping never failed him, but he was struggling at every stride to get a footing in the treacherous shifting ground.

At the water the second time, where Kerstin hit the front, I watched with extremely mixed feelings as Gaillac, who had once been almost tailed off, swept past and up to the leaders.

Taxidermist's owners, Mrs Cath Walwyn and Mrs Priscilla Hastings, had been sorely tortured by doubt before they at length decided to run. They are, of course, devoted to the horse and my orders were clear – not to persevere if the going had robbed him of his chance.

He jumped the last fence on the far side less perfectly than most and now as the leaders drew away I came within an ace of giving up. Two things decided me to continue: passing the farm Taxidermist's stride began to lengthen, and still far in front I saw Madden wave his whip as Mandarin began to tire.

Perhaps there was still some hope but as Kerstin swept on with Caesar's Helm and Gaillac at her heels it seemed a forlorn hope indeed. Taxidermist hates to gallop downhill (his hind feet sometimes even strike his elbows) and I do not believe he made a yard of ground until the second fence from home.

As the last loomed up we were closing with Mandarin but the others had already landed safe and Kerstin must have been at least ten lengths to the good. Knowing my horse's stamina (my own was dwindling fast) I thought he might be placed, but victory seemed as remote as the moon itself.

Few who saw it will easily forget what happened next. I shall remember with wonder and gratitude all my life. If ever a horse deserved John Masefield's famous words it was Taxidermist at this moment. He indeed was

'Ready to burst his heart to pass
Each gasping horse in that street of grass.'

Gaillac and Caesar's Helm might have been rooted to the ground and twenty yards from the line the fantastic possibility of catching Kerstin became real for the first time.

Six yards to go ... five ... four ... and I thought we had her. But no. Surely the post had come too soon. To Stan Hayhurst, who had ridden a perfect race, it seemed that Kerstin had held on. I agreed. The all-seeing camera proved us wrong.

Poor Kerstin! She looked better than ever and, more than likely thought the race was over before the end. Had there been no camera the judge could only have given a dead heat. Perhaps after three and a half miles that would have been the fairest result.

But Taxidermist did get his nose in front and, to do so, achieved the impossible. There was no question of judgement. We could not have been an inch nearer than we were at the last fence and only an exceptional horse could produce such speed at the end of such a race.

For Fulke Walwyn this was yet another triumph of the trainer's art and for Taxidermist's grateful rider yet another gift from the Fates who have already smiled on him more than any man deserves.

To have won the Imperial Cup, Whitbread and Hennessy in the same year was not a bad achievement for any jockey let alone a balding amateur exponent of the Old English Lavatory Seat. But that Hennessy was extra special on account of the effect it had on my father – pushing eighty by then – who stood near the last fence to watch the race and was so excited by what he saw that he described the experience in a note:

Today was one of the most exciting if not the most exciting I've had. John was to ride Taxidermist in the Hennessy Gold Cup at Cheltenham, and as the going was soft we did not know whether they would run him until the numbers went up...

They charged the first two jumps near the stand like a cavalry brigade and soon disappeared into the mist. When they came round the first time John was in the middle of the bunch but on or near the rails. After the turn for home they were more strung out and he was perhaps sixth or seventh. Kerstin was leading by then but I only listened for Taxidermist's name.

Between the last two fences I heard the announcer say he was making up ground and as he came at the last he was fifth or sixth. On landing he quickened at once and got to fourth and seemed to be going best of them all, but the leaders – Kerstin still leading – were about ten lengths ahead.

I thought John would be third, Marjorie said he might be second. We then hurried up to the winner's enclosure and found an enormous crowd of excited people, among them Mrs Whitbread, who said John had won. But as Taxidermist was in the second enclosure and there seemed to be a lot of people standing round Kerstin in the first, I could not believe he had really won.

They seemed to be giving a cup to somebody, possibly Mrs Hastings and Mrs Walwyn, but I thought it might be for second.

John had disappeared into the weighing room before we got there. Many people gave different accounts but Mrs Whitbread stuck to it that they had announced that John had won. I would not believe it and was nearly crying with excitement and anxiety so we hurried back to the lawn, and there I saw the number 5 at the top. Later we saw the official photo which showed a win by the shortest of short heads, but unmistakable.

I did not see John until he rode out for the next race but one, but I stood at the exit from the saddling ring to make certain. I saw him and gave him a word. It was the most marvellous finish I ever saw.

The most exciting day of my father's life?

Well, of course it cannot have been. He had fought Germans and/or Turks for three years in the First World War, winning a DSO and twice being mentioned in dispatches. He had been a judge for twenty-five years, including Nuremberg – and one of his beloved Guernsey cows Flintham Duchess won a championship at the Royal. Nevertheless, true or false, in all the circumstances, as you can imagine, they were nice words for his son to read.

7

'Just trot and hang on to the neckstrap'

I have mentioned my courting Ginger Dennistoun's daughter Victoria – 'Tory'. In May 1959 we were married at the Inner Temple Church, with Martin Jacomb as best man. I had a pretty memorable stag night – except that 'memorable' is not quite the right word, because not many of us could remember much about it: certainly not Gay Kindersley, who got back to his wife Magsie so heavily smeared with lipstick and smelling of cheap scent that she turned up two days later at the wedding dressed in black. Piers Bengough, who became Her Majesty's Representative at Ascot, was in an even worse state than Gay, and I have a photograph of him slumped across the table to prove it!

After our honeymoon in Italy, Tory and I went to live with Ginger and Nancy Dennistoun at Antwick, but this was not a long-term success, and after six months we rented a cottage in Childrey belonging to Joy Bassett. At this time Tory was expecting our first child, Patrick, and all the time we were looking for a more permanent home. In 1960 we found Marndhill, a house the other side of Wantage near Lockinge and Ardington, which was really too big for us but had a marvellous garden. Our second child, Sara, was born a year later, and it was at this time that we had the great good fortune to employ Nanny Butler, a marvellous lady who brought up the children with, I think, just the right mixture of love and discipline. When we moved to Marndhill they both started riding. Patrick never really took to it, although he did once or twice ride to his school at Larch Lloyd's house in Lockinge where he and Sara had in common with the dual Gold Cup winner Best Mate the privilege of being taught by Henrietta Knight. Of course, she had not acquired Terry Biddlecombe yet, but she was already – in the days before she turned her abilities to training racehorses – a brilliant teacher.

But brilliant teachers do not come cheap, and to supplement our income we took in the occasional lodger – notably a fresh-faced youth with a passion for racing who was riding out locally and needed a regular billet. His name was Brough Scott, and from the days when I first knew him he has brought to everything he pursues an enthusiasm and intelligence which have long been a source of envy. We rode against each other on countless occasions and have, over the years, found ourselves in the same employment on several occasions – notably, of course, with ITV and then Channel Four Racing. In 1978 Brough became a trustee of the Injured Jockeys' Fund (a position he still holds), and I am proud to have considered him a friend for so long.

I was busy riding out, not only with Ginger and Bob Turnell but with anyone else who seemed at all likely to give me a ride. When I met Jakie Astor – through Tom Egerton, who, like Jakie, had horses with Dick Hern at West Ilsley – I little suspected that he would become one of my most generous and prolific suppliers of rides.

Jakie – fourth son of the second Viscount Astor and son of Nancy – had just installed Dick Hern as his private trainer in place of Jack Colling at West Ilsley, the famous stables and gallops which he bought and was later to sell to the Queen. (It was the Queen's purchase of West Ilsley which lay behind the sale to Sheikh Hamdan Al Maktoum of her broodmare Height Of Fashion, who after being sold by Her Majesty became the dam of Nashwan, Unfuwain and Nayef.) When I first knew him Jakie was selling his geldings and potential jumpers – among them, sadly, the great stayer Trelawny and, only a short time before the events I am about to relate, the brilliant hurdler Persian War. I have always wondered what would have happened if the triple Champion Hurdler has stayed in Jakie's hands for a bit longer. What a thrill it would have been to school him – but then I reluctantly come to the conclusion that I would not have got half as much out of him as his regular jockey Jimmy Uttley.

Meeting Jakie on the downs above Lambourn one day, I asked him to dinner at Marndhill. Ginger and I happened to have had a fairly serious row riding out that morning, at the end of which I told him never to darken the doors of Marndhill again, and accordingly we locked all the doors after Jakie arrived and were just sitting down to dinner when Ginger turned up. Ginger later explained that he could not bear to be left out when such an important potential owner was being entertained, but I'm not sure whether that excused his method of entry – commando-style, crashing through the dining-room window, upsetting at least one candle and setting the curtains on fire. Jakie, who knew Ginger of old, took all this in his stride.

This was not a particularly satisfactory start to our trainer-jockey relationship, but when Jakie started training at his Bedfordshire home Hatley we managed to fulfil one of his great ambitions – to saddle a winner with his first runner. This was a tough little horse called Dashing, and although the prize for the Fakenham novice hurdle he won was a princely £120, it was worth a very great deal more to Jakie and me. The night after Dashing's success I slept in a bedroom at Hatley, the wall of which was covered with a cupboard full of huge ledgers. They turned out to be the deeds and rent books of the New York property on which the Astor family's fortune was founded…

Over the next ten years or so I had wonderful fun riding Jakie's horses, and schooling them at Hatley. Most of our outings were at East Anglian courses, and one notable day at Fakenham I was knocked out in a hurdle race fall. The racecourse doctor wanted to take me to some local hospital, but Jakie insisted on Addenbrookes at Cambridge. It was a Bank Holiday and the ambulance was forced to go at a funereal pace in the holiday traffic – with Jakie cursing himself for prolonging the journey and, he thought, putting my life in danger. Needless to say he wasn't doing any such thing.

When we reached Addenbrookes I was examined for the umpteenth time with the by now boring routine of reflex tests, and early next morning a grand-looking surgeon came in with a class of students behind him. After doing the tests all over again he turned to his pupils and pronounced: 'Either this man has got very slow reflexes, or he is dead.' Loud laughter from the class, not echoed by me. I had a coveted ride on Bullock's Horn in the Grand National coming up but in the event I was forced to miss the race, and among many other letters of consolation I got one from my great literary hero Siegfried Sassoon. I wrote him a letter of thanks and have always cursed my idleness in not taking up his invitation to meet when I got out of hospital.

At that time Jakie was still married to his first wife Chiquita, the beautiful Roman Catholic daughter of a South American diplomat. The sad thing was that she did not like the country life of Hatley and would much rather have been living in London. At the time of their wedding in 1944 his mother, who objected strongly to Chiquita's Catholicism, flatly refused to attend. Later Chiquita became one of her favourite daughters-in-law, but Jakie was upset at the time and said that he would have reservations about attending his mother's funeral! I never knew Lady Astor, but clearly she was not a lady to be trifled with. When Jakie heard that she might write her autobiography, his suggested title was *Guilty but Insane*. In fact, when she suffered her final illness she asked her son, 'Am I dying or is this my birthday?' 'A bit of both' was Jakie's reply. (Jakie kept his sense of humour to the very end of his own life in 2000. 'The best thing about dying is that you don't have to pack,' he said.)

I would often arrive at Hatley quite late at night, to be greeted by Jakie's marvellously smooth and Jeeves-like butler Leonard. At weekends there would probably be a party often including William Douglas-Home, Arthur Marshall, Tom Egerton and others of Jakie's friends, many of them from Cambridge. Most of these I got on with well, but on one memorable occasion I had a fairly major disagreement with Lord Rothschild. The ladies had left the dinner table, and finally this famous scientist became so unkind to another guest that I could not bear it and stormed out into the drawing room. 'I can't take that bloody man!' I exclaimed, not noticing that his wife Lady Rothschild was among my audience. Luckily she quite agreed – and so did Jakie.

Evenings at Hatley were invariably memorable, often with a pretty high standard of conversation. Roy Jenkins, with whom Jakie had made great friends during his time in Parliament, was often there in later years, and so was Woodrow Wyatt, chairman of the Tote. Jakie never really enjoyed the House of Commons, and only stood in the first place to please his mother: the politician he most admired was Aneurin Bevan, not a popular choice among his Tory colleagues. To make matters worse, he deeply disapproved of

Anthony Eden's policy at the time of Suez and ignored the whips, taking the view that the Government's actions were 'unnecessary and wrong'.

Jakie never spoke much about his own war, but was almost certainly one of those people who believed in deeds and not words. In fact he joined the SAS and was closely involved in the communications on which the success of D-Day depended.

About halfway through the time I knew him he suddenly took up flying and installed an airstrip at Hatley. Like everything else he did, perfection was the aim, and we had many happy flights until the accursed Parkinson's Disease began to make itself felt. Jakie faced it with typical courage, for quite a while not admitting that it was affecting him. By that time I had given up riding in races and so we saw less of one another, but he remained one of my best and most beloved friends, a 'proper person' in all the senses of that much argued-over expression. (It was Jakie who suggested that my autobiography were it ever to be written, should be entitled *Bumping and Boring* to reflect the riding and writing sides of my life. But the publishers of the current volume vetoed the idea, on the perfectly understandable grounds that the last word of such a title might be uncomfortably close to the truth!)

In 1976, after he and Chiquita had separated, Jakie married Susie Sheppard. His third wife Marcia de Savary was, among many other things, a talented sculptress and I am glad to remember that during Jakie's last months a commission to do a one-and-a-half-times life-size bronze of a horse was awarded to her. The bronze stands outside the National Stud in Newmarket, and will always remind me, like so many other things, of Jakie and our time together.

Ginger Dennistoun was a past master at getting a horse fit, who liked nothing better than laying one of his horses out for a decent punt. In August 1948 he was planning to give a horse of his named Prompt Corner a quiet run round in a selling handicap at Haydock Park, with a view to getting the horse a lower weight in a later race when the money would be down. Shortly before the race he sought out the trainer Keith Piggott, whose twelve-year-old son Lester was riding The Chase in the same race, to tell him that Prompt Corner, ridden by Davy Jones, was 'not off'. In his autobiography Lester described what would turn out to be an historic occasion:

Apparently Ginger Dennistoun decided late on that Prompt Corner should try his best after all, then changed his mind again when he was unable to get his money on, so the last instruction to Davy Jones was to go easy. As The Chase and I took up the running close home Jones, just behind me, was screaming 'Go on! Go on!' – which is just what we did, winning by a length and a half.

So Ginger had played a part in bringing Lester the first of the 4,493 winners he would ride in Britain.

My father-in-law lived up to his nickname in several different ways. His temper, not all that difficult to rouse, was definitely on the warm side, and although generally obedient to the Rules (when he approved of them) there were some – those governing selling races, for instance – which he neither approved of, nor, if he could get away with it, observed!

Ginger, whose hair, until it went grey, was the appropriate colour, had an unerring eye for a horse and was a first-rate stableman and, except on the rare occasions when his judgement was distorted by betting, a skilful all-round trainer. He had saddled High Point to win two Imperial Cups in the early 1950s, when that race was still by far the most valuable and hotly contested handicap hurdle of the season.

One of Ginger's favourite manoeuvres was to buy a few cheap or cheapish yearlings at the autumn sales, test them at home and, if one showed a bit of ability put it in the weakest possible race – and back it to the hilt.

For most of the 1950s one of Ginger's most reliable assistants in his sorties against the bookies was a grey called Fellhound, whose owner Ben Smith also owned Broadway Motors, a big garage in Wantage, not far from Ginger's yard. Tough as old boots and a bold jumper, Fellhound went wonderfully well for Harry Sprague, and the combination was hard to beat in handicap hurdles when the money was down. But the handicapper did not show Fellhound much mercy and one obvious alternative was a switch to novice chasing. The only snag about putting Fellhound over fences was that Harry his best friend and most effective companion in arms, was a hurdles specialist who rode over fences only in exceptional circumstances. (His most famous victory over the larger obstacles came in the 1959 Whitbread Gold Cup, when the effort of forcing Done Up to short-head Mandarin so exhausted Harry that he threw up while returning to unsaddle – and later discovered that in the process he had ejected his false teeth! Done Up's trainer Ryan Price had to go and scrabble around in the dirt – and eventually found them.)

Fellhound's first novice chase was definitely not exceptional enough for Harry but

Ginger had the ideal substitute ready and willing.

Dave Dick had never ridden Fellhound in a race, but Ginger had known him since he won the Lincoln on Gloaming in 1941 as an apprentice. Now, though pushed to do much less than eleven stone, Dave would ride anything, and he and Fellhound might have been made for each other. First time out over fences, in fact, they were narrowly beaten – by Bob McCreery and Gold Wire – but that was just for practice.

There was still a jumping course at Birmingham in those days, and in his second attempt at steeplechasing Fellhound took to the straightforward fences there like an old hand. Eight years old and nearly white by that time, he made not a single mistake, jumping through the Birmingham smog like a ghostly stag.

You need a bit of luck in racing, and Ginger's guardian angel must have been busy that afternoon: he not only contrived to have a hard-drinking sportsman called John Fox-Strangways at Birmingham, but also saw to it that he was deeply impressed by Fellhound's polished jumping.

'Who on earth trains that? He must be a real expert,' said Fox-Strangways – and promptly had Ginger pointed out and introduced. 'Will you buy me a horse?' were almost his first words – but the next, unfortunately made it all too clear that this was no Sheikh Mohammed-type transaction. 'You can go to five hundred quid if you must,' said Fox-Strangways, 'but the cheaper the better.' So with those somewhat unpromising orders in mind, Ginger went off to the sales in Dublin.

A bay yearling colt by Guersant caught his eye, largely because of its walk. But in any case, Ginger liked horses by Guersant, having had one which, though no flying machine, was tough and game. Barbizon (not yet named, of course) strode round the Ballsbridge ring as if he owned it. The girl leading him was only just in control, and although the bay yearling had not much flesh on his bones, those bones looked to be put together in more or less the right order.

Rather surprisingly Ginger's first bid looked, for a while, like being the last – and in the end 120 guineas was enough to gain the day. But economy was still the watchword, and Ginger shipped his purchase home as cheaply as possible, by ferry. The new owner could certainly not complain of extravagance!

Sadly Barbizon's first step on British soil was not a happy one. Prancing out of the box on to the platform at Challow Station, he landed, as luck would have it, squarely on Ginger's toe. Luckily the yearling had no shoes – but it still hurt quite a bit. Through clenched teeth the wounded trainer gave his orders. 'I'll ring the vet now. He'll be there when you get back. Ask him to cut [geld] this so-and-so there and then.'

So, for better or worse, poor Barbizon's stud career ended before it had a chance to begin. Judging by his antics when he first appeared on the gallops, it was probably just as well: who knows? In fact, his dam had been best at two miles and two of his half-sisters were jumpers. So imagine Ginger's surprise and delight when, almost the moment he was backed and ridden away the still unfurnished, backward-looking 120-guinea purchase began to step out as if he had been doing it for years. He matched strides not only with the other two-year-olds, but quite soon with a three-year-old as well. Finally still reluctant to believe his luck, Ginger asked Fulke Walwyn if he could come and work one morning at Lambourn. Security was, of course, a first priority and Fulke, well aware of Ginger's need to have the occasional punt at a good price to keep the wolf from the door, promised faithfully to have only lads he could trust in the gallop.

I was never told the name of Barbizon's companion, but whatever it was, he was ridden right out and finished at least four lengths behind, with Barbizon still on the bit. They had only gone about four furlongs, but both Fulke and Ginger were smiling as they turned away and the atmosphere at breakfast was distinctly cheerful.

I have always thought that moments like that – when an untried horse suddenly shows unmistakable ability – must be among the brightest spots in a trainer's so often bitterly disappointing life. Of course, the glow may not last. 'Morning glories' can blind the most experienced eye. But that first flash of real promise, even if it turns out to be dross, must make the birds sing louder and the sun shine bright.

There were only five runners in the Sunbury Selling Stakes at Kempton Park on Saturday 7 May 1960. I can still remember the date, as it was one of the rare days when almost everything went right.

Ginger had engaged Willie Snaith to ride Barbizon and, conscious of the fact that Willie was a cheerful soul, always apt to be the life and soul of any party, told him in the parade ring (but not before!) that this was no joyride. By that time Barbizon, who opened in the betting at 8–1, was being heavily backed. As a very amateurish 'commission agent', equipped with pockets full of readies, I scurried around the bookmakers trying to take the longer odds, and was eventually able to report the placement of £400 at an 'average' of 6–1, of which I was rather proud, as his starting price was 11–4 favourite. Ginger, on the other hand, did not think much of my efforts and always claimed that his own 'agent' had done far better.

The race went very smoothly Barbizon was given a lead for three furlongs by Scobie Breasley on the third favourite Mickey Walker, but took over two furlongs out. Mindful of his 'be serious' instructions, Willie rode him out to the line and beat Mickey Walker by eight lengths. Not altogether surprisingly Ginger had to go to 1,300 guineas to buy his horse back.

Barbizon won his next two races easily and started at 4–1 *on* when finishing third in the Champagne Stakes at Salisbury but ran only once as a three-year-old. Then, in the late summer of 1961, Ginger started schooling him over hurdles. Having by this time married the Guv'nor's daughter, I had (very slightly) improved my prospects of getting rides. Only very slightly though, because, as he made clear almost every morning, Ginger's opinion of my talent in the saddle was only a little more favourable than Fulke Walwyn's 'Old English Lavatory Seat'. But he had 'used' me once or twice and, by riding out pretty regularly at Antwick, I did my level best to enter his good books.

Just the same, it was an almost complete surprise when, one night at the poker table, or rather, as we got up from it to go to bed, Ginger growled, 'Ride Barbizon tomorrow morning.'

I had only ridden the bay once or twice, and was well aware, even then, that holding him together tested my strength and ability to the limit. But you can get lucky, and the Fates were smiling that day. Cantering over three flights of hurdles, Barbizon not only settled calmly but met all three in his stride and jumped them like an agile veteran. Of course, I knew it was too good to be true – and so, no doubt, did Ginger. But he left me on and, better still, let me ride in Barbizon's first seven 'real' races. We won two of them and were second twice, but all the time, win or lose, I knew all too well that there was more, much more, to come, if only I was strong enough to get it.

I have often wondered since if what Ginger and I did that season was 'dishonest'. Barbizon ran nine times – beginning with three justifiably educational sighting shots, in the third of which, the Hedge Hoppers' Hurdle at Newbury we finished seventh. A clairvoyant racereader in *Chaseform* ended his comments with the words 'good effort'! Clairvoyant because, next time out at Wincanton, I was beaten only half a length by Starborne, out of whom Derek Scott got demonstrably more than I did out of Barbizon.

That was the first time he made me feel really inadequate – simply unequal to the task of pulling him together. I felt it again at Windsor, but that was against one of Peter Cazalet's cracks. A few weeks later, back at Wincanton, Barbizon gave my morale the boost it badly needed by winning comfortably but the question mark was still there in my mind.

I knew the answer – another (stronger) jockey – and, painful though it was, I ended up reluctantly discussing the problem with my father-in-law. Barbizon was entered in a valuable race at Hurst Park, the charming course next door to Hampton Court which, so sadly is now a housing estate. The race was called the Grey Talk Hurdle, and always attracted a good-class field. 'I might get Fred,' said Ginger – and in that context there was only one Fred.

So F. Winter went up in the frame – and that put me one ahead of the bookies. Because I *knew* that Fred's skill and, more important, his strength, would enable and/or galvanise Barbizon to run the race of his life – at least a stone in front of anything he had done before over hurdles.

'Headway from 6th; led going to last, driven out.' I can't quarrel with *Chaseform*'s description of the race – and I especially like their account of the betting: Barbizon '11–2 (touched 8–1)'. He did indeed 'touch 8–1', and Mr J. Lawrence touched it too. For the second time in Barbizon's career I knew more than the bookies. It has very seldom happened since and is not all that likely to happen again. But I am still deeply grateful to Barbizon and Ginger Dennistoun, who made it possible.

The ideal situation, before you have a bet, is to know something about the race – or the horse you are going to back – which, for whatever reason, is unknown to the rest of the world, or at least to the bookie with whom you are betting. Of course, this gives you an advantage, arguably an 'unfair' one. But if, in the ultra-competitive world of horse-race betting, you are going to start worrying about things like that, you would unquestionably be better advised to stay at home, and keep your money in your pocket.

Jockeys are notoriously unreliable tipsters, and in my experience trainers are not much better. But you can, I believe, use your knowledge of jockeys, and their ability – or lack of it – to work out results and winning distances, particularly if you happen to have been involved. I used, for instance, to have a fair idea, after a race, how near I had come to getting the best out of whatever I was riding. Nine times out of ten, the answer (without false modesty) was 'nowhere near'. Even at my fittest, I often found myself getting uncomfortably tired, especially on something which pulled to begin with and then needed holding together and driving.

But that deplorable weakness did turn out, in one or two cases, to pay dividends. On Barbizon, for instance, I *knew* that Fred Winter's presence on his back would improve him by several pounds – and lengths – and was able to benefit from that inside knowledge.

Betting on a race in which I was myself riding was, of course, strictly forbidden, but had it been allowed I would certainly have risked a few shillings on my partner in the four-mile National Hunt Chase at Cheltenham in March 1959. Sabaria, owned and trained by Bob Turnell, absolutely trotted up – a particularly sweet victory as Bob had been so kind and helpful to me over the years. For amateur jockeys the National Hunt Chase was – and is – one of the biggest events of the season. It is also a race with a long and venerable history: it was first run in 1860, and in its early years the venue would move from course to course; its settling at Cheltenham in 1911 signalled the start there of what we now call the National Hunt Festival.

In his younger days Sabaria had got loose on the road, galloping for miles before being caught; as a result his forelegs took on the shape of two pillar boxes. He was a big, long-striding horse who was brilliant if he met the fence right; the danger came when he misjudged. I'd love to have ridden him in the Grand National: he ran in the race in 1960 (fifth behind Merryman II) and 1961 (thirteenth of fourteen finishers).

On the work front, in 1959 I was approached by *Horse and Hound* to become its new racing correspondent, taking on the venerable *nom de plume* Audax. I was only the third Audax in the magazine's history following in the distinguished footsteps of Arthur Portman (who had founded *Horse and Hound* in 1884 and was still Audax when killed by a bomb in 1940) and David Livingstone-Learmonth. Writing a 3,000-word piece for a weekly magazine started out as quite a chore compared with my more familiar task of composing much shorter pieces for the *Telegraph*, but I soon grew to appreciate the opportunity to write about events and issues on which I'd had a few days to reflect.

My bread and butter, however, continued to come from the daily paper, and a story which I took particular pleasure in filing appeared on 3 March 1962:

The sun came out today just before the Corinthian Handicap Chase. Perhaps it was an omen, as for Taxidermist too the clouds rolled away and soon, with his famous final sprint, he at last put behind him three long years of defeat and disappointment.

It was in February 1959 that Taxi last won a race – when he beat Linwell at Newbury. On the strength of that, with Saffron Tartan scratched at the last moment, he started favourite for the Gold Cup, only to fall when in touch with the leaders five fences from home.

I have often wondered how much that luckless fall (he made no mistake but landed in a patch of mud) may have cost my old friend. For Linwell, whom he had just beaten four lengths, was a good second and Roddy Owen came from far behind to win very much in Taxi's style.

The question was never to be answered, for after that Gold Cup outrageous fortune lost no time in loosing off its slings and arrows.

The first was a serious liver complaint, the second a strained tendon, and the third a flaw in Taxi's wind. He was fired on both forelegs, tubed, then Hobdayed, and when at last at Windsor he finally got his head in front fortune, in the shape of a valid objection, intervened again.

I make no apology for repeating the story. It explains a little how I felt when he passed the post today and it explains the applause that welcomed him back. When a horse with this record gives away 21lb, four years and a beating it is surely, however humble the race, something to shout about.

The runner-up to whom Taxi was giving the weight and the four years was a highly promising six-year-old named Carrickbeg, of whom we shall hear more – a great deal more! – shortly.

The 1959 Cheltenham Gold Cup, for which Taxi started 4–1 favourite, was my first ride in the most prestigious race of the jumps season, and the sense of disappointment when he knuckled over at the fifth last, when going as well as any of his rivals, was acute. I felt I might never have as good a chance again – and I didn't. Indeed, I never again had a ride in the Gold Cup.

But if opportunities to compete at the very highest level were strictly limited, there were still plenty of good horses for me to ride.

Rosie's Cousin was a brilliant hunter-chaser and perhaps the best jumper of a steeplechase fence that I ever sat on – positively spring-heeled, he would pick up outside the wing of a fence and fly. But in a way he was an infuriating horse, as he scarcely stayed three miles even on fast ground and a flat course such as Stratford, and when he reached the limit of his stamina he would just die on me, which meant that the knack was to build up a big enough advantage in the early part of the race to coast home once the tank ran dry.

One day at Taunton in 1962 we were on the verge of beating the great hunter-chaser Baulking Green, about a fence in front of that wonderful old campaigner with less than half a mile to go. But Taunton has notoriously sharp bends and it had just rained on the firm ground – and poor Rosie's Cousin lost his footing on the turn into the straight. Falling on the flat is always worse than falling at a fence, and that one hurt more than most.

Rosie's Cousin was never beaten when partnered in point-to-points by Mrs Pat Tollitt, daughter of his owner Major Rushton, and after winning yet another race dropped dead under her while coming back to scale.

Another splendidly agile horse was Don Verde, whom I was asked to ride in a novice hurdle at Worcester in October 1960 by a new young trainer named Peter Walwyn – cousin of Fulke. Don Verde duly won, thus granting Mr J. Lawrence the distinction of having put one of the great trainers of the age on the first rung of the ladder he was to climb so memorably notably with the 1975 Derby winner Grundy whose battle with Bustino in that year's King George VI and Queen Elizabeth Diamond Stakes at Ascot remains one of the most stirring Flat races I ever witnessed. But even the most

)VER–UNDER THE PONY'S NOSE

MIND my nose, sir!" A pair of flashing heels with one led eye upon them show that e are more ways than one of ng company at the hurdles. pony thought this way the est yet.

aking a toss neatly in this pic- is John Lawrence, son of the Geoffrey and Lady Lawrence.

Mince Pie in stubborn mood at the pony hunter trials at Purton, 1935

Aged seventeen in 'Pop' (Eton Society) finery

The Eton boxing team, with me seated, far right

My father outside Hill Farm, Oaksey, which he bought in 1919 and where I still live

My mother at Epsom races

Three sisters and Mince Pie — Libby in the saddle, Robby on the left and Jenny on the right

Taxidermist in his glory year, 1958: *above*, catching Mandarin (Gerry Madden) at the last fence of the Whitbread Gold Cup at Sandown Park *(Empics)*; and, *below*, in an apparently impossible position going to the last in the Hennessy at Cheltenham

Trapeze II taking advantage of my seven-pound allowance when winning at Plumpton on New Year's Day 1958. The other horse in the picture is third-placed Clapper (Alan Oughton) *(Empics)*

Sabaria wins the 1959 National Hunt Chase at Cheltenham *(PA Photos)*

Rosie's Cousin winning at Stratford in March 1963 *(Bernard Parkin)*

Before the ceiling fell in: Pioneer Spirit in full flight at Cheltenham, December 1964. In second place on French Cottage is Bill Tellwright, unaware of the prize about to fall into his lap *below (Bernard Parkin)*

Thames Trader strolling home in the inaugural Moët et Chandon Silver Magnum at Epsom on August Bank Holiday 1963 *above (PA Photos)*

Taxidermist and me (stripes) about to depart from the 1961 Grand National at Becher's Brook first time round *(Empics)* — then walking away as Colonel Volchkov legs up Vladimir Prakhov to remount Reljef *(Associated Press)*

Commiserating with Beltran, Duke of Alburquerque, after the fifty-seven-year-old had finished third on Tuscan Prince in the Dick McCreery Cup at Sandown Park, March 1976 *(Hulton Archive/Getty Images)*

At Deauville in 1969 with John Ciechanowski

'The perfect ride': Happy Medium sails over the last to win the Benson and Hedges Gold Cup at Sandown Park, December 1971 *(E.G. Byrne)*

Carrickbeg over the last in the 1963 Grand National — with nemesis, in the form of Pat Buckley and Ayala, at our shoulder

Tuscan Prince with me in his prime — airborne on his way to winning at Sandown Park, January 1972 *(E.G. Byrne)* — and in his venerable old age at Hill Farm, Oaksey *(Kit Houghton)*

Proud Tarquin heroic in big-race defeat on consecutive Saturdays in April 1974: *above*, caught by Red Rum at the final fence of the Scottish Grand National, and *right*, edging towards — but never touching! — The Dikler at the last in the Whitbread *(S.K.R. Photos)*

With John Francome, in and out of the saddle: *left*, on Naughty Boy upsides John on the winner Osbaldeston tracking Richard Pitman (left) and Stan Mellor at Kempton Park, December 1971, and *right*, doing my homework for Channel Four Racing at Chester, while my hirsute colleague as usual seems to be studying the female form *(Gerry Cranham)*

With the beloved Patron of the Injured Jockeys' Fund at Newbury, November 1985 *(Bernard Parkin)*

The pride of my bathroom wall *(George Selwyn)*

A day with the Mid-Surrey Farmers' Drag, with my great friend Edward Cazalet (right)

Athletic pursuits: *above*, paragliding on the Injured Jockeys' Fund holiday in Tenerife *(Peter Dun)*; *below*, skiing in Aspen, Colorado, with Evelyn Jacomb (left) and Chicky; *right*, in training for the London Marathon in 1983 — encouraged by a bewhiskered tricyclist

My children Patrick and Sara

My wedding to Chicky in March 1988, with the happy couple flanked by Patrick (left), Mark Crocker (seated), Clare Crocker and Patrick Crawford (behind)

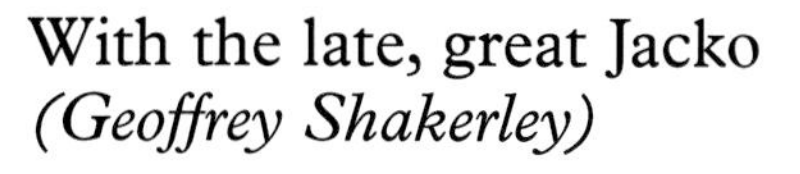

With the late, great Jacko
(Geoffrey Shakerley)

Patrick's daughter
Cleopatra, with Muff

Sara and Mark's son Alfie riding work on Murphy when aged eight

Plaid Maid — 'Rosie' — after winning yet another Exeter steeplechase, with Jane King and her admiring jockey Tony McCoy.

Future Ascot and/or Cheltenham Gold Cup hero Carruthers with his mother, his proud co-owner and Vicky How *(Chicky Oaksey)*

distinguished trainers must start somewhere, and I am proud to have ridden P.T. Walwyn's first winner.

But I'm sorry to say that Don Verde, who won several other races, also gave me one of my saddest racing days. I don't claim he would have *won* the County Hurdle at Cheltenham in 1961, but he would certainly have been in the first three or four, and it was the fearless leap that he threw at the last flight of hurdles, standing back just inches too far, which thrust his front feet through, instead of over, the top bars of the flight. He broke a leg and was put down on the spot.

Before he started to concentrate on the Flat, Peter trained a good few jumpers, among them a very decent chaser named Royal Spirit, on whom I won a few races.

In November 1962 I mentioned briefly in *Horse and Hound* 'a fine big five-year-old' whom the great Irish trainer Tom Dreaper had taken the bold step of sending across to Cheltenham to make his steeplechasing debut after a few highly promising – but far from spectacular – outings over hurdles. At the same period the big hope – in many senses – for English steeplechasing was another immensely promising young horse named Mill House, a giant whom everybody in Fulke Walwyn's yard had been talking about for months. Like everybody else I thought Mill House was wonderful, and it was no surprise to see him power home to win the 1963 Gold Cup from Fortria. At the same meeting the 'fine big five-year-old' trained by Tom Dreaper, whose name was Arkle, won the Broadway Chase in astonishing fashion, as I described in *Horse and Hound* before moving on to join in the debate about the comparative merits of these two young phenomena:

Arkle's victory in the Broadway Chase was a heart-warming sight for any lover of a good horse, whatever his nationality.

No real doubt existed that Arkle was a good horse – and the opposition was not all that impressive. But the way Arkle dealt with it had to be seen to be believed.

Coming to the third last sandwiched between Brasher and Jomsviking, Arkle jumped it less well than either of his rivals and looked for a moment in grave danger of getting squeezed out.

At the next fence, too, he gained no ground, and in front of me a partisan with an Irish air groaned – whether from heart or pocket or both I could not tell – 'Begod he's beat.' But the next ten seconds made him eat his words.

Without a visible signal from Pat Taaffe, without the slightest apparent effort, Arkle was a dozen lengths clear. He simply shot from between the two English horses like a cherry stone from a schoolboy's fingers. It was done in less than 50 yards and neither of the others was stopping.

It is, of course, both tempting and downright useless to make comparisons between this performance and that of Mill House in the Gold Cup. In my opinion Mill House is, at present, a better and faster jumper than Arkle – but further than that I would not go.

One can only pray that both keep sound and well until they meet – and hope that whenever and wherever that meeting takes place we will all be there to see it.

There has, in my short memory been no comparable pair of six-year-old chasers in training at one and the same time, and if they are ever to come to the second last together in a Cheltenham Gold Cup the man who would, at this moment, predict the outcome with confidence is either a fool or has second sight.

But in the immediate future in that spring of 1963 a horse taking an even more prominent place in my thoughts than those luminaries was a dark brown gelding with a huge white blaze down his face – in fact, the very horse which Taxi had beaten at Kempton Park. His name was Carrickbeg.

Taxidermist had given me my first two rides in the Grand National – he fell at first

Becher's in 1961 and pulled up on the second circuit in heavy ground which he hated in 1962 – but with that stalwart now on the verge of retirement, I could see no readymade National winner on my horizon – not even an Aintree ride with halfway reasonable prospects.

I cannot remember exactly how the idea of my taking a half share in Carrickbeg came up. My old friend Gay Kindersley was plagued by a recurrent dislocation of the shoulder and had, I think, just been operated on by Bill Tucker – the great orthopaedic patcher-upper of 71 Park Street. There was some doubt about the long-term effect of this operation, and it certainly left poor Gay with some pretty horrific-looking scars. But in any case, much as he too longed to ride in the National, there was clearly no hope of that for a year or two. And the point was that Gay had just come by a six-year-old gelding – and not just any old six-year-old either.

By the time he turned seven in January 1963, Carrickbeg had won four chases including the 1962 Kim Muir at Cheltenham, and finished fourth in a Hennessy second to Frenchman's Cove in the 1962 Whitbread and second, on other occasions, to both Mill House and (as we've seen) Taxidermist. He was practically as old a friend of mine as his owner! Anyway Gay kindly sold me a half share on the condition that, at least until he recovered, I should do the riding.

Then, of course – good old England! – the weather closed in, and everything was frozen off from New Year's Day 1963 to March.

My first ride on Carrickbeg was therefore in the Leopardstown Chase. With England frozen solid, he had not run for five weeks, and I had been leading the life of Riley – or rather of Soapey Sponge: ten wonderful days hunting in Ireland.

At this point I had better make a confession. It is that all the most thrilling and satisfying experiences of my fox-hunting life – as well as some of the most embarrassing and painful ones – have come from horses rather than hounds or, for that matter, foxes.

Of course, the fox and hound play essential parts, and I wish I understood them better. I respect and envy those to whom every cry of a hound or a note of a horn brings an immediately recognisable message – the experts to whom one clever, successful cast means more than five minutes across the best of Leicestershire, Limerick or Tipperary.

But each man to his taste. For me the high point of any day's hunting is always apt to be the delight, hard to describe but harder still to exaggerate, when you meet a big fence right and your horse picks up, lands safe – and sails away ears pricked, looking for the next one.

So it was partly the pressing need to get fit for my Grand National ride on Carrickbeg, and partly a previously unfulfilled ambition to ride over the Irish banks which took me to southern Ireland.

We had, to begin with, the best possible guide and mentor – the marvellous, incorrigible Pat Hogan, by far and away the best man across country I have ever seen. Wherever we went hunting (including days with packs of whose staff our critical host did not altogether approve – 'He has a *reed* in his horn, would you ever believe it?') Pat was treated (or anyway behaved) like an honorary field master. It was just as well, since the order, in any worthwhile hunt, was always the same: the fox, the hounds, P.P. Hogan, cantering at ease on a long rein, the huntsman (provided that he had been wide awake when they found!), a select half dozen, which in those days usually included Alan Lillingston – and the rest of us, strung out like also-rans in a selling chase.

The day I remember best of all began, like so many Irish days, in the pub of a village (probably either Knocklong or Elton) not far from Hospital. When Thady Ryan and his Scarteen 'Black and Tan' hounds arrived, jumping powder (port and brandy was the recommended mixture for nervous English beginners) had been on offer for quite a while. As we moved off – just to remind us that this was Ireland – a cheerful stray donkey called Joey joined the hounds. 'Jumps like a buck, too,' someone said – but a little boy recaptured Joey before he could confirm that warranty.

I forget the name of the gorse where we found, but remember every detail of the bank over which Pat Hogan – 'Just trot and hang on to the neckstrap,' he had advised – promptly disappeared. The landing side was ominously invisible but Tango, the smallish bay cob Pat had hired for me from the infinitely reliable Willie Gleason, either had periscope eyes or did not care.

Bounding gaily across the first ditch, he landed with a crash in the mess of blackthorn and bramble which separated it from the second. That was two yards wide, deep and full of water but, after a moment's pause to untangle his feet, Tango cleared it with equal ease. It was only thanks to Pat's advice about the neckstrap that I was still, more or less, in tow.

Have you ever seen Jim Meads's picture of the Black and Tans leaving covert in full cry? It makes you feel sorry for the fox, and that's how they were going now. After a dozen more fields and what felt like a hundred varieties of bank, our particular ginger-whiskered gentleman had the good sense to pop down a hole.

With the hounds well back, one of Thady's terriers was called for – a splendid rough-coated desperado, white with a few black patches. His name was Jacko, and on account of what followed I have named my last two black and tan terriers in his honour. Because when, thanks to Jacko (which would, of course, now be against MFHA rules), the fox emerged, the first obstacle in his path was what I think they called a 'corporation ditch'. Roughly the width of Aintree's Chair Fence and full of black smelly water, it guarded a smallish but substantial bank and was, I now understand, something to do with the local dairy.

The fox got over somehow and so did most of the hounds, but just as I was asking Tango for his solution to this new problem, Jacko (the terrier) took off under Tango's nose. The space that he cleared was a caution to see, but with three-inch legs he could hardly be blamed for landing a bit short.

Tango was in mid-air by then – and he was even less to blame for being distracted by a small white figure struggling for a foothold on the far bank. Horses don't tread on dogs if they can help it, and I shall always believe that Tango sacrificed himself (and me!) for Jacko.

The sacrifice, though not fatal, was a real one, because with gravity against him, Tango toppled slowly over backwards into the ditch. You've heard about situations in which 'everything goes black'? Well, this was one of them. The mud closed over both our heads, and for the rest of our stay I was known as 'The Coalman'.

By the end of a marvellous afternoon's hunt in which I only fell off once more, Tango (who never turned his head all day) was nearly dry and we hardly smelt at all. I shall never forget the Black and Tans and, if I did, there is Jacko Mark III to remind me.

But there was, of course, a more serious purpose to be achieved in Ireland than enjoying myself hunting, and Carrickbeg ran well enough in the Leopardstown Chase to keep the Grand National dream alive. Running third to Owen's Sedge (owned by Gregory Peck) was encouraging, but his pre-National outing in the Kim Muir at Cheltenham ended with my being deposited on the floor at the fifteenth fence after he had blundered when still very much in contention.

In the middle of February I had written in the *Telegraph* about Carrickbeg's Aintree prospects, finishing with the perfectly reasonable view that 'Victory would of course be sweet, but if we get round safe and finish not too far away there will be no complaints.'

Not too far away. Six weeks later that phrase had a new resonance for me.

8

'Blue skies, clear light – and the greatest horse in the world'

Taxidermist and Carrickbeg would certainly figure high on any list of the horses who have meant most to me in my life, and since other equine heroes were, like those two, racing in the 1960s, this seems an appropriate point to pay homage to them.

Pride of place goes – predictably – to Anne, Duchess of Westminster's Arkle, without a shadow of a doubt the best steeplechaser I ever saw. I never witnessed Golden Miller or Easter Hero in action in the flesh, and Prince Regent had been robbed of his prime by war when I listened on the Hill Farm radio to his heroic third under twelve stone five pounds in the 1946 Grand National.

Of course, you cannot realistically compare the stars of different generations, but for three seasons Arkle was *the* complete steeplechaser – further ahead of his contemporaries than any other chaser we have known, and certainly in my opinion, capable of turning any Grand National run in his lifetime into a procession. Since he never fell and practically never made a serious mistake, the Aintree fences would surely have been no problem – provided, of course, that he steered clear of interference and unavoidable bad luck; but his owner resolutely refused to entertain running her great horse in the National, so my theory was never put to the test!

It is true that there was, for a short time, perhaps two seasons, one horse who might have been capable of disputing Arkle's supremacy. Until he was tragically crippled and handicapped by brucellosis, Flyingbolt, two years younger than Arkle, trained like him not far from Dublin by Tom Dreaper and ridden by Pat Taaffe, had form over fences – and on at least one occasion over hurdles – which, as both English and Irish handicappers agreed, put him within two pounds of his great stable companion. They never met in public – and although Pat Taaffe never doubted or questioned Arkle's supremacy, he would have hated having to make a choice between them.

In his fascinating and all too brief autobiography *My Life – and Arkle's*, Pat describes the one occasion they 'schooled' over fences together. For both him on Arkle and Paddy Woods on Flyingbolt it was, by the sound of it, a genuinely terrifying experience, with neither horse prepared to give an inch and neither jockey able to remember ever crossing steeplechase fences any faster. They jumped – or galloped over – four fences, drawing from Tom Dreaper the heartfelt pledge, 'That's one thing we shall *never* do again.' They never did – but although at two miles Pat thought Flyingbolt just might give 'Himself' a race, Arkle would always have been his choice, at any distance. Under pressure, Pat reluctantly ended his comparison with these words: 'In fact, I am sure that there was at least a stone between them. Over two miles, of course, it would have been a very much closer thing, but Arkle would still have won.'

But do not ever forget that Flyingbolt was still only seven years old at the end of his triumphant 1965–6 season, when in six months between 2 October 1965 and 11 April 1966 he won, in sequence, the Black and White Gold Cup at Ascot, the Massey Ferguson Chase at Cheltenham, the Thyestes Chase at Navan and the NH Two Mile Champion Chase (now the Queen Mother) at Cheltenham, and after finishing a close third in the Champion Hurdle the *following day* went home to Ireland to defy twelve stone seven pounds in the Irish Grand National over three and a quarter miles. 'Poor Flyingbolt,' Pat Taaffe wrote: 'What can one say about him? Certainly he was as good at seven as Arkle was at the same age.'

So maybe my claim for Arkle's superiority over all other steeplechasers should be made with that proviso. It now seems to be accepted that brucellosis may at least have contributed to the end of Arkle's active life, and late in 1966 Flyingbolt certainly suffered an attack of the same mysterious disease.

I remember an October day at Cheltenham that year when, carrying twelve stone seven pounds as usual, Flyingbolt started an odds-on favourite to give twenty-one pounds to four inferior rivals in the two-and-a-half-mile National Hunt Centenary Chase. Odds of 7–2 on might have looked quite attractive to big punters in Flyingbolt's heyday but the price had been 5–1 on when betting opened, and there were not many takers. Sadly we soon saw why. Flyingbolt led for five fences and was still in with a chance of sorts three fences out. But by that time, in the old days, the others would have been struggling. Instead, this time Tibidabo and Gort went away to fight out the finish while behind them the big chestnut who had so often dominated the Cheltenham hill floundered up it forlornly.

It should also be said that Flyingbolt does not sound nearly as attractive a character as Arkle. As Pat Taaffe wrote in his book: 'You could leave a child in Arkle's box – but no man in his senses would ever go into Flyingbolt's.'

As it happens I did, once, ride Flyingbolt – when he was twelve years old and, after the brucellosis, well past his prime.

After a few years with Ken Oliver – for whom, incidentally he gained his last victory – Flyingbolt spent his last two seasons in training with Roddy Armytage, for whom I regularly rode out. Having no idea of the arrival in the yard of a famous new inmate, I arrived (a little late) one morning to be told, a bit sharply: 'Get on that chestnut over there.' It seemed rather a long way up, but neither the height of the horse nor the distinctive white face – a broad blaze stretching from above his eyes to the tip of his muzzle – made me register that this was the great Flyingbolt.

There was, in those days, a gallop above East Ilsley which ran for five or six furlongs uphill to a small circular wood, around which you could continue as many times as you were instructed. 'Up and once round' were my orders that morning – but my trusty steed did not appear to hear them. I held him, more or less, up the hill – but then...

Oh dear. Maybe he was looking for Arkle. Round and round and round that wood we went – four times in all, I think – with Flyingbolt not exactly running away but me not exactly in control either! It was only after I had eventually got him to pull up that

I learned the identity of my steed.

Arkle, given the chance, might well have run away with me in the manner of his celebrated stablemate. But he never ran away with his owner. The Duchess loved riding him and, when he was out at grass, lying down on summer holiday she used to sit beside him in the field. Not many racehorses would let you do that.

The facts of Arkle's glittering career are well enough known to need only brief repetition here: winner of twenty-two of his twenty-six steeplechases, including the Cheltenham Gold Cup in 1964, 1965 and 1966; Hennessy Gold Cup in 1964 and 1965; Whitbread Gold Cup and King George VI Chase in 1965; and Irish National in 1964. But perhaps his greatest ever victory came in none of those famous races, but in the Gallaher Gold Cup at Sandown Park in November 1965. Here he faced – for the fifth and, as it turned out, final time – Mill House, whose rivalry with Arkle had so brightly illuminated chasing in the mid-1960s. They had first met in the 1963 Hennessy, when Mill House powered to a conclusive victory after Arkle had stumbled on landing over the third last fence – the final open ditch – and had managed only third. But Arkle won the famous 1964 Gold Cup showdown by five lengths, slammed Mill House into fourth place in the Hennessy later that year and beat him out of sight in the 1965 Gold Cup. Their meeting at Sandown Park – when Arkle conceded no less than sixteen pounds to his old adversary – produced one of the most enjoyable race reports I ever filed for the *Sunday Telegraph*:

Blue skies, clear light – and the greatest horse in the world. Sandown had all these today and as Arkle came home alone in the Gallaher Gold Cup it had much more besides. For all the normal rules and theories about racing were being shattered. The impossible was happening before our eyes. We were watching a miracle in the shape of a horse. It was in the end an effortless victory one of the easiest, Pat Taaffe says, in Arkle's whole career.

But that hadn't always been how it looked. For one heart-stopping moment down the railway straight Mill House had his hour – and never let it be forgotten. Superbly ridden by David Nicholson, the big horse stormed away from Arkle over the three close fences.

It was like the good old days of his supremacy and, glancing back at least four lengths to Arkle, even the most convinced began to doubt.

But we couldn't see inside Pat Taaffe's head – or inside Arkle's heart. There all was calm and confident. 'I hoped he'd take a rest,' said Pat. 'But he never really stopped pulling.'

What Arkle felt no one can say – but perhaps, since he is a kind-hearted horse, it was pity for his old rival.

And round the final turn England's hopes, so high a moment earlier, were dashed for good. In a dozen easy strides Arkle swept up beside Mill House.

Before the Pond he was in front, and as he landed over it the stands were shaken by a mighty cheer. It wasn't by any means the first.

Both horses were clapped in the parade ring. Arkle was applauded walking down to canter to the start and – something I've never heard before on an English racecourse – a roar greeted the field as they passed the stands *first time round!*

By that stage Arkle was in front and had shown once again that extraordinary intelligence is among his many qualities. For down the back side, as Mill House sailed along ahead of him jumping the others silly, the favourite settled calmly well behind at ease in Pat Taaffe's hands.

But Arkle has been to Sandown before. He knows where the finish is and galloping around towards the Pond not bothering to count he decided it was time to go.

For 100 yards Taaffe was a passenger and

yet again poor Mill House saw beside him the form he must by now hate more than death itself.

It did not, to his eternal credit, stop him trying. But second time round the same thing happened and that was just too much.

David Nicholson, humane as well as skilful, did not persevere and Rondetto, running a marvellous race for a horse probably not yet fully fit, passed Mill House landing over the last to finish second. As he did so Arkle was nearly home.

Scarcely ever off the bit, he won by 20 lengths in record time (the first horse ever to break six minutes over three miles round Sandown) and made no shadow of a mistake.

'Weight will stop a train,' said Tom Dreaper afterwards – but 16lb had not made an ounce of difference today and I do not really see how Arkle can ever be handicapped again.

To describe his greatness fully no words or comparisons are adequate. He is not just the best I ever saw, he is like something from another world.

When they made him I suspect they threw away the mould – so long may he live and flourish – a delight to watch – a thing to marvel at – a miracle.

Only six horses ever finished in front of

Arkle over fences – and only one, Mill House, was giving him weight. Of the others, Happy Spring was receiving twenty-four pounds when second to Mill House (with Arkle third) in the 1963 Hennessy, Flying Wild got thirty-two pounds and Buona Notte twenty-six pounds in the 1964 Massey Ferguson, Stalbridge Colonist thirty-five pounds in the 1966 Hennessy and, last scene of all, when Arkle broke a pedal bone in the 1966 King George VI Chase, Dormant, receiving no less than twenty-one pounds, was all out to beat him a hard-fought length.

On the 1966 Hennessy form, don't forget, the results of the next two Cheltenham Gold Cups, in which Stalbridge Colonist was beaten a total of less than two lengths (at level weights) by Woodland Venture and Fort Leney strongly suggest that if a sound, fit Arkle had had the opportunity of matching Golden Miller's five-Cup record, he would have won both those races with about two stone in hand. He would have been twelve years old for the next (1969) Gold Cup – but so was What A Myth, who won it. Even the late Ryan Price, who trained that tough old stayer, would not, I think, have rated him within *three stone* of Arkle.

But it is my own assessment that of all Arkle's wonderful performances, the finest may have come in one of his very few defeats – his third place in the Massey Ferguson Gold Cup at Cheltenham in December 1964. Just seven days earlier he had left an exhausted Mill House (who received three pounds) trailing home fourth, beaten nearly thirty lengths in the Hennessy. A three-pound penalty raised Arkle's weight at Cheltenham to twelve stone ten pounds – and, instead of going home, as usual, to Ireland, he and his entourage spent the intervening week at Anne, Duchess of Westminster's Eaton Lodge in Cheshire.

No one suggests that the accommodation was any less luxurious or comfortable than Arkle's own box at Greenogue – but the fact remains that these were unfamiliar surroundings; and, as you can imagine, the Duchess's sporting Cheshire friends were not likely to pass up this golden opportunity for a respectful visit to the best steeplechaser they were ever likely to see. Of course, Arkle was perfectly accustomed by then to the homage and adoration of his countless fans. Who knows, they may even have been a distraction and cheered him up. The Hennessy after all, had been a far from effortless victory.

However that may be, the Massey Ferguson differed in two other, quite possibly more serious, respects from the Newbury race. It was run over only two miles and five furlongs

– the shortest distance Arkle had attempted for two years – and, even more to the point, the opposition was definitely stronger.

That opposition included the lovely grey mare Flying Wild, trained in Ireland by Dan Moore for the US Ambassador Raymond Guest, owner also (lucky man) of L'Escargot (the only horse apart from Golden Miller to win both the Cheltenham Gold Cup and Grand National) and Derby winners Larkspur and Sir Ivor. I rode Flying Wild in a race once, but sadly my only clear memory of her is a mental picture of her elegant forefeet vanishing *between* the top two bars of a hurdle. She had stood back a full stride too soon – and, two inches higher, would have gained us at least two lengths. Instead, poor lady she turned a violent somersault – and my memory of the incident ended there.

But this fine mare, winner of a Cathcart Chase and several other good races, over hurdles as well as fences, was getting thirty-two pounds from Arkle at Cheltenham – giving him no mean task even by his uniquely high standards.

Another of Arkle's rivals was Buona Notte, trained by Bob Turnell for Jim Joel and ridden by Johnny Haine, and at that time very much the rising star of the chasing world. He had won six of his eight chases the previous season – culminating in a victory over the subsequent Gold Cup winner Fort

Leney in the Totalisator Champion Novices' Chase at Cheltenham (the race we now know as the Royal and SunAlliance Chase). Buona Notte had also beaten Dunkirk and just about every other up-and-coming chaser worth the name. To give him twenty-six pounds was a Herculean task, even for Arkle.

So Buona Notte and Flying Wild were no ordinary pair to have snapping at your heels. Nor were the others simply there to make up numbers. The Hennessy second Happy Spring, an old rival of Arkle's, was beaten when he fell at the last and The O'Malley had probably always been just out of his depth. But the Paddy Sleator trained Scottish Memories, who was fourth in the end, two lengths behind Arkle, had already won twenty-four races. This was no ordinary handicap steeplechase.

Up with the leaders all the way Arkle, an odds-on favourite as usual, had jumped with his usual blend of accuracy and boldness. But he never got far ahead, and between the last two fences Flying Wild thrust her grey head past him. Buona Notte, at her quarters, seemed to be going best of the three – but jumping is still the name of the game. Buona Notte measured the last fence well enough – but still hit it an inch or so too low. At such moments, with all to play for, angles, inches and split seconds suddenly count double –

and, for Johnny Haine and Buona Notte, this time they simply did not quite add up. Mr Joel's lovely horse came down a bit too steep for the speed he was travelling, slipped, sprawled and lost a few priceless ounces of momentum.

It is the memory of the next few moments which convinces me that this may have been Arkle's finest hour. If ever a chaser had an excuse for sulking, or hoisting the white flag, this surely was it. For the second time in seven days – with two longish journeys in between – Arkle had been asked to gallop and jump his heart out, carrying around two stone more than his opponents. And now, with the Cheltenham hill to face, two of them came and jumped past him. For ninety-nine chasers out of a hundred that, I believe, would have been the end. But not for Arkle.

'Led 13th till approaching last,' the form book reads – then 'rallied near finish'. My only quarrel with *Chaseform*'s observer is those two restrictive words 'near finish'. Arkle had been rallying – fighting back – ever since the other two went past him, and, still gaining as they reached the post, he kept fighting to the bitter end, but to no avail. Flying Wild beat Buona Notte a short head, with Arkle just a length further back in third.

Arkle *never* surrendered in his life – and, of

all his brilliant victories and against-the-odds defeats, that Massey Ferguson Gold Cup was, for me, the bravest and the best.

But the race had a sad postscript. Buona Notte, though narrowly beaten in the Massey Ferguson, looked every inch a future champion and seemed poised to crown the careers of his owner and trainer, two of the most faithful supporters British jumping has ever had. But, as Bob and Mr Joel knew from long experience, perfect happy endings are all too rare. After falling next time out at Newbury when made favourite to beat Mill House, Buona Notte fell again in his next race, the Great Yorkshire Chase, and this time his injuries were fatal. He was still only eight years old. Johnny Haine, who died so prematurely in 1998, did so in a house (in the village of Crudwell, close to Oaksey) called Buona Notte. He had named all his houses in honour of 'the best horse I ever rode in a race'.

As Pat Taaffe would have been the first to admit, Johnny Haine's flat-race polish on Buona Notte contrasted starkly with his own slightly agricultural style of finishing up the Cheltenham hill. Pat was also out-manoeuvred – and, at least by the look of it, outridden – by Stan Mellor when Arkle failed so heroically to give the grey Stalbridge Colonist thirty-five pounds in the 1966 Hennessy. Stan's tactics that day were to stay precisely in Arkle's slipstream – so that, until he pulled out to challenge, the great Irish horse could not see the approaching threat. As soon as they were safely over the last Stan pulled out Stalbridge Colonist to mount a furious finish, and they collared Pat and Arkle close home and won by half a length.

But tactics and the finish are not everything and Pat Taaffe, the only man who ever rode Arkle in a steeplechase, was also responsible, don't forget, from first to last, for his (almost always) impeccable jumping.

There is an amazing footnote to the story of their famous partnership – because, if the Jockey Club's current medical regulations had been in force, I honestly believe that Pat would almost certainly never have sat on Arkle's back.

When a much younger (26-year-old) Pat Taaffe regained consciousness in a Dublin hospital after a dreadful fall at Kilbeggan in 1956, the question in the mind of the surgeon attending him, Mr Bouchier-Hayes, was not so much 'Will he ride again?' as 'Will he live?' A badly fractured skull was just one of Pat's multiple injuries, and he remained unconscious for five days. Even after a convalescence which lasted more than a year, no doctor connected with racing would, nowadays, have considered letting him ride a horse in a steeplechase; but they see such things differently in Ireland – or did in those days, anyway.

Tom Dreaper gave Pat two 'comeback' rides at Navan, the first of which deposited him in a ditch! Two days later, when the yard had two fancied runners, Rose's Quarter and Dizzy, in England, Pat, still lacking confidence in his own fitness and ability, begged his Guv'nor to get someone else. 'If you don't ride them they don't run,' was the trainer's reply – and for once the story had a happy ending. Both horses ran – in the Pathfinder and Emblem Chases at Manchester – and both won; and from that day on, Mr Dreaper never, if Pat was fit and available, 'got someone else'.

But not even Pat Taaffe could protect Arkle from the injury which ended his racing career on 27 December 1966, when he cracked a pedal bone in the King George VI Chase at Kempton Park, was caught by Dormant close home and beaten a length, and then could scarcely hobble back into the unsaddling enclosure. I was riding at Wincanton that day and can still recall as if it were yesterday the sheer disbelief with which we heard the news in the weighing room. Arkle beaten by Dormant? It made no sense. But it was true, of course, and racing would never be the same again.

As I suggested earlier, the exact cause of Arkle's final illness – the stiffness which persuaded his vet Maxie Cosgrove and devoted owner Anne, Duchess of Westminster to have him put to sleep on 31 May 1970, has never been diagnosed with absolute certainty. Brucellosis may have been partly to blame – or, perhaps more likely arthritis started by the broken pedal bone he suffered in his last race.

In the following weekend's *Horse and Hound* Audax was moved to point out the irony of Arkle's death occurring shortly before the Derby:

It is a slightly sobering thought that, in under three minutes this week, a three-year-old colt will, by galloping 12 furlongs on the flat, have earned nearly as much (£60,000) as the total (£75,000) Arkle won by galloping almost 100 miles and jumping 500 fences and hurdles.

Such are the topsy-turvy values of modern racing – but it wasn't for money that Arkle ran his heart out. He did it because he had been bred for the job and taught to do it well by kindly men whose kindness and skill he was glad to repay.

He did it because he loved his own speed and strength and agility – and perhaps because he loved the cheers they brought him. He was, more certainly than any other Thoroughbred I can think of, a happy horse who enjoyed every minute of his life.

In that sense perhaps the human race did

repay some small part of the debt it owed him and at least when his life ceased being a pleasure it was quickly and humanely ended.

But mostly the debt remains unpaid. We can only try to pay it by remembering Arkle as he was – brave in defeat, magnificent in victory and gentle in repose.

Now he is gone and we must search for others to warm our blood on winter afternoons, to fill the stands and set the crowds on fire. No doubt we shall find them – but they will be pale shadows of the real thing. For those who saw Arkle will never forget the sight and, until they see another like him, will never believe that two such miracles can happen in a lifetime.

It was a tragedy that Arkle, who loved and revelled in the admiration and affection of his fans, was able to enjoy them for only just over two years. If you have not read it already Ivor Herbert's definitive book *Arkle* is an absolute must for any lover of a good steeplechaser – and, mercifully it was published before the unfortunate decision was made to have the great horse's body removed from his grave on the Duchess's estate at Bryanstown and his skeleton displayed in the Irish Horse Museum in County Kildare.

Having seen the skeletons of several racehorses, including some great ones, I still find it very hard to understand the Duchess's decision to have Arkle's disinterred and 'reconstructed'. I have not seen the result and do not intend to. I so much prefer to remember the greatest of them all as Ivor Herbert describes his grave:

Arkle's old pony friend Meg did not long outlive him and, by the end of August she was buried beside him in their grassy grave. It is surrounded by a banked hedge of daffodils in the garden at Bryanstown, halfway between their own stable and what is now called Arkle's Field. The stone above her grave reads simply 'Meg, A Good Hunter'. Above Arkle's, facing the rays of the southern sun, is an even more simple memorial. As befits the last home of the greatest steeplechaser of all time it just states his name.

If Arkle and Flyingbolt were the two best chasers I ever saw, third place would go to a horse somewhat less fêted in the jump racing annals but one who holds a special place in my affections, not least on account of his local associations. For Pas Seul was born in Crudwell – the village just two miles from Oaksey which had already been the birthplace of one Gold Cup winner: Gay Donald, Cheltenham hero in 1955. I apologise to those who know Pas Seul's extraordinary story – but I believe it is worth telling one more time.

Pas Seul's dam, Pas de Quatre, was bred by the great Beckhampton trainer Fred Darling, but had the misfortune to be born not long before the Second World War. Like so many other professional racing men, Mr Darling found himself with a lot of blue-blooded potential in his yard, but precious few opportunities to turn it into prize money. He sold Pas de Quatre for a virtual song to a farmer friend of his called Harry Frank – and that is where Crudwell comes back into the story.

Mr Frank, whose family all loved horses and hunting, lived on the border between the countries of the Beaufort and VWH hunts, half a mile from the village of Crudwell. His son Andy and daughter Judy found Pas de Quatre a bold if slightly erratic hunter – but in any case their father, keen to exploit her pedigree, sent her to a local stallion called Gay Light.

From the first Pas de Quatre was a shy breeder – and, it seems, a somewhat clumsy mother. She (literally) dropped her first foal in a field, and Gay Donald had a 'wall' eye all his life to prove it! (Gay Donald was, incidentally one of the easiest – and least widely expected – winners in Gold Cup history. A 33–1 outsider in a field of nine for the 1955 running, he was ridden by Tony

Grantham and ran clean away with the race to win by a long ten lengths. Halloween, never at his best round Cheltenham, was second with the previous year's winner Four Ten third. Crudwell, ridden by Dick Francis on this occasion, was among the also-rans.)

Sadly for Harry Frank, the fact that Pas de Quatre had now become a potentially valuable and desirable brood mare did not alter her apparent reluctance to get in foal. In between ineffective coverings she spent a lot of her time out hunting – and was, in this period, quite often ridden by Bob Turnell. 'She was an erratic old girl,' I remember him telling me, 'but tough as old boots – and brave.'

In the spring of 1953, after yet another apparently unproductive union – with a horse called Erin's Pride – Harry Frank lent the mare to Gay Donald's owner Mr P. J. Burt, on the understanding that his girl groom could ride her in hunter trials and point-to-points. So Pas de Quatre, already the mother of one Gold Cup hero, spent six or seven weeks competing in two ladies' races and three hunter trials! She did not win; but that, as it turned out, was not altogether surprising.

Sadly Mr Burt then died and the mare went home to Crudwell. 'What are you going to do with her?' Bob Turnell asked Harry Frank, whose realistic reply was:

'Shoot her – unless you want her.' Bob, who was in the process of setting up as a trainer, remembered the courage Pas de Quatre had shown him out hunting with the Beaufort. Losing no time, he accepted Harry Frank's offer and sent her to the Littleton Stud – and was delighted to hear next day that she had been satisfactorily covered by Royal Tara.

With Pas de Quatre, of course, that did not mean a lot – but the next message from Littleton meant a very great deal more. 'You know that mare of yours we covered the other day?' an astonished stud groom said on the telephone to Harry Frank: 'Well, she is about to foal!' This time there was no mistake – and Pas Seul, a horse who was to stir the hearts of many and break the hearts of some, slipped quietly into the world.

For the first two years of his life Pas Seul was turned out at Harry Frank's farm near Crudwell – with another young horse bred by Bob Turnell: a year-older grey called Seringapatam, who has already featured in these pages, disappearing over the horizon in a deluge with Taffy Jenkins and his electric spurs. Seringapatam and Pas Seul ran together for so long – and became such mates – that when Bob came to take the grey home there was, he said, 'an almighty fuss!' 'You had better take the other one too,' said Harry Frank – and a price of £600 was agreed. Bob immediately rang John Rogerson to tell him he had bought him a Gold Cup winner. Although a bit surprised to learn that Pas Seul was still only a yearling, Mr Rogerson accepted – and never had cause to regret it.

For the rest of his life Bob Turnell was convinced that Pas Seul was not only the best, but '*miles* the best horse I ever had and one of the unluckiest too. Should have won three Gold Cups. He was just too brave. The fences were stiffer in those days – and, worst of all, those bloody dopers were about.'

Well, of course, these things can only be a matter of opinion. But Pas Seul certainly looked all over a winner going to the last fence of the 1959 Gold Cup. He had just hit the front, going best of all, when for some reason he decided to treat the obstacle as if it was six inches high. Three years later, in 1962, Bob is convinced that Pas Seul – and his Champion Hurdle hope The Finn – were 'got at' in the week before Cheltenham.

When reading accounts of these disasters you must remember that old habits of suspicion die hard. However that may be, in the light of what happened at Cheltenham, Bob Turnell remained convinced, to his dying day that both Pas Seul and The Finn were doped. 'It finished The Finn for months,' he told me. 'Pas Seul was so strong and healthy that he got over it quicker. But he ran three stone below his best on Gold Cup day.'

I also remember Bob telling me of a meeting he had with Sir Noel Murless, who of course trained Pinturischio, famously nobbled when ante-post favourite for the 1961 Two Thousand Guineas and Derby. The great Flat trainer described to Bob how his colt was found to be blistered around the mouth. 'Just like Pas Seul and The Finn,' Bob said. 'We had turned them out for an hour and thought they must have eaten some nettles.'

Before that 1962 Cheltenham Gold Cup, Pas Seul drifted in the betting from 10–11 to 9–4 and he finished fifth behind Mandarin who was, as we are about to see, in the middle of the golden period which ended with his historic bitless Grand Steeplechase in Paris.

Pas Seul had won the Gold Cup in 1960, narrowly beating Lochroe, but probably his greatest performance came in the Whitbread of 1961. Carrying top weight of twelve stone in a field of twenty-three including Mandarin and Taxidermist, Pas Seul was stopped in his tracks by a fallen horse at the Pond Fence three from home, but recovered to win comfortably giving that year's Grand National winner Nicolaus Silver twenty-one pounds. Arkle apart, it was probably the best weight-carrying performance by a steeplechaser since the war.

One summer day in 1954 – the year after Pas Seul had been born and three years before Arkle came into the world – a small, extremely fat bay gelding arrived from France at Fulke Walwyn's yard in Lambourn. Beside the big handsome chasers at Saxon House he looked insignificant and, reporting his safe arrival to his owner Madame Peggy Hennessy the trainer said, without much enthusiasm, that he had never seen a fatter three-year-old.

Eight years later, in the outskirts of Paris, the same horse, dirty, sweating and desperately tired, pushed through a huge, excited crowd thronging the winner's enclosure at Auteuil. Beside his head there dangled a broken, useless bridle and on his back sat the greatest steeplechase jockey in the world. Not an ounce of fat remained on the horse's wiry battle-scarred body and he looked as insignificant as ever. But from all sides men and women with tears in their eyes pressed forward to try and touch him. They looked like people who had seen a miracle – and perhaps in a way they had. The horse's name was Mandarin and this, briefly is his story

He was born at the Hennessy family's stud in Normandy. His sire Deux Pour Cent won the Grand Prix de Paris in 1944 and his dam Manada won two small hurdle races, also in France. She had only three foals before she died and the eldest of them, Manuscrit, was already in training with Fulke at Lambourn when Mandarin arrived there. He had, in fact, already won the Cotswolds Chase at Cheltenham, with Devon Loch behind him.

Any equine newcomer to a big racing stable is at once carefully weighed up by the lads – his appearance, the price paid for him and anything his relatives may have accomplished. Mandarin at first glance looked distinctly unhopeful. Being home-bred, nothing at all had been paid for him and, although Manuscrit had shown himself a pretty useful horse, there was certainly no great rush for the honour of 'doing' his younger brother. In the end John Foster got the job – largely because he, like Mandarin, had only just begun his apprenticeship and had, therefore, to take what was given him and be thankful. 'Mush', as he is always known, had sole charge of Mandarin, and if (which is now unlikely) anyone wanted to criticise a hair of the horse's coat, they had better not do it in Mush's hearing.

Having learned the bare rudiments of good behaviour (he was always a pretty hair-raising ride at home), Mandarin began his education as a jumper. He showed precious little promise, and his progress – or lack of it – was littered with a trail of broken schooling hurdles. If he met one bang in his stride all might be well – if not, he went straight on, kicking the bothersome thing to blazes on the way.

Small wonder that when, at Newbury on 10 December 1954, Mandarin first appeared on a racecourse, no great advance publicity heralded the event. Ridden by Gerry Madden, the little Irishman who was to play so great a part in his life, he started at 20–1, jumped badly – and pleasantly surprised everyone concerned by finishing a respectable third. The winner was a chestnut called Axim, and as Fred Winter unsaddled him he little knew that only a few yards away stood the horse destined one day to carry him so gloriously. The two were to team up for the first time at Sandown the following season – but by then Mandarin had already shown that, however inaccurate his jumping, he at least knew how to gallop.

Indeed, he won his next race, a novice hurdle at Kempton Park, ridden by Johnny Gilbert, and gave that great jockey what he himself called 'one of the roughest rides of my life'. But despite hanging, pulling, and flattening more hurdles than he jumped, Mandarin won by five lengths – and although he failed in his only other race that year, Fulke Walwyn retired him for the summer confident that at least he would earn his keep.

For most of the next season, however, that confidence steadily waned. The little horse stubbornly continued to treat his hurdles as if they were made of thistledown, and against the experienced handicappers he now met, such carelessness was costly.

Six times Mandarin ran without success for several different jockeys. Then, at the Grand Military meeting of 1956, he was ridden for the first time by the man with whom, above all, his name will always be linked.

It is probably sentimental to read too much into that first meeting with Fred Winter. I certainly cannot tell you how Mandarin performed – as, having ridden my first winner under Rules that afternoon when Pyrene won the hunter-chase, I was in far too deep a rosy haze to notice anything around me! But the fact remains that they won, and that Mandarin jumped rather better than ever before. So perhaps at least the seeds were sown of that priceless understanding which, six years later, was to bring them, without a bridle, round the twists and hazards of Auteuil.

Nevertheless, at the end of by far the least distinguished season of his life, Mandarin's future hung in the balance. Fulke Walwyn, whose own highly successful riding career included some crashing falls, is not the man to risk a jockey's neck unnecessarily. Judging both by past performances and by his comparative lack of size and substance, Mandarin's chances of jumping big English fences looked slender, to say the least. In conference with Madame Hennessy it was quite seriously discussed whether the best thing might not be to send him back to France. It was touch and go – and if the decision had fallen otherwise the rest of this story would be written either in French or, more likely not at all.

Instead, thank heaven, Walwyn decided to have at least one try; and so, after plenty of schooling (some of it fairly nerve-racking for those concerned), Mandarin, with Gerry Madden up, sallied forth for his first steeplechase – a handicap at Ludlow. He made no serious mistake and finished strongly to be third. His trainer breathed again; and, by the end of that season, he had, in place of a wild, far from outstanding hurdler, just about the best and most consistent novice chaser in the land.

In seven races with the best of his generation, Mandarin was never worse than second. Ridden mostly by Michael Scudamore, a supremely tough, brave horseman and father of Peter, he won three times – including in March 1957 the three-mile Broadway Chase at Cheltenham (predecessor of the Totalisator Champion Novices' Chase which Buona Notte won, and now the Royal and SunAlliance Chase).

It was in these early days, no doubt, that Mandarin learned the highly individual style of jumping that was to take him to his marvellous record of fifty-two races with only one fall. Small and light-framed for a chaser, he always relied on agility rather than strength, twisting and screwing his body to escape from predicaments that, for a bigger and less well-balanced animal, would surely mean disaster.

He did, of course, make his share of mistakes – among them those which probably cost him two Gold Cups and an earlier Grand Steeplechase de Paris – but although his jockeys often had to cling on by their eyelashes, they always felt that, somehow, Mandarin wouldn't let them down. Fred Winter said that he was by no means an extravagant jumper – not like, for instance, Saffron Tartan or Frenchman's Cove, who loved to stand far back.

'But if,' said Fred, 'you left it to him, he would get you there and you wouldn't have lost much ground.'

At the end of that first season's chasing, Mandarin made the first of four attempts in what was to be his unluckiest race – the Whitbread Gold Cup at Sandown. For the next three years he came to the last upsides in front with only one to beat. Three times he was run out of it up the hill – beaten a neck by Much Obliged in the inaugural running in 1957, four lengths by Taxidermist (whose victory I have described in narcissistic detail in Chapter 6) in 1958 and, in one of the finest finishes ever seen at Sandown, a short head by Done Up in 1959.

The first narrow failure against Much Obliged showed not only that Mandarin, then a novice, could hold his own with experienced chasers – but also that he stayed for ever. So when his owner's family firm, the famous brandy house of Hennessy staged their own Gold Cup at Cheltenham early the next season in November 1957, Mandarin was understandably one of the favourites.

That race was the first in which I clearly remember what since became, for me and for many others, the most moving sight in British racing – the sight of Mandarin at war, muscles straining and head thrust out, struggling to stave off the hated spectre of defeat. That day at Cheltenham, it is true, the real hero was Linwell who, conceding sixteen pounds, looked sure to win a hundred yards from the line. Mandarin had hit the last fence hard, and to catch and beat the reigning Cheltenham Gold Cup winner up the hill took all his resolution. He was, however, getting an awful lot of weight.

His next big task – set to *give* the brilliant Lochroe seven pounds in the King George VI Chase at Kempton Park on Boxing Day – would, one felt, surely be beyond him. And so it seemed to Gerry Madden as, with a full circuit still to go, he had to push and drive the little horse to stay near the leaders. But neither Mandarin's jockey nor anyone else knew then the huge reserves of strength and stamina that lay hidden inside that lean and wiry frame. Ounce by ounce, stride by stride, Mandarin produced it now until, at the last, even Lochroe could do no more. Mandarin won in the end by a length, and I shall always believe that in terms of merit this was one of his most extraordinary feats.

Rested until March, Mandarin was made favourite for the 1958 Gold Cup. But now, for the first time since he started chasing, his jumping let him down. No one will ever know just what happened at the thirteenth fence, but he and Linwell blundered simultaneously – and this time neither jockey stayed aboard.

Two weeks before that ill-starred race the writer, riding a horse called Taxidermist for the first time, had taken part in a gallop with Mandarin on Sandown racecourse. The track was a sea of mud and Taxi, hating it, finished at least two fences behind his famous stable companion. Had a crystal-gazer foretold that day the finish of the 1958 Whitbread Gold Cup, I would have called him a raving lunatic.

Yet, two months later, the impossible came true. On the rock-hard ground he loved and receiving twenty pounds, Taxi and I sailed into the last alongside Mandarin – and sprinted clear up the famous hill. In case anyone now thinks less of Mandarin because of that defeat, I can tell them that, in his prime, with the conditions to suit him, the horse was never foaled who could have given Taxidermist twenty pounds. But that is another story.

Now the clouds of misfortune which darkened so much of his life began to gather over Mandarin's head.

Beaten again behind Taxi in the 1958 Hennessy Gold Cup, he could only run third in that year's King George VI Chase and, walking back very lame, was found to have fractured a bone in his hind leg. No doubt one of those acrobatic recoveries of his had done the damage, but just the same, Mandarin kept on jumping and galloping. That was, probably his first experience of real pain and, like all the agonies that followed, it utterly failed to daunt him.

The bone healed too slowly for another attempt at the Gold Cup, but after a tune-up over hurdles at Cheltenham, Mandarin had his third and most heroic crack at the

Whitbread. Far behind on Taxi, I did not see the finish, but it was only in the final yards that Harry Sprague, at his irresistible best, forced Done Up's nose past Mandarin to win by a short head.

Coming so soon after a serious injury this desperate struggle would have been more than enough for most horses, but for Mandarin the season was not over. That summer he, a Frenchman born, set sail again for France to run in the Grand Steeplechase de Paris at Auteuil. For three of the four tortuous miles the unaccustomed obstacles worried him not at all. Then, pulling hard as usual, in front and, I shall always believe, with the great race at his mercy he suddenly checked at a staring post and rails with water showing beyond it.

No one could blame a horse trained under English conditions for looking twice at such an obstacle, and before Mandarin could recover the damage was done. Six horses swept past and he lost a dozen lengths. After that, to fight back as he did into second place – beaten just a few yards in the end – was itself a famous victory. For the first time – but not the last – I stood with tears in my eyes watching him unsaddle at Auteuil.

Next season, by which time he was rising nine years old, it looked as if the strain of so many battles might be beginning to tell. 'Well in' this time at the weights, Mandarin squeezed home only by inches to beat the veteran Pointsman for his second King George VI Chase in December 1959 – something he would normally have done, so to speak, with one hand tied behind his back.

Perhaps the comparison is not a bad one, for Mandarin returned to Lambourn lame again. This time the tendon was badly strained and he had to be fired.

The old story used to go that after this unpleasant operation no horse ever comes back to within a stone of his best, and for much of 1960–1 season there was no shortage of gloomy prophets who shook their heads over Mandarin as an example of that pessimistic theory.

In fact, Mandarin did run a few races below his normal standard in 1961; but the reason was not his damaged legs. Because now, when he needed the luck most, it deserted him yet again. In his second race at Chepstow that old agility misfired for the first and only time. Hitting a fence halfway up, he turned a complete somersault: as Gerry said afterwards, 'The first thing to hit the ground was his tail.'

Up to that time no race, however hard, and no injury however painful, had ever daunted the little horse's spirit. But now, as Fulke Walwyn discovered the first time he schooled at home after the fall, that one horrid moment of surprise and shock had shattered – or at least badly dented – Mandarin's confidence.

Next time out, losing ground at almost every fence, he was beaten by Frenchman's Cove, and although he did go on to win a minor race at Sandown, the old fire was not there. In the Great Yorkshire Chase in January 1961 he jumped better, but by now the public had virtually written him off, and he was allowed to start as an outsider for the Cheltenham Gold Cup. The betting public were right – but only just! Again it was faulty jumping, not lack of ability that held him back. Up in front all the way Mandarin hit the two vital fences at the top of the hill, lost his place completely and was left with over twenty lengths to make up on Pas Seul and Saffron Tartan – probably the two fastest chasers in the world. Of those twenty by a supreme effort of determination and stamina he recovered all but four and a half – and as Saffron Tartan staggered home exhausted, Mandarin was catching him with every stride. It was, in all the circumstances, an unbelievable performance which, had we but known, set the stage for the last, most glorious chapter in this strange, eventful history.

Because, although Mandarin could still not win his 'unluckiest' race, the Whitbread, the 1961 running of the Sandown race – in which he finished sixth behind Pas Seul – turned out to be the last time he was beaten. One of the reasons for this was undoubtedly the fact that Fred Winter was retained as stable jockey by Fulke Walwyn. Fred could not ride him when he won the 1961 Hennessy owing to a broken collarbone, but Willie Robinson, who took his place, was not available thereafter, and so it was Fred who rode him to win the Walter Hyde Chase at Kempton Park in January 1962 and then the Cheltenham Gold Cup – beating Tom Dreaper's Fortria – that March.

And so to Paris, for a second attempt at the Grand Steeplechase on Sunday 17 June at the age of eleven. Fred Winter, Dave Dick, Joe Lammin (Fulke's head lad) and I walked round the Grand Steeple course on the morning of the race and wondered afresh at the many turns and countless opportunities for losing your way. The Grand Steeple is, roughly two figures of eight in opposite directions, then one whole circuit outside both. There are four bends of 180 degrees. It was a daunting prospect – and we were not, of course, thinking of going round them with neither brakes nor steering!

After walking the course I contacted the British Embassy to confirm an arrangement I had made to file my piece for the following morning's *Daily Telegraph* from there. The piece, when duly sent in a state of high excitement a few hours later, described the most remarkable horse race I had – and have – ever seen:

Without a bridle – with only his own great heart and Fred Winter's matchless strength to keep him going – Madame K. Hennessy's Mandarin this afternoon became the first English-trained horse to win the Grand Steeplechase de Paris at Auteuil since Silvio in 1925.

The bit broke in Mandarin's mouth after only three fences and for three twisting, hazardous miles Fred Winter had neither brakes nor steering. So when in the end, unbelievably Mandarin thrust his head across the line in front, we who were here knew beyond doubt that we had seen a feat of courage, skill and horsemanship never excelled on this or any other racecourse.

For a few dreadful moments however – staggering dazed and hoarse from the stands – we did not know if this was victory or just a bitter heroic defeat. A photo had been called for.

Then the right number was in the frame, and as Winter and Mandarin pushed their way back through the wondering crowd a cheer went up – from French throats as well as English – that would have made the Irish yell at Cheltenham sound like a feeble whimper.

Forty minutes later the incredible Winter was back in the same enclosure, having won the Grand Course de Haies for four-year-olds on Beaver II. For a French jockey I imagine this would be a formidable double. For an Englishman in these circumstances it simply proved what we already knew – that Fred Winter has no equal in the world.

But once more this was Mandarin's day and as he bounded past the stands, a gay determined bundle of fire and muscle, already up in front and pulling Winter's arms out, there was no hint of the disaster to come.

The little horse was wearing his usual bridle, the one with a rubber-covered bit in which he won both the Hennessy and Cheltenham Gold Cup last season. But going to the fourth (a privet fence nearly six feet high) some hidden fault appeared, the bit parted and Winter found the reins loose and useless in his hands.

'What could I do?', he said afterwards to Bryan Marshall. 'I couldn't steer him, I couldn't stop – and I was much too frightened to jump off!'

In fact, of course, the thought of giving up occurred neither to horse nor jockey. On they went, pitching dangerously over the big water, and it was not till the second circuit that we in the stands realised the desperate situation they were in.

Desperate indeed it was! Quite apart from the near impossibility of steering without reins round this tortuous figure-of-eight, Mandarin, a horse who always leans hard on his bridle, must have felt horribly ill at ease and out of balance. As for Winter, his task defies description.

'I could give him no help at all,' was how the jockey put it, and no doubt by his own high standards that was true. But if ever I saw a horse given all possible assistance it was Mandarin today and I do not believe any other man could have got him there.

Round most of the bends Winter managed to keep a horse or two outside him, and the French champion Daumas, upsides on Taillefer when the bit broke, did his best to help.

Close up fourth down the far side for the last time Mandarin flicked cleanly over the post and rails that undid him three years ago – and then, at the junction of the courses, the worst all but happened.

For three strides coming to the turn it seemed Mandarin was going to run out the wrong side of a marker flag. His own good sense and some magic of Winter's kept him on the course, but the hesitation had cost precious lengths and round the last bend he was only fifth, six lengths behind the leader.

'Just wait till Fred gets him straightened out.' Dave Dick's voice beside me was much more hopeful than confident. But a moment later, going to the Bullfinch, two from home, the impossible began to come true.

With all the stops pulled fully out, Mandarin's head appeared like a bullet through the dark-brown barrier – and by the last, answering, as he has always done, Winter's every demand, the little hero was actually in front.

He made no mistake and landed perhaps a length clear, but up the long run-in, hard and brilliantly though Winter rode, like a man sculling without oars, Mandarin was tiring. Inch by inch Lumino crept up and at the line not one of us could really be sure.

But all was well and as Mandarin walked away dog tired, his faithful attendants quite speechless with delight, the dreams of his owner, Madame Hennessy had been realised.

At an age when many jumpers are past their best, and after many hardships, her wonderful horse had come back to triumph in the land of his birth – to a triumph even finer than any in his long career.

For Fulke Walwyn, too, it was a moment never to be forgotten. After the Gold Cup, at Cheltenham last March, there seemed to be no more fields left to conquer. Understandably Mandarin's devoted trainer had grave doubts about subjecting him to another gruelling race in Paris – but he can sleep sound tonight (if he sleeps at all) in the knowledge that the risk so boldly taken has so brilliantly come off.

I never expect to be more moved by a man and a horse than I was by Winter and Mandarin this afternoon. Separately they have always been superb. Together, today taking disaster by the throat and turning it into victory they have surely earned a place of honour that will be secure as long as men talk, or read, or think of horses.

Mandarin had in fact broken down on one of his forelegs when making that rapid change of direction by the marker flag, so his victory was even more heroic than we had thought at the time. He retired in triumph – to be fêted at Wembley the Horse of this or any other Year.

That retirement had not lasted very long when Fulke accepted an invitation for Mandarin to attend a farmers' club dinner in Aylesbury at which I was also invited to read my account of the Paris race. The room was crowded, with two long tables virtually back to back, and no one thought to call for silence for the grand entrance of the guest of honour.

When Mandarin's lad Mush Foster led him into the hall the assembled farmers gave a deafening cheer – at which the poor horse, who had certainly never heard anything like it before, whipped round and might have gone anywhere. In fact he went straight down between the two tables, towing Mush behind him, and out of a small door down three steps into the kitchen. Those chefs may well have been some of the most frightened in the world at that moment.

But no harm was done and Mandarin's poor old legs were none the worse. He was, in any case, retired, and Fulke used to ride him at exercise until he decided that it was much too dangerous!

At the end of his career Mandarin had won far more prize money than any other English-trained jumper. But it is not for that that he will be remembered; it is because, for eight hard years, he faced and overcame disaster, shrugged off pain and failure, ignored the whims of fortune and, at last, forced it to smile upon him. He was the bravest of the brave, and if men breed horses for a thousand years they may never find another like him.

9

'Hope you get something to write about'

The Grand National first registered in my infant mind two days before my eighth birthday in March 1937, when my nanny organised a sixpenny sweepstake on the race. At that point I had no idea what the Grand National was, let alone that I would ever ride in it, and the name on my ticket – Royal Mail – meant nothing much to me either. But after we had crowded round the radio at Hill Farm to hear Evan Williams bring Royal Mail home three lengths ahead of Cooleen and I had pocketed the five shillings in the pool, I was hooked, and the stranglehold which the great Aintree race exerted on my imagination grew steadily tighter over the years. (In 1937 I had no way of knowing, of course, that Evan Williams would breed Taxidermist, the best steeplechaser I ever rode; and I certainly did not know that Jack Fawcus, who rode the runner-up, would, two years later, be taken prisoner in France with my future brother-in-law Freddy Burnaby-Atkins!)

From then on I won many an imaginary Grand National on the nursery rocking-horse and on Mince Pie, but I had reached the ripe old age of thirty-two before I got my first ride in the real thing – on Taxi himself in 1961.

At his very best Taxi would have been the ideal Grand National horse – well endowed with stamina and class, and a wonderfully accurate and clever (as opposed to flamboyant) jumper. I used to dream of unleashing the final charge which won him the Whitbread and Hennessy Gold Cups, and on the right – fast – ground he would have been a formidable proposition on Aintree's interminable run-in. By March 1961 he was still only nine years of age – but he had not won for over two years, and was, truth to tell, past his best: a condition doubtless reflected in his starting price of 40–1.

So we set off with more hope than confidence. Approaching Becher's Brook, the sixth fence, we were baulked three strides from take-off by a riderless – and, incidentally, blinkered – horse called Tea Fiend. Taxi, like the brave, agile and careful jumper he always was, 'fiddled' neatly to meet the fence dead right – but because of lost momentum landed half a stride short. At any other fence in the land it would not have mattered a damn. But this was Becher's and, landing against a 45-degree counterslope – the 'lip' of the brook – at thirty miles an hour, a horse needs the balance of an Olympic gold medal-winning gymnast to stay on his feet.

I have a photograph which shows the angles involved including the one at which we landed. As when hitting a fence, it is the sudden deceleration that matters. Unless you, the rider, anticipate it – and take all necessary precautions in far less time than it takes to read those words – you tend to be ejected like a spent cartridge case. In John Hislop's book *Steeplechasing* there is a sequence of line drawings by the author's great friend John Skeaping which illustrates, with amazing clarity, the correct way to cope when your horse hits a fence and, equally clearly the wrong way – complete with undesirable consequences. But understandably I was not in a position to consult the book as Taxi pitched on landing over Becher's, and off I tumbled.

As I sat there lamenting my luck, there came a resounding thump beside me closely followed by a loud and robust curse in Russian. The latest victim of Becher's was none other than my new friend Vladimir Prakhov, and how this indefatigable Russian jockey came to be prostrate beside me on the Aintree turf requires a little explanation.

A former Russian premier, Georgi Malenkov, had been a guest of the redoubtable

Mrs Mirabel Topham, whose family firm owned Aintree racecourse, for the 1956 Grand National, the year of Devon Loch's disastrous, unexplained fall fifty yards from the winning post and certain victory. Possibly Malenkov saw that notorious incident as proof that literally anything can happen at Aintree – because five years later (one year after the first televised Grand National in 1960) the Russian racing authorities suddenly entered three horses in the race: Epigraf II, Grifel and Reljef. Just a little more fact-finding reconnaissance would have told them that their two actual runners (Epigraf II was withdrawn) would both be lumbered with top weight of twelve stone – in the belief that the British handicapper 'had no access to their form'. That ridiculous rule has, thank heaven, now been modified – but in any case, Grifel and Reljef did not, at first sight, strike terror into either the handicapper or their rivals.

The newborn *Sunday Telegraph* was keen to establish the credentials of its first racing correspondent – which position I had recently added to my duties on the daily paper – and as I was due to have my own first National ride that year I was dispatched to Moscow (plus interpreter) to assess the Russian challenge. My interpreter was a charming former White Russian called Boris who, as he told us at Heathrow, had got out of Moscow by the skin of his teeth in 1919 and had not been back since. To say he was nervous about the reception he could expect from the KGB would be a grave understatement. Happily (for him) he quickly discovered the ideal anaesthetic in vodka – and was quietly under its influence shortly after take-off. As it turned out, the Russian chef d'équipe, a tough-looking cruiserweight called Volchkov (of whom more later), spoke excellent English and was well able to interpret between us and the two jockeys, Brian Ponomarenko and the then reigning Russian champion, Vladimir Prakhov.

We had brought several not-too-horrific films of past Grand Nationals and, apart from the crowding at some of the early fences, there was nothing to spoil the sleep of the two jockeys, each of whom had ridden more than once in the great Czech cross-country race the Grand Pardubice. One thing they enquired about was remounting – because apparently in the Pardubice they have squads of strong-arm thugs down by the difficult fences ready to load the poor little so-and-sos back on! Well, we tried very hard to convince them of the old weighing-room adage that 'There are fools, bloody fools, ****ing idiots – and people who remount in a steeplechase!' Except perhaps at the last few fences, once you are down or unseated in a Grand National that, ninety-nine times out of a hundred, is that. We tried really hard to convince them – and, as you'll see, we failed.

So it was that the first man to land beside me at Becher's was my (by then) good friend Vladimir. I was just about to start commiserating in my fluent Ukrainian when from out of the crowd on the take-off side sprang Colonel (probably a KGB rank, we decided later) Volchkov. Heedless of my cries of 'Niet, niet!', he grabbed poor Vladimir and hoisted him back aboard. The unfortunate Grifel set off towards the next (to become notorious six years later as Foinavon's fence) but then, to my delight, Vladimir pulled him up and addressed some words to his superior on the ground. I hoped he was telling him to jump in the Mersey – but not a bit of it. What he actually said was: 'Comrade Colonel, will you please pick up my whip?'

When it was handed back Vladimir continued on his way, and got all the way round to the water jump. He was, I can tell you, a real game boy – and I have good reason to believe that an ex-chambermaid at the Prince of Wales Hotel in Southport would confirm that view. She, like the rest of us, wished Vladimir could stay on instead of going home. These were the days of Stalin, don't forget, when unsuccessful Russian sporting teams were not exactly guaranteed a red-carpet welcome. We tried in every conceivable way to confirm Vladimir's safe arrival – but all in vain.

Then, by a little long-range miracle, early in the year 2001 word came through from a holidaymaking ex-reader of my Audax columns in Horse and Hound. He claims to have been introduced to a Vladimir Prakhov who, although over seventy (I should think so too) is not only alive and well but a successful trainer of Flat racehorses down by the Black Sea. If any interested party who knows him ever happens to read this book, I would be eternally grateful for his address and, if possible, telephone number.

I am ashamed (well, only slightly) to say that Vladimir and our search for him have found their way into one of my most used after-dinner stories. With apologies to anyone who has heard it more than once, this is roughly how it goes.

Letters, cables and telephones having failed to contact the missing Prakhov (which rhymes with a rather rude Anglo-Saxon dismissal beginning with 'f'), I thought I had surely cracked the problem when my nephew Geoffrey joined the Foreign Office and found himself posted to Moscow. Geoff left England with instructions to leave no stone unturned – and under no circumstances to come back without news of the much-missed Prakhov.

I am sure he would have succeeded – but for an unhappy incident at his very first embassy dinner. Geoffrey of course, was extremely junior – but, though a long way below the salt at this dinner, he found himself sitting next to an amazingly attractive dark-haired Russian lady. She, it transpired, did not speak much English so, since Geoffrey had only beginner's Russian, conversation was minimal. But when their eyes met she did not take hers away and when, as the vodka flowed, his hand fell on her knees, she did not take that away either. After another glass or two, my nephew, a bachelor in those days, was beginning to think that this might signal a much better-than-expected start to his stay in Moscow when the lady spoke for the first time – in English, and a surprisingly deep voice. 'Don't show surprise when you get to my balls. I'm Fotheringay-Phipps, MI5.'

I was back on board Taxi for a second National attempt in 1962, but the ground that year was far too soft for the old horse's liking, and we were becoming increasingly detached from the leaders when I pulled him up after jumping Valentine's Brook second time round.

So Carrickbeg in 1963 was my third ride

in the Grand National, and by a considerable margin my most promising.

A few days before the race the late Clive Graham – Peter O'Sullevan's famous comrade-in-arms for the BBC television racing coverage – telephoned: 'How would you like to go round Aintree in a helicopter, and tell the BBC audience how it really feels to ride in a Grand National?' Clive, at his charming and persuasive best, made the whole thing sound like a picnic – and, to be honest, I had never worked for the BBC before and was flattered by the invitation.

On the other hand, I had only ridden in two Nationals. Twenty-eight fences, one fall – really an 'unseated rider' – and one pulled up was my fairly pathetic record. I could see at least a dozen jockeys booked to ride the following Saturday who fitted Clive's blueprint a whole lot better than I did. But 'He either fears his fate too much – or his deserts are small.' The great Montrose, who wrote those words, never had to make a fool of himself on television, but he was surely right. In any case, I had borrowed more money than I could afford to buy the half share in Carrickbeg, and was only too well aware that the wages the *Daily Telegraph* pays junior racing correspondents do not include the costs of racehorse ownership!

So I said I would try, and turned up at Aintree early on the Tuesday morning, to find the BBC helicopter parked on the spot where four days later the big-race field would line up for the start.

Carrickbeg had ten stone three pounds to carry, which, since I wanted to use a seven-pound saddle, meant being not more than nine stone seven stripped by Saturday. Everything except whip and crash helmet count on the scales, and my light boots, breeches and (woolly) colours added up to about three pounds. I was determined not to need any last-minute sweating, so when I reported for BBC duty I was hungry as well as nervous – and, as always when wasting, in a quite unnecessarily bad temper.

Racecourses on non-racing days are seldom hilarious places, and in March 1963 the Aintree stands and buildings were a grey, depressing sight. Mrs Topham had not yet sold the course on to developer Bill Davies, but the empty stands somehow already had a condemned look about them – as if they had been forewarned of all the hiccoughs, quarrels, duff commentaries, 'last' Nationals, false sales, alarms, excursions, chaotic starts and bomb scares on the horizon. How could they know that salvation was also coming – in the shape of Red Rum, Crisp, Aldaniti, Ivan Straker and Seagram (the company even more than the horse!)?

The helicopter itself, waiting complete

with underbelly camera, did nothing much to raise my spirits, but the pilot was a cheerful veteran who turned out to have known my beloved brother-in-law Hugh 'Cocky' Dundas.

The running (or pseudo-riding) commentary which I had laboriously scripted the day before sounds pitifully inadequate now, though it did, I suppose, have its moments...

To jump Becher's well is like no sensation I know. You seem to hang suspended for a heartbeat. The reins slip wildly through fingers. Now – sit back and wait for the shock of landing...

After one helicopter circuit we landed to take a break, and I was unwise enough to wonder aloud whether we were flying low enough to give a proper 'jockey's eye' view of the action. I have never forgotten the pilot's reply. 'Look,' he said, 'when you hit one of these fences on your bloody horse, they just cart you off on a stretcher and some pretty nurse tucks you up in a hospital bed. If *we* hit one they scrape us off and put what's left in a bag...' On reflection, I saw his point.

At what I thought was the end of our filming session we touched down by the last fence. 'Right, that's it,' I told the pilot. 'Thanks very much. I'm off to my hotel for a drink and a hot bath.'

But not a bit of it. 'Oh no,' said the eager-beaver director – who had hitherto played little noticeable part. 'You must do a finish...'

So, heedless of my pleas that there seldom is a finish worth speaking of in the Grand National, he insisted – and, needless to say this was the only bit I had not scripted. Tired, hungry and with my temper deteriorating, I ad-libbed:

Round the last elbow into the straight, and now, with the winning post in sight, the final dregs of stamina are draining fast for horse and man alike. A hundred yards to go, and perhaps another's head appears at his knee. The final effort – a deafening crescendo as they cheer him home. At last it's really over...

Well, I make no claim to second sight, but four days later that awful imaginary scene of being caught close home bloody well came true. Carrickbeg did jump the last in front and, passing the Elbow – where the National run-in angles to the right – we did seem to have it to ourselves. But Pat Buckley blast him, had not given up. Neither had his mount Ayala and, though probably just as tired as Carrickbeg, he ran on doggedly to pass us a few yards before the post and win by three-quarters of a length.

I had little time to feel the crushing disappointment of 'so near and yet so far', as I had to file my report for the *Sunday Telegraph* within minutes of returning to weigh in. I dismounted, rushed into the changing room to wipe the worst of the Aintree mud off my face, then, still in my riding colours, ran across the Ormskirk Road to the house from which I had made an arrangement to file the story.

Three quarters of a mile from home today the dream of a lifetime seemed to be becoming true before my eyes. 'Go on John, you'll win!' – the speaker, as I passed him before the second last, was Pat Buckley on Ayala. He thought it was true too.

But half a minute later as Carrickbeg and I tired together in the final desperate 50 yards, it was he and Mr P.B. Raymond's gallant chestnut who dashed our hopes.

It was, I think, setting out on the second circuit that the thought of victory first entered my head. Carrickbeg had long since made the fences look and feel like hurdles and, after jumping the water well behind, he moved up outside his field turning away from the stands with a surge of power that warmed my heart.

At Becher's second time round he made

one of the few mistakes I remember, and for an awful moment his big brave head seemed to rest on the quarters of another horse stumbling in front of us. But then, somehow, we were clear, and at the Canal Turn, as Ayala blundered badly Carrickbeg nipped inside him like a polo pony.

Now there were only a handful ahead, and as the fences flicked by we pulled them back, one by one, until four from home, when for the first and only time in this hectic, wonderful race, fate took a hand against us.

Out And About had been in front from the start, but now, three lengths ahead of Carrickbeg, he ploughed low through the fence and fell. Seeing him go my horse, for once, failed to pick up when I asked him and, as he landed in a sprawling heap, had to swerve and struggle round his fallen rival.

At the time it did not seem to matter for, coming on to the racecourse, I saw Gerry Scott pick up his whip on Springbok. The favourite could do no more and, before the second last, we were past both him and Ayala, upsides in front with Hawa's Song, and the stands looming ahead like the shores of a promised land.

It was a sight that has been with me day and night for months – and now, seen in reality, will never, never be forgotten. You can only just hear the crowd, a murmur from afar, and the thing I remember best is a big chunk torn out of the last fence – and thinking, whatever happens, I must steer clear of that.

But Carrickbeg made no mistakes. I can't remember how he jumped it – but there we were, safe on the flat, and the winning post still a hundred miles away. Until now I had not felt tired. The horse had done it all and still, halfway up the run-in, as we straightened round the final elbow, he was strong and galloping under me.

At this stage, Pat Buckley told me later, he never thought Ayala could get there. As for me, he might have been in another world – all that mattered was the post, nearer and nearer now, stride by agonising stride.

But then it happened – nothing much, invisible from the stands – but there 50 yards from home I felt Carrickbeg sprawl and change his legs. The rhythm was gone, and hard as I strove to pull him together, the last dreg of his stamina – and mine – had drained away.

It still seemed possible – but then, like Nemesis, the worst sight I ever expect to see on a racecourse, Ayala's head appeared at my knee. He and Pat Buckley had never given up and must have struggled like heroes to make up four lengths from the last.

But they did, and poor Carrickbeg, with no more help available from me, staggered home gasping, his job gallantly done, the prize so very nearly his. Seven years old, a mere beginner by chasing standards, he had run the race of a lifetime – and there will, perhaps, be other years. But whether there are or not, I will never, never forget the ride he gave me today the instant ungrudging way he answered my every call, his strength and courage when things went wrong, his featherlight agility when they didn't.

The hours and minutes before a National are always hell and today when we left the warm and dark haven of the weighing room, a cruel wind bit through thin breeches to drive one's heart deeper still into one's boots.

Threading through the crowd towards the ring, every word of encouragement is welcome. Today Bobby Petre was one of the last to wish me luck – and since he was the last amateur to win (Lovely Cottage in 1946) I took it gratefully as an omen of good fortune.

The huge field took even longer than usual to sort into line and all the time, striving to keep your fingers warm, cold, stiffness and fear made it difficult to smile. 'Hope you get something to write about,' someone said.

'Who's coming with me on the outside?' Dave Dick as usual sounded cheerful, and I followed him to the right of the field alongside Tony Biddlecombe on Wingless.

Starter Alec Marsh (who knows how it feels) did not keep us waiting long and soon the Melling Gate flashed by with the first green and grim ahead.

I did not see Magic Tricks fall there and, tracking Mr Jones in the second group, Carrickbeg jumped it like a bird. He hit the third – and that more than anything filled me with confidence, for his head came up instead of down, like the safety net on an aircraft carrier.

Becher's was nothing – a soaring joy with scarcely even a pause on landing – but at the 10th a ghastly crash beside me spelt the end for Connie II – a harsh reminder that this was no happy-go-lucky picnic.

Mostly they seemed to be jumping well (22 finished, so they must have), but as Out And About led us past the stands the Chair loomed up and Wingless, riderless in front of Carrickbeg, gave me a nasty moment.

But all was well and now, I thought, it's time to get a bit closer. Michael Scudamore told me he tried to follow on O'Malley Point as Carrickbeg made his ground, but couldn't – and, galloping up the middle to get the clearest possible view, we closed on the leaders stride by stride.

I think it was Loyal Tan on whose back we so nearly landed over Becher's. He had up till then given Terry Biddlecombe a wonderful ride – an example, like Carrickbeg himself, of how a horse who ran deplorably last time out can rise above himself on the day.

As if remembering the Canal Turn from first time round, Carrickbeg swerved like a boomerang in mid air and, without help from me, got a couple of priceless lengths. It was here that Pat Buckley must have sat tight as sticking plaster – for Ayala carved a hole big enough for a London bus.

Springbok, I think, was just behind us at this stage, but I really cannot say for sure. From then on, you see, it was all a marvellous, jumbled dream – a dream that only became a nightmare seconds before the dawn...

Even as I was dictating that report, over in Ireland Thady Ryan was anticipating a good evening at my expense. I've already mentioned that I had more fun with the Black and Tans than any other pack, and after one particularly thrilling day followed as usual by a well-lubricated evening, I rashly promised to give them a slap-up 'Thank You' party if (which I certainly did not expect) Carrickbeg happened to win the Grand National. They do not forget that sort of promise in Ireland – and, on the afternoon of National day, Thady was persuaded (rather against his will and better judgement) to suspend operations so that the rest of the field could pause to listen to the race at a convenient pub.

Thady was not much of a racing man himself, and I gather that he and the first whip stayed on their horses with the hounds – only just able to hear the radio commentary. But they heard the roar when Carrickbeg came over the last in front – and when we passed the Elbow halfway up the run-in some of the throng in the pub, like many in the crowd at Aintree, thought it was all over. 'He's won, he's won!' they shouted to Thady – and, believe it or not, without waiting for the actual finish, he and the whip rode off with the hounds to draw the next covert! 'At least we thought we were sure of a good party,' Thady told me later – and I've always felt ashamed of letting them down.

Five days later I was able to recollect the race in a good deal more tranquillity when composing a much longer account for my weekly column in *Horse and Hound* – the tone of which seems to suggest that, if anything, the disappointment became more rather than less acute with the passing of time:

There are 494 yards between the last fence and the winning post in the Grand National at Aintree – and, for about 480 of them, I was, last Saturday afternoon, the happiest man in the world. But the last battle is the only one to count – and for that, for those final, ghastly 14 yards, Carrickbeg and I had nothing left. So there, in a split second, the dream of glory became a nightmare and Pat Buckley swept past on Mr P.B. Raymond's Ayala to win the great steeplechase.

The pair of them won it fair and square because, together, with certain defeat staring them between the eyes, they had the courage and endurance to go on fighting what was an apparently hopeless battle.

A horse with slightly less bottomless stamina than Ayala, or a man slightly less strong, fit and determined than Buckley would never have been able to seize the chance when it came.

At the time – at that bitter moment when Ayala's head appeared at my knee – I wished them both at the bottom of the deep blue sea. Now, with admiration and only a little envy I salute them for winning, deservedly a truly wonderful race...

That scruffy little man outside the gents in Piccadilly Underground station who accused me of being 'tired before yer 'orse' might well, I suppose, have been a *Horse and Hound* reader who had been struck by the sheer honesty of my description of the finish: His stride had still not faltered and, straightening round the elbow halfway home with the roar of the crowd rising to a crescendo in our ears, the only feeling I remember was one of wild, incredulous hope that the dream first dreamt on a nursery rocking-horse long ago was really coming true.

Until this moment, sustained by my horse's strength and by the heat of battle, I had felt no real physical strain, but now, all at once, the cold, clammy hand of exhaustion closed its grip on my thighs and arms.

Even to swing the whip had become an effort, and the only thing that kept me going was the unbroken rhythm of Carrickbeg's heroic head, nodding in time with his stride. And suddenly even that was gone.

With a hundred yards to go and still no sound of pursuit, the prize seemed within our grasp. Eighty, seventy, sixty perhaps – and then it happened. In the space of a single stride I felt the last ounce of Carrickbeg's energy drain away and my own with it. One moment we were a living, working combination, the next, a struggling, beaten pair...

(Come to think of it, it was Tommy Weston – who won the Derby on Sansovino in 1924 and on Hyperion in 1933 – who coined the phrase 'tired before yer 'orse'. But I console myself with the reflection that Tommy did not ride in all that many four-and-a-half-mile steeplechases!)

In the days following the race I received dozens of letters – including plenty from total strangers – offering commiserations for my near miss. I was particularly flattered to get a charming note from the great trainer Cecil Boyd-Rochfort, and one from Pat Buckley's father Joseph, thanking me for my kind words in *Horse and Hound* about his son's riding!

With the heat of battle cooled, I was able to reflect on the race. Any worthwhile jockey on a fancied horse gets to know all he can about the probable behaviour of his opponents. In a National, I always tried to make a mental note of horses with a proven record at Aintree. Of course it doesn't always work, but in those days you felt a lot safer over the early fences tracking a Wyndburgh or Team Spirit than you do behind a first-timer with no experience at Aintree.

Of the forty-six ranged against Carrickbeg and me in 1963, one about whom I (and everyone else) should certainly have known one all-important fact was Josh Gifford's mount Out And About. Then an eight-year-old, he had considerable ability – but negligible brakes. The National was Out And About's first race in England, but he was already a winner of four Irish chases – despite almost always running away over the first few fences! All of us should have known that – and should therefore also have known that Out And About was one to steer clear of in the last half mile. Sure enough, off he and Josh went when the tapes went up – at a gallop no horse could be expected to keep up for four and a half miles.

Rather surprisingly they were still in front after a whole circuit, and in fact were only headed at Valentine's (three after Becher's) second time round. It was then, still going strong on Carrickbeg, that I should have had the sense to keep well away from Josh and his tearaway steed. Obviously there was a big chance that Out And About would soon be tiring. In fact, as Josh told me afterwards, he scarcely got off the ground at the fourth from home – crashing through it just above the guard rail and leaving a gaping hole.

Poor Carrickbeg had, until then, made only one mistake, a minor one at the third fence. An open ditch, nearly (but not quite) as big as The Chair, the third has always seemed to me one of the National's most testing obstacles. At this point, so early in the race, your horse may still be puzzled by the unfamiliar material with which the obstacles are made. Furze and broom look nothing like the tidy birch of Cheltenham or Sandown. Unlike all the plain fences in the National, which were sloped on the take-off side in 1960, the open ditches still stand upright. A horse running at Aintree for the first time will never have seen, let alone been asked to jump, anything like them before. Carrickbeg did not get quite high enough for perfection at the third, but instead of going down his head came up, and it was, for me, an infinitely reassuring sight. After it, Carrickbeg took care of himself – and me – with an unbelievable mixture of boldness and agility. He was, don't forget, only seven years old and seeing the famous fences for the first time in his life. Several times, during the second half of the race, I remembered the wise advice of his trainer, Don Butchers. 'My only worry is that you will get too confident. He'll make you feel so safe you'll go to sleep and tumble off.'

Well, I did not do that, but I did something almost equally idiotic by staying 'in line ahead' behind Out And About. We were not exactly on his tail when he fell, but the best jumper in the world will go for a gap if it is offered. Worse still, after scrambling through the debris of Out And About's demolition job on the fence, poor Carrickbeg was forced to make yet another deviation – round Josh and his prostrate steed on the landing side. We must have lost at least five lengths, three-quarters of our momentum – and, most important of all, the energy needed to get it back.

It was then that I lost my head. Needless to say this was, for me, a brand new experience. Only my third Grand National ride, and here I was, three fences out, on a horse still full of running. And then, to be all but brought down and lose your position completely – the chance of a lifetime thrown away it seemed.

Oh, if only I could have that chance again, how differently I would treat it! There was, I should have realised, still a long, long way to go. Well over half a mile from the third last – five hundred yards of it flat, featureless run-in. Suddenly for the first time in ten minutes, your horse has no fence to concentrate on, nothing to take his mind off aching legs and burning lungs.

Having since completed (very slowly) a London Marathon, I know a little how Carrickbeg must have felt in those last painful miles. And, unlike him, don't forget, I had no clumsy monkey on my back, trying to make me go faster. But he answered my every call so well when, in my ignorant panic, I picked him up, that we were in front before the last.

Carrickbeg certainly looked a winner at that point, and halfway up the interminably long run-in, he still felt like one to me. Which is why I am convinced that if only I'd had the sense to sit quiet and let Ayala (or Hawa's Song) lead me part of the way home, the first two places would have been reversed. You can write the words *If Only* on my gravestone – and I wonder how many beaten National jockeys have said that. Incidentally my old friend and co-owner Gay Kindersley never once complained. He did not, I hope, belong to the 'tired before yer 'orse' school of thought – or if he did, like the good, sporting friend he was, he never said so.

Ayala never won another race and practically never finished a steeplechase course again. By contrast, next season Carrickbeg gave weight and a beating all round in quite a good handicap chase at Sandown Park. He was still only eight years old – but had jarred a tendon first time out at Towcester and broke down landing (with a clear lead) over the last at Sandown. He still won that race decisively – but pulled up hobbling lame. Leading him back up the Rhododendron Walk was, I think, the saddest moment of my whole race-riding career. Poor Carrickbeg deserved at least one more shot at a Grand National, but was never sound enough to run again.

Team Spirit, who won the National at his fifth attempt in 1964, had finished eleven lengths behind us the year before. Carrickbeg, who would have met him on much the same terms at Aintree, enjoyed a happy retirement hunting with the Mid Surrey Farmers Drag, of which Gay Kindersley and his father were joint masters. A bold jumper to the end, he gave me one marvellous day with that hospitable and sporting pack.

In 1964 Peter Rice-Stringer kindly offered me the ride on an eleven-year-old called Crobeg. He had been trained by Bob Turnell for Jim Joel – but when I asked Bob about his jumping, the answer was not exactly designed to fill you with confidence. 'Flat and low,' said Bob. 'Flat and low – that's how I remember him.' The form book did not cheer me up much either. Crobeg had won a few races for Mr Joel, but had not crossed the winning line in front for some years and, on Bob's advice, the owner passed him on. Now he was owned by Mr M.J. Richardson, a sportsman, thrilled, his trainer said, just to have a runner in the National.

Well, he had a fair run for his money. Crobeg, a rather washy chestnut, had enough sense to work out that 'flat and low' might not be altogether advisable at Aintree, and jumped round safely enough to finish ninth, but without lighting too many fires in my heart. Five letters of his name were just about the only things he had in common with Carrickbeg...

That 1964 race was won, as I've said, by Team Spirit at his fifth attempt – a real triumph of equine durability and, on the part of his owners, sporting perseverance. It gave Team Spirit's trainer Fulke Walwyn the rare double honour of having both ridden a

National winner (Reynoldstown in 1936) and trained one. It was also a popular transatlantic triumph because the winning syndicate of owners included two Americans, Ronald Woodard and John K. Goodman. Willie Robinson brought Team Spirit from a long way back to catch John Kenneally and Purple Silk close home. Carrickbeg and I sympathised with John and Purple Silk.

The 1964 Grand National was notable for several other reasons. It was preceded by two tragic accidents, one on the racecourse and one beside it. In the latter, an aeroplane bringing five enthusiasts to watch on National day crashed near the Canal Turn, killing all five. They included the celebrated author and journalist Nancy Spain.

A few weeks earlier, at Aintree's Yuletide Meeting, the universally popular ex-champion jockey Tim Brookshaw had suffered injuries in a hurdle-race fall which left him a paraplegic. In the National itself, Edward Courage's Border Flight gave Paddy Farrell a dreadful fall at the Chair – a fall in which, like Tim, he suffered paralysing injuries to his spine. As you will see in Chapter 12, these two disasters inspired Clifford Nicholson and Edward Courage to start the Farrell-Brookshaw Fund – which grew into the Injured Jockeys' Fund.

In 1965 I was delighted and flattered when the royal trainer Peter Cazalet offered me the Grand National ride on his very good chaser Kapeno. But in his warm-up race, the National Hunt Handicap Chase at Cheltenham, not only did Kapeno fall at the water (a fence I had been trying, for years to get removed or at least made harmless), but he, or someone else, also contrived to put a foot in my stomach! Walking back with a severe tummy-ache, I watched the finish – in which Fort Leney under one of Pat Taaffe's most forceful and agricultural rides, tried in vain to give Rondetto eleven pounds. I remember thinking, as Sir John Thomson's gallant horse was belaboured up the hill, that Fort Leney probably felt about the same as I did.

Fort Leney turned out, in fact, to have strained a valve in his heart; I had merely ruptured my spleen. Needless to say I missed the National – in which Kapeno, ridden by Dave Dick, was crossed and brought down when going strong at Becher's second time round.

But the 1965 race was a chapter in one great story and the beginning of several others. Fred Winter, who had already ridden two National winners, Sundew in 1957 and Kilmore in 1962, took out a licence to train in 1965 and, in his very first year as a trainer, joined Fulke Walwyn and the other jockey-trainer double achievers by saddling the American Maryland Hunt Cup winner

Jay Trump to win at Aintree. This was an extraordinary triumph, against extraordinary odds. With coughing rife in Lambourn, Jay Trump had to be isolated for weeks before the National. His rider Tommy Smith had never ridden at Aintree and scarcely at all in Europe. But he had the assistance of Fred Winter, a truly great jockey – with a will to win perhaps even stronger than Tommy's! That is saying a good deal; but together, despite the American's almost complete inexperience of European conditions, Tommy and Jay Trump overcame all the difficulties – and Aintree into the bargain.

Halfway up the run-in, in fact, they nearly threw the race away. Challenged by Pat McCarron on Freddie, Tommy Smith picked up his whip – and Jay Trump hung away from it in protest. 'Put it down, Tommy put it down!' – of course, in the uproar of a fierce Grand National finish no one could hear Fred Winter's agonised shout from the top of a crowded stand. But somehow, by some miracle, the message got through. Tommy did put down his whip and Jay Trump did run on. They got home by three-quarters of a length – and twelve months later, Fred Winter brought off yet another double when Anglo, whom he trained for Stuart Levy beat poor Freddie a second time. Anglo, incidentally had bucked

Tommy Smith off the first morning he arrived at Uplands, Fred Winter's Lambourn yard...

I pulled Solimyth up behind Anglo – and the following year, 1967, 1 was actually at Aintree the day before the National. 'Taffy' Jenkins, by now a trainer, had very kindly booked me for the big race to ride a ten-year-old he trained called Norther – and I was glad to do so. Norther, after all, had won a Welsh National and gave me other good rides. Keen not to let Taffy down, I planned to walk the course again on the Friday and, in addition, there was Friday's selling race. As I've already mentioned, my then father-in-law Ginger Dennistoun was in the habit of buying a few cheapish yearlings at the autumn sales each year and then, once he'd identified the quickest, having a bit of a punt on it at one of the early mixed or Flat race meetings.

Well, in 1967, our 'trials' – held in secretive seclusion at the crack of dawn on the Greendown gallop above Letcombe Regis – strongly suggested that a Golden Cloud filly called Curlicue was much the best we had at Letcombe. On firm ground the day before the National she had only eight opponents in the seller – and I wanted to be there early just in case there were any fancy prices to be had. Needless to say there weren't. An Irish shrimp called Blue Spider was made favourite – with Curlicue second choice at 7–2. I got what little 4–1 there was, and took not much notice of a strong, rather leggy bay trained by Tim Molony.

Curlicue went off in front – and was running on really well when this bay thing challenged her half a furlong out. They went by the post together and, with no photo finish at Aintree in those days (the camera was, I believe, available but, for some reason, not in use!) we had to wait for the judge. You couldn't really blame him for calling a dead heat – but that meant we got only the odds to half our stake. It was the first but by no means the last time that Red Rum – for he was the leggy bay – cost me money!

Whenever breeding experts start pontificating about bloodlines and stamina, incidentally it is always tempting to call their attention to Red Rum, the only horse, so far, to win three Grand Nationals. He was bought by Tim Molony to win that five-furlong Aintree selling race (as a two-year-old!) and did precisely that.

The next day Norther gave me the second-best ride I ever had in a National – at least as far as we got. Starting out on the second circuit, he was one of a larger than usual bunch of survivors, most of whom – the optimists among us, anyway – were beginning to fancy our chances. There were, it is true, these three loose horses up in front, and of course you always watch loose horses carefully to begin with. But they seemed to be minding their own business, and when they led us out over second Becher's running and jumping straight as railway lines, well, we more or less forgot them...

The fence after Becher's, the seventh and twenty-third in a Grand National, is kicked to pieces first time round and, if you get that far again, looks the least significant obstacle of the entire race. But that, for some unknown reason, was not how it looked in 1967 to a loose horse with the ill-omened name of Popham Down. He lived up to his title with a vengeance – jumping Becher's like a stag, but then careering across from left to right and mowing down the leaders like a machine gun. By the time Norther and I arrived, there were horses everywhere – one of them lying directly in our path.

Norther did his level best, jumping his fallen rival clean as a whistle. The leap was flawless; the landing rather less so. Norther came down in what was left of the fence itself – and I jumped it really well. With apologies to Will Ogilvy. 'The space that I cleared was a caution to see,' and I touched down – without a horse – close beside my good friend Stan Mellor. Stan had not by then ridden his historic thousandth winner, but his total was well over nine hundred, and you don't achieve that without learning a thing or two. One of the very first lessons a jockey is taught is that, after falling, you should curl up in the smallest possible ball with your head tucked in – until the storm rolls by. (In Stan's worst fall, at the second flight of the first-ever Schweppes Gold Trophy run, in those days, at Liverpool, he fractured his jaw and skull in fourteen places – and still got married to Elain three months later!)

Now, on the other hand, with horses going arse-over-tit on every side and the evident promise of more to come, he decided to break the well-known rule – and *run*. With no time for discussion and no inclination to argue, I followed his excellent example. Unfortunately a cameraman captured our flight – but at least the sub-editor in charge of the *Telegraph* sports page pictures had a heart. 'S. Mellor and Mr J. Lawrence running in search of their horses', he put under the picture in Monday's paper – one of the kindest and least accurate captions I have ever seen: the one thing we were *not* running in search of at that particular moment was our horses.

John Buckingham and Foinavon – once a stable companion of Arkle when owned, like him, by Anne, Duchess of Westminster – were the only ones to get through the carnage at the twenty-third without falling. They stayed doggedly in front and came home in solitary glory at 100–1. Foinavon's trainer, John Kempton, had, quite understandably not thought it worth his while to come to Aintree. But he saddled the winner of a hurdle race at Worcester – so almost everyone was happy.

Before the 1968 race, Terry Biddlecombe and I were amazed to find Brian Fletcher, due to ride the much-fancied Red Alligator that afternoon, sitting in the steam room – the hottest part of the Southport Turkish Baths. We both knew that Brian, who in any case then resembled a refugee from Belsen, could easily do ten stone. 'What the hell are you doing in there?' Terry asked – and got the amazing reply: 'I'm wasting to do nine stone on a three-year-old in the last.'

Well, the last race that day was a Flat race – so this, from a jump jockey with a real chance of a Grand National victory was a pretty surprising reply. It was the work of a moment with us to buy Brian a glass of champagne and get him out of the steam room – into which experienced 'wasters' (like Terry) would only go in the first place to open pores and start the sweating process. The recommended treatment worked. Red Alligator trotted up and, if only Ginger McCain had not jocked him off Red Rum, for what has always seemed to me an inadequate reason, Brian Fletcher would now have four Grand Nationals to his credit.

Falling at Valentine's on Master Mascus, my mount in Red Alligator's race, I found myself sharing the Brook with a great friend – the gallant Polish amateur John Ciechanowski. Once Fegentri champion amateur of Europe, John got out of Warsaw a short head in front of the Germans in 1939. Just as he reached the eastern border of Poland, the Russians came in – and when, after many close shaves and hazardous adventures, he reached Paris, where his father was a diplomat, the French capital fell to the Wehrmacht! John spent the rest of the war driving a British tank for the Free Polish Armoured Division, and if you ever want to bore an explosive hole in your ceiling, just ask John who he likes best: the Germans or the Russians...

Another brave feat of the 1968 Grand National was achieved by the 68-year-old American grandfather Tim Durant. He had to remount the eleven-year-old Highlandie – but still finished the course, the oldest jockey ever to do so. Tim's achievement – at his third attempt – won him a case of champagne from the bookies, and a contribution of £500 from them to the Injured Jockeys' Fund!

I had dinner with Tim the night before his triumph and learned his extraordinary story.

Over six feet tall and good-looking with it, he was bankrupted by the US stock market crash in 1929 and went to Hollywood, hoping to turn his height and good looks into money. Sadly he found all the parts for tall, handsome young men already filled.

'But, John,' he told me, in his Gary Cooper drawl, 'there was still some scope if you looked good and could talk a bit. But above all, you must not have a name the gossip columnists knew. There was room, you could say for a reliable and, above all, *anonymous* escort.' I think they call them 'walkers' these days; Tim was quite hurt, I remember, when I suggested 'gigolo'.

Anyway filling the role, whatever you call it, Tim went out with a lot of famous names – including Paulette Goddard and Greta Garbo, with whom, Tim said, he played tennis. 'Just tennis?' I am ashamed to have asked – and, I suppose, I got the answer I deserved. 'John,' said the oldest man ever to complete the Grand National course, 'John, the men that lady liked to consort with were men you and I would not willingly invite to dinner.' The mind boggles a bit – but I still have a dream of entertaining Garbo to dinner at Hill Farm, Oaksey. Sadly it turns into a nightmare at midnight – with all her best friends hammering on the door.

The most powerful man in Hollywood in Tim's time, he told me, was undoubtedly

Charlie Chaplin and, as it happened, Tim took Paulette Goddard to a party at which she was introduced to the great man. Chaplin, it seems, had never met Miss Goddard before – and that was the end of the story. 'He fell for her – and next day he offered me a job as his press agent. Chaplin was a huge name in Hollywood at that time, and one way and another I never looked back...'

I did not ride in the National in 1969 or 1970, but had a very good run round on Regimental in 1971 – he finished ninth behind last-gasp winner Specify – then missed out again in 1972 before playing a minor role in the most astonishing National of modern times in 1973. My ride was Sir John Thomson's Proud Tarquin, who gave me so many memorable moments – good, and, through no fault of his own, less good – in the saddle. On 31 March 1973 he served, as my *Sunday Telegraph* report put it, as 'the perfect mobile grandstand':

The last cruel yards of Aintree's quarter-mile run-in claimed yet another victim yesterday. And as Mr Noel Le Mare's Red Rum caught Crisp close home to win the 1973 Grand National, one of the saddest, as well as the finest, chapters had been written in all the great race's eventful history.

For Sir Chester Manifold's Crisp had

come from the other side of the world to teach us Pommies a lesson we will never forget.

From the first fence to the last he blazed a glorious lonely trail. In the end, though beaten by a weight no horse has carried to victory since 1936, he earned a sort of immortality wherever men admire brave horses.

But if, which God forbid and I don't for a moment believe, this was the last Grand National, it more than lived up to its reputation, with not one, but two, supremely romantic stories.

For the race's other heroes, Brian Fletcher and Red Rum, were fulfilling the dream of a lifetime for the eight-year-old's octogenarian owner.

Mr Le Mare had three dreams in fact: to marry a beautiful woman, become a millionaire and win the National. The first two came true long ago and last year, buying Red Rum for 6000 guineas at Doncaster, he laid the foundations for the achievement of the third.

But when you have just ridden around the greatest steeplechase course in the world it is inevitably horses you feel for more than people.

And so, with apologies to Mr Le Mare, to Brian Fletcher and Red Rum, I come back to Crisp and his rider, Richard Pitman.

To me, peering ahead from Proud Tarquin's back through a kaleidoscope of hooves and tails and colours and flying brush that is the National, Richard was, almost from the start, just a speck on the horizon...

...and through the race that speck became ever more tiny as Crisp went further and further ahead. By the Chair, in front of the stands at the end of the first circuit, he was all of thirty lengths clear, by second Becher's the margin was even greater, and by second Valentine's he was almost a fence in front of his rivals of whom only Brian Fletcher on Red Rum was mounting any semblance of serious pursuit. Crisp was still twenty lengths clear at the last fence, but Red Rum, galloping relentlessly and in receipt of no fewer than twenty-three pounds from his quarry caught him in the shadow of the post to win by three-quarters of a length.

As I wrote in the *Sunday Telegraph*:

If there was any justice in the National, which there never has been, Crisp would surely have got the reward he so richly deserved.

Red Rum and Brian Fletcher deserved it too, of course. For they alone had the strength and speed and determination to attempt what looked so hopeless a task. But this will be remembered as Australia's Grand National, and the wonderful lop-eared ten-year-old who made it so will, as I say, never be forgotten.

The time of the race – 9 minutes 1.9 seconds – shattered Golden Miller's 1934 record by almost nineteen seconds, and I'm convinced that in finishing a noble seventh Proud Tarquin beat the Miller's record as well.

By the time Red Rum scored his historic third victory in 1977 I had retired from the saddle, but I did ride against him at Aintree twice more after 1973 – on both occasions on Edward Courage's wonderful horse Royal Relief, a top-class performer over two miles who twice won the Two-Mile Champion Chase (now the Queen Mother Champion Chase) at the Cheltenham Festival.

There was a widely held theory that horses who excelled over two or two and a half miles somehow managed to find extra reserves of stamina over the four and a half miles of the National – Gay Trip, winner of the 1970 race under Pat Taaffe, was essentially a two-and-a-half-mile horse, and Crisp, who failed so gallantly in 1973, had won the Two-Mile Champion Chase in 1971 – but Royal Relief never had much opportunity to put that theory to the test. In 1974, the year of Red Rum's second victory he fell at the first fence, and the following year he got only as far as the seventh, by then familiarly – if not yet officially – known as 'the Foinavon fence'.

Eleven rides, got round four times and finished a close-up second on one these. Not a bad record, I suppose, and the thrill of riding in the race never diminished.

But my view of the vital place which the Grand National at Aintree played in our country's life, while shared by millions, was not enough to protect the race from the vagaries of other people's attitudes, and the whole story of the long-drawn-out threat to the race and the campaign to save it for posterity is, for the most part, a sorry tale.

The land on which Aintree racecourse is situated belonged to Lord Sefton, but from the mid-nineteenth century was leased to the Topham Company who took over the running of the course and the racing. In 1949 Lord Sefton sold the course to the company which from 1937 had been chaired by the redoubtable Mrs Mirabel Topham.

In 1964 Mrs Topham announced that she was selling Aintree to a property firm called Capital and Counties – and that could mean only one thing: the end of the Grand National, as the huge racecourse site disappeared under God knows how many houses. The sale was hotly disputed by Lord

Sefton, who, when parting with the racecourse in 1949 to solve a little 'cash flow problem' had imposed an injunction that during his and Lady Sefton's lifetime the land should be used only for racing or agriculture.

It took Mrs Topham just three years to get that restriction dismissed, by the House of Lords (with costs to Mrs T.). That gave the 1966 and 1967 runnings of the great race the unwanted – and a long way from confirmed – soubriquet of 'The Last Grand National', and my *Sunday Telegraph* report of the 1968 running concluded with these words:

Whether rumours yesterday about the future of the racecourse have any foundation or not, I cannot believe that either Liverpool or England can afford to let the National die.

Despite those high-flown sentiments, the rumours persisted and the position got worse. While the legal wrangle wore on and on, the facilities at Aintree deteriorated – why should Mrs Topham keep them up to scratch if the stands were about to be demolished? The racing public was voting with its feet. Attendances plummeted, and even on National day the running of the greatest and most historic steeplechase in the world hardly lifted the gloom which pervaded the place.

By 1973 Mrs Topham had cleared the last remaining legal obstacles, and announced that she had sold the land to property developer Bill Davies. Two years later Mr Davies was on the verge of selling on to another prospective owner, but that deal fell through, and the days of the National continued to look distinctly numbered.

Hope appeared in the shape of Ladbroke's, and in 1975 the biggest bookmaker in the land made an arrangement with Davies to lease the racecourse for seven years – which at least gave the race enough life for Red to register that unique third victory in 1977. On the day of Grittar's victory in 1982 – at the end of the seven years – the Jockey Club launched a public appeal to raise £7 million by 1 November that year: a sum which would both secure the purchase of the land from Davies and secure the National's future. The deadline came and went and the money had not been raised; but eventually Davies agreed to accept a considerably lower figure, and, through the good offices of the distillery company Seagram, which came forward to offer such generous support of the National that the appropriate funding could be found, Aintree passed into the care of Racecourse Holdings Trust, a subsidiary of the Jockey Club. At the press conference in

1983 announcing that the Grand National was at last safe, Ivan Straker, chairman of Seagram in the UK, was kind enough to declare that it was one of my (many!) articles in the *Telegraph* about what an outrage it would be if the race were allowed to die which inspired him to intervene.

Beyond regularly writing about the cause, I did my bit for the appeal, including making a trip to Saratoga in upstate New York – oldest and undeniably the loveliest of American racetracks – with Lord Vestey, the Jockey Club's chief organiser of the campaign, Fred Winter and Dick Saunders, who when landing the 1982 race on Grittar became, at forty-eight, the oldest winning National jockey ever. The campaign had from the start been a public relations disaster – as I wrote when in the thick of things, 'timed with all the delicacy of a midwife boiling water at a wedding', and seen in many quarters as rich men taking round the begging bowl – but in Sam Vestey it at least had a leader of considerable wisdom and tact, one able to build up a decent relationship with the perceived villain of the piece, property developer Bill Davies – who, after all, simply and perfectly understandably just wanted to cut his losses and get out.

My boldest, or most foolhardy contribution to the campaign to save the National was to run in the London Marathon, which I did to support the appeal – along with Brough Scott, my friend Rupert Lycett-Green and the racing journalist Tim Richards – in April 1983. I started training in January and considered myself in reasonably good shape at the start, but that feeling did not last long. In fact, I have always reckoned since, that covering those last five miles along the Embankment (Brough and I had promised each other not to walk!) was just about the only genuinely 'brave' thing I have ever done. I was fifty-four years old, my back ached, and the pain of each stride reminded me how much the next was going to hurt – and that there were hundreds more to come. Somehow I managed to complete the twenty-six-mile course in under four hours – three hours fifty-one minutes, to be precise.

But the pain of the most agonising strides throughout those final miles was soothed by the cause for which we were (barely by then) running; and, if I needed any inspiration, I had only to think of that feeling which Carrickbeg had given me for the first 480 of those famous 494 yards.

10

'It wasn't exactly a spare ride on Arkle'

Not long after Carrickbeg's – well, all right, Ayala's! – 1963 Grand National, Gay Kindersley persuaded the great champagne house Moët et Chandon to sponsor a Flat race for amateur riders over the Epsom Derby course and distance. Intended as a gesture of gratitude for the generous hospitality which we British amateurs had so long enjoyed all over Europe and the world, the race was run on August Bank Holiday Monday and entitled, rather elegantly the Silver Magnum.

In its early days, I have to admit, the conditions of the race were rather loosely drafted – leaving loopholes easily exploitable by sharp-eyed trainers. Two of the first three winners had at least a stone in hand – but although I rode them both, I promise the 'loophole' was not devised by me! And although in the end the first winner, Thames Trader, won decisively enough, his victory was preceded by what you might call – at least for his rider – a character-forming experience.

Thames Trader was trained by one great expert, Staff Ingham, for another even greater, Stanley Wootton. Staff, in fact, was one of several famous and highly successful jockeys who started their careers as apprentices to Mr Wootton; Charlie Smirke, Ken Gethin, Joe Marshall and Jackie Sirett were other graduates of the Wootton Academy at Treadwell House.

An expert judge of form and, when he thought the price was right, a fearless punter, Mr Wootton saddled eighty-four winners in 1924, and the following year bought Epsom's Walton Downs gallops for a reported £35,000. In 1969 he earned – or certainly should have earned – the undying gratitude of British racing by making over the whole property to the Horserace Betting Levy Board. Epsom is now one of twelve racecourses owned (not, admittedly without the occasional expression of public discontent) by the Jockey Club, through its subsidiary the Racecourse Holdings Trust.

Not long before the first running of the Silver Magnum I was summoned to Epsom to ride Thames Trader in a gallop, and my orders from Staff Ingham were perfectly clear: 'Sit in behind Jimmy [Uttley who was riding Thames Trader's galloping companion] until you see Mr Wootton and me. Then just let him stride on as you pass us.' Well, I did my best, but Thames Trader, a big, handsome seven-year-old with a mind of his own, thought otherwise. The Six Mile Hill gallop at Epsom is not as long as its name suggests, but halfway up it I could see Messrs Wootton and Ingham all too clearly The trouble was that, far from 'sitting in behind' Jimmy Uttley, Thames Trader and I were soon about a hundred yards in front.

Jimmy was then a few years short of his three Champion Hurdle triumphs on Persian War but already established as a high-class dual-purpose Flat and hurdle pilot. He is also a nice, kind-hearted man who has since become a friend – and, I'm sorry to say a beneficiary of the Injured Jockeys' Fund. He had, in fact, already warned me that Thames Trader 'can take a bit of a grip' – and was no doubt unsurprised to see me about to bore a hole in the horizon! I passed my expert audience doing my level best to look unconcerned, but needless to say they were not fooled for a millisecond. 'I think you should try riding a couple of holes shorter,' was all Staff Ingham said afterwards.

Heaven knows what he thought would happen four days later in the race, but in those days starting stalls had not yet been introduced to British racecourses, and by allowing Thames Trader to miss the break by two or three lengths I was able to tuck his nose in the tail of an opponent and persuade him to drop the bit. He came down to Tattenham Corner calmly enough, and once in the straight outclassed and outpaced his opponents to win by three lengths from Marchakin, ridden by Sir William Pigott-Brown. Bob McCreery rode the third, and Gay Kindersley was unplaced. Another rider who finished well behind was a young man named B. Scott.

When I steered Thames Trader into the winner's enclosure, Stanley Wootton greeted me with the words: 'Scobie could not have ridden him better.' Since Scobie Breasley was at that time well on the way to his fourth jockeys' championship and a rider of singular artistry I took these generous words as a signal that my ineptitude on the gallops had been forgotten – or least forgiven.

I am almost shamefaced to report that the next two Silver Magnums went just as easily to the partners of Mr J. Lawrence. King Chesnut, trained by Arthur Budgett, won by six lengths in 1964, and Prince Hansel, trained by David Thom, by the same margin in 1965. Prince Hansel made all the running (he was, to be honest, running away with me throughout) and my only worry during the race was how to pull him up after the winning post – a concern, incidentally which had likewise troubled the Australian jockey Pat Glennon with a somewhat more prestigious Epsom winner earlier that year, the great Sea Bird II in the Derby itself!

The course at Epsom falls away soon after the winning post and terminates rather abruptly in a fence, but Prince Hansel proved amenable enough after his stroll on the Downs, and my concern was unfounded.

Having won the first three runnings of the Silver Magnum, it was to be another eight years before I landed the race again – on Sol'Argent in 1973, who got home by a mere length from Petty Officer, ridden by Philip Mitchell – now a trainer, and himself a four-times winner of the 'Amateurs' Derby'.

But my time in the saddle in the early 1960s had its less triumphant moments, and the day of Arkle's battle with Flying Wild and Buona Notte at Cheltenham in December 1964 is etched indelibly in my memory for a reason much more painful than the great horse's defeat.

In the second race that afternoon, the Whaddon Handicap Chase for amateur riders, I had the ride for Roddy Armytage on a grey gelding named Pioneer Spirit. Having twice seen the horse jump round Plumpton in style, I had accepted readily when Roddy's wife Sue had offered me the ride at Windsor a couple of days before Cheltenham. I longed, in any case, to see Arkle again – and, with only a small field in

Pioneer Spirit's race, all seemed set for a happy and exciting afternoon.

The prospect looked even better when Pioneer Spirit turned downhill for home, well in front and with the race safely in the bag. There had been only seven starters, and of those only two, Bill Tellwright on French Cottage and myself on the grey were still standing. I was many lengths clear – and will never know the true explanation for what happened next. All I can say is that somehow, by some strange optical delusion or rush of blood to the head, I suddenly seemed to be heading for a hurdle, instead of a fence. 'You've gone the wrong way' I thought, and yanked poor Pioneer Spirit to a standstill – pulling a muscle in my back in the process – and then shouted at Bill a warning which, with a look of mingled pity and contempt, he very sensibly ignored, sweeping past to go on and win the race.

I got Pioneer Spirit going again and, pulsating with embarrassment, pushed him up the hill to take second place. We had started second favourite so the crowd, understandably were not amused – though surprisingly few seemed to think I had done it on purpose. The stewards presumably did not think so either, since they only fined me £25. I know it does not sound much now but, considering inflation and the inadequate income of a recently married amateur, I promise it felt quite painful enough at the time. So did the muscle in my back – and then having to describe poor Arkle's heroic 'failure' for the *Daily Telegraph* was just about the last straw.

After I had driven gloomily home through a swamp of self-pity a huge drink and a hot bath seemed the only solution. Back at Marndhill, I ran the bath and poured the drink. Then my sister Jenny rang up to commiserate: apparently the whole disaster had been described in clinical detail on the BBC! Well, of course it took me some time to tell her how quickly my mind had worked, and of course when I returned to the bathroom the bath had run over. I shouted downstairs to my four-year-old son Patrick to see if any water was coming through the ceiling – and just as he shouted back that all was well, the ceiling fell in.

Roddy Armytage trained in the next village, East Ilsley and it was there that I went, cap in hand, next morning to apologise. At that early stage of his career any winner at Cheltenham would have been extremely welcome for Roddy and I do not claim that he greeted me with open arms. But we have been friends ever since, and he kindly allowed me to ride work and schooling for him for several years even after I gave up riding in races. It was thanks to Roddy and Sir John Thomson that I had the enormous pleasure and privilege of riding the two full brothers Proud Tarquin and Tuscan Prince, to say nothing of Lean Forward (on whom my daughter Sara won several point-to-points) and Prince Tino. All these were out of Sir John's great brood mare Leney Princess, of whom we shall hear more later.

One Wednesday in late March 1966 I was phoned by a Scottish permit holder (that is, a trainer who handles horses for his or her immediate family) named Colin Alexander, asking me to ride his horse Subaltern in the Foxhunters' Chase at Liverpool – run over nearly three miles of the Grand National course – the following day. I'd never met Mr Alexander, but any chance to ride over those famous Aintree fences was not to be passed up, and although my knowledge of the twelve-year-old Subaltern was sketchy to put it mildly I readily accepted. After all, Carrickbeg was, at that time, the nearest I had come to riding a winner around the National course, and I was keen to get on the scorecard.

Subaltern started at 100–7 (14–1 in today's betting parlance) and as we made towards the first fence I felt a twinge of anxiety at setting off around that fearsome circuit on a horse I had never sat on before. I should not have worried, as Subaltern had previous experience at Aintree, having finished third in the Foxhunters' the previous year when ridden by Ken Hutsby. Ken's father had owned Subaltern at that time, but then sold him to Mr Alexander, so this year Ken was on board a horse named Wonderment – which word would make a good description of the look of exasperation and surprise on Ken's face when, leading the field as we turned for home, he swivelled round and saw his old partner rapidly closing and then sweeping past him. Subaltern stayed on stoutly up that accursed run-in to win by half a length from a horse named Chaos – and give me my first winner over the Grand National course.

I had to wait seven years for my second. Some time in 1970 Bob Turnell phoned and announced: 'I've got a hunter for you to ride. I think he's the slowest horse I've ever had in the yard.' After I'd had my first experience of Bullocks Horn I started to see what he meant. Owned by Mrs Nan Barker, whose husband Gar was a celebrated hunting man with the VWH, and named after a covert not far from Oaksey. Bullocks Horn was a good old jumper, but you had to work really hard throughout a race to keep him involved.

We struck up a useful partnership, and by the time we lined up for the 1973 Foxhunters' Chase, Bullocks Horn and I had already been placed in the race, having finished six lengths behind Bright Willow in 1971. Even better, we came to Aintree fresh from having won the other big hunter-chase of the season, the Foxhunter Challenge Cup at Cheltenham, albeit after a stewards' enquiry. It's never much fun being beaten by a head in a four-mile chase (as the Foxhunter then was), but that's what I thought had happened at Cheltenham after a ding-dong battle up the hill with Bear's Slipper, ridden by my good friend Bill Foulkes. The sounding of the stewards' enquiry bell as we returned to unsaddle came as a surprise – I had never even contemplated an objection – but so, when we were shown it, did the head-on film. Bill and Bear's Slipper did appear to bump Bullocks Horn quite badly – and had won only by a head. When asked by the stewards what I thought of the film I was able to reply rather smugly but with a clear conscience: 'Well, sir, I think it speaks for itself.' The stewards felt the same – and I don't think Bill has forgiven me yet...

At Aintree, Bullocks Horn was preferred in the market only by the top-class hunter-chaser Credit Call, who had won the race the previous year with his indefatigable owner Chris Collins.

Chris, now a veteran member of the Jockey Club, had made himself a leading amateur rider (champion in the 1965-6 and 1966-7 seasons) by sheer determination in the face of physical disadvantage: at well over six feet tall, he was hardly in the accepted mould of a jockey. Mind you, that determination manifested itself in other areas of his life, too. When he was about to sit the exams to qualify as a chartered accountant, his father expressed some scepticism about the chances of his passing. 'Not only will I pass,' the aggrieved son responded, 'but I'll finish in the top ten in the country.' His father gave him good odds against such an outcome and a bet was struck – and Chris duly collected, having finished second! He rode Mr Jones to come third behind Jay Trump and Freddie in the 1965 Grand National, and made headlines in 1973 when riding Stephen's Society to win the Velka Pardubice, that extraordinary Czech steeplechase which apart from one fence always struck me as cross-country hunter trial.

Credit Call was probably Chris's best horse, and started a worthy favourite for the 1973 Foxhunters': an intended run in the Grand National had been scuppered by a setback in training, and he was re-routed to the hunters' race which seemed – and, since that was the year of Crisp and Red Rum, undoubtedly was – a less demanding option. Bullocks Horn gave me a wonderfully smooth ride all the way round, hardly touching a twig, and going to the last fence was one of five or six still in with a serious chance. Then Credit Call appeared on our inside, only to fall away beaten in the next few strides, but as we battled up the run-in a new danger appeared in the shape of Dubaythorn, ridden by the great John Thorne – who at the age of forty-six was older even than I was. Both horses and both riders were all out, but we held on to win by a head. (John's finest hour came up that same run-in as a fifty-four–year-old eight years later, when on his wonderful hunter-chaser Spartan Missile he was narrowly beaten by Bob Champion and Aldaniti in that emotion-charged Grand National of 1981. Less than a year after that John was killed in an accident at the Bicester point-to-point, a terrible loss to the sport.)

But the afternoon that Bullocks Horn won the Foxhunters' was not all good news. An hour and a half before that race I came within an ace of fulfilling my great ambition of riding a winner in the colours of the Queen Mother. I had ridden for the beloved patron of our sport in the past, and to this day still regret not winning the 1964 four-mile National Hunt Chase at Cheltenham on her gelding Sunbridge, trained by Jack O'Donoghue. Sunbridge was a dour stayer and an excellent jumper, two qualities which could be put to good effect in a marathon race like the National Hunt Chase, and my plan was to settle him out the back and gradually bring him into the race as other horses tired late on. But going out on to the final circuit he saw daylight, picked up the bit and started jumping flamboyantly passing two or three horses in the air at three fences running. The result was that I found myself in the lead much earlier than I wanted, and Sunbridge was run out of it in the final half mile, finishing third behind Dorimont. When I met the Queen Mother after the race I apologised wholeheartedly for my failure to stick to the game plan, but the great lady as ever in her best Devon Loch mode, exclaimed: 'Oh, don't worry about that!'

At Aintree that afternoon in 1973 her grey gelding Inch Arran had an outstanding chance in the Topham Trophy – the day's other race over the National fences – and with half an hour to go before the race her jockey David Mould had not arrived at the course. There must have been a distinct shortage of top-class riding talent without a commitment in the Topham, as Jim Fairgrieve, trainer Peter Cazalet's head lad who was in charge that day as his guv'nor was mortally ill back at Fairlawne, approached me and asked if I could take over.

I excitedly changed into those famous

blue and buff colours and was queuing up to weigh out when – to my chagrin and no doubt to Her Majesty's great relief, and with a timing which the US cavalry never bettered – David appeared. His brother's brand new Jaguar had boiled over on the motorway and by the look of them its passengers were close to the same temperature by the time they arrived in the Aintree weighing room. I ruefully stripped off the royal colours and handed them back to their rightful owner – then watched with only a little regret as Inch Arran proceeded to win the Topham Trophy. I never did ride a winner for the Queen Mother.

Exactly what David Mould's reaction would have been had he arrived at Aintree the wrong side of the clerk of the scales's deadline and seen a mere amateur getting the leg-up on Inch Arran, I shudder to think. He had robust views about amateur riders ('bumpers', in the parlance then current), and was never – in my hearing at least! – shy of expressing them.

'The only thing I ever say to a bleeding bumper is, "Get out of the ****ing way"' was one of his more moderate utterances; given the chance, he could be much more eloquent – almost talkative in fact! One December day at Sandown, for instance, we had a slight disagreement at the Pond Fence, three fences from home and often a crucial stage of any steeplechase. I was riding Tuscan Prince, who always wanted a lot of daylight, and switching in search of it I may just possibly have altered course a bit sharply across the bows of the Fairlawne candidate. David thought so anyway and over the last two fences the unprintable riot act he read me certainly lasted longer than six words!

The winner was gone beyond recall by then, but as we pulled up – with me second and David an admittedly hard-done-by third, the last words I remember from Mrs Mould's eldest son were, 'All you ever 'ad was a few ****ing brains – and now they're gone.'

On another, happier occasion, when pouring rain and big fields turned the inside of the Sandown hurdle course into a quagmire, David wisely steered wide and I was the only one in a field of fifteen to follow his example. We must have gone fifty yards further than the others – but up the final hill we had horses and they didn't. It so happened that mine (I think it was a horse of Jakie Astor's named The Bugler) happened to have about a stone in hand of David's. As I passed him after the last, he deigned for once to break his rule about not talking to amateurs. 'You *cunning* old ****,' he growled, and those four words meant more to me than a dozen purple paragraphs of uninformed praise in the next day's paper.

I had, incidentally won my first Foxhunters' at Aintree as Mr John Lawrence and my second as Lord Oaksey as I had succeeded to the title when my father died at the age of ninety in August 1971. I became not only the second Baron Oaksey but the fourth Baron Trevethin, as my father had succeeded to the latter title when his brother, my Uncle Trevor, had died unmarried in 1959. Along with the titles came the family motto *Pur fel dur* – 'Pure as steel' – and the arms, officially described as:

Per chevron arg. and gu. two crosses raguly in chief of the last and a lamb in base holding with the dexter forefoot a banner and staff all of the first, the banner charged with a cross couped az.

The crest is 'A dragon's head erased sa. between two bugle horns counter embowed or.', and the supporters 'Dexter, a Guernsey bull; sinister, a hart, both ppr.'.

And they say the language of racing is impenetrable!

I have always loved roulette, and when in Lake Tahoe, Nevada, during my American trip in 1953 I saw a man lose half a million dollars betting *'en plein'* on the number 32.

When I left, the little white ball had – he and the croupier said – avoided 32 at least two hundred times, and this genial maniac, a Texan with a dash of Red Indian blood, was still betting the thousand-dollar maximum.

Well, I know it is ridiculous, but ever since I have felt a certain 'loyalty' to *trente deux, pair et passe*. Actually my favourite bet is *zéro et les deux voisins* – zero and the numbers on either side of it, 32 and 26. I like being able to see the ball approaching this (zero is, of course, a different colour) slightly more visible three-number 'target'. But I have to admit that, so far, the method has brought me more grief than glory.

After riding in a Fegentri hurdle race at Baden Baden in the late 1960s, for example, a group of us – including, I am pretty sure, my old friend Piers Bengough, later Her Majesty's Representative at Ascot – fetched up at the local casino with, in my case anyway a distinctly limited supply of funds. With what was, quite definitely a last throw, I plonked my few surviving marks on 32 – and, unbelievably up it came. The equivalent of nearly £200 to the good, I bought my wife Tory a small but rather charming watch at the airport shop next morning and, I regret to say popped it, undeclared, into my pocket.

The journey home was no problem – nor were the next eighteen months. But then

Tory was coming back from a week's hunting in Ireland when one of her party got into a heated argument with a particularly short-tempered customs official at Heathrow. Tory was minding her own business on the fringes of the row when this irascible and officious ferret, now thoroughly on his mettle, suddenly asked her: 'Where did you get that watch?'

It seems (if only we had known) that dutiable goods like watches carry a special mark if the duty has been paid. Needless to say the surface of our watch was virginal.

Poor Tory's perfectly honest reply – 'My husband gave it to me' – might still have been OK, if only I had been sensible enough to follow her honourable (and truthful) example. Instead, hearing that the watch had been impounded, and furious with myself for being tripped up over such a minor smuggling peccadillo, I gave my first interrogator a cock-and-bull story about a present from the grateful and generous German owner for whom I had been riding at Baden Baden.

Sir Walter Scott was dead right about 'the tangled web we weave! When first we practise to deceive'. Mine was pretty threadbare to begin with, but it took the Customs and Excise bloodhounds nearly a year and (I'm ashamed to say) God knows how many taxpayers' pounds to disprove it.

I was summoned to London twice to repeat my story and by this time was feeling distinctly shifty. The tabloid papers were not half as bloodthirsty in those days as they have since become, but as the son of a law lord, a *Daily Telegraph* hack and so-called amateur rider, even I could think up some pretty colourful headlines to describe my conviction as an untruthful smuggler of watches.

By this time – ten months after the event – I was on quite good terms with my chief interrogator, Blair by name but, according to reliable recent research, absolutely no relation...

Anyway ringing to fix yet another encounter – our third – Mr Blair sounded positively friendly. 'Just one more little chat to clear things up' was how he put it and, lulled into a positive pea-soup fog of false security I invited him to my club in London.

No doubt, in its time, St James's Street has seen quite a few criminals brought to book. But as we sat down with our drinks in the upstairs card room at Brooks's – one table has a semi-circle cut out of it to accommodate Charles James Fox's stomach – I doubt if many lawbreakers have approached their doom with such mistaken confidence.

'Now, Mr Lawrence, if you could just tell me, once again, how you acquired this watch?' With a sinking heart (not much liking the size of the file he had taken out of his briefcase), I trotted out my 'grateful German owner' alibi.

'Well, yes,' said Mr Blair – and that was when he opened the file. 'According to our research, this watch was manufactured in Essen in 1967 and sold, wholesale, to its makers [Avia was the trademark, I think] in Dortmund on 16 July 1968. It was next sold, retail, in the airport shop at Munich, on 4 May 1969, the day you left that same airport on a BEA flight to London.'

No doubt my jaw was near the floor by that time, and a lame reply about circumstantial evidence proving nothing got me nowhere. 'I am sorry to say,' said Mr Blair, 'that my superiors think it proves enough.'

It was then – almost certainly not for the first time – that the august walls of Brooks's heard the words, 'Anything you say will be taken down and may be used in evidence against you.'

The cards, you could say were well and truly on the table, and, not before time, I then faced the uncomfortable task of telling my parents, family – and, worst of all, solicitors.

My cousin (and godfather) John Barstow was then senior partner of Trower, Still and Keeling, an old established New Square firm of high repute which only very occasionally earns (or anyway deserves) the less flattering title of 'Slower, Still and Sleeping'.

As luck would have it, John was on holiday and my 'confession' was answered by a junior, much less experienced partner. 'Sorry to hear of your trouble,' he wrote. 'The case will be heard at Uxbridge on such and such date. I have briefed Jeremy Hutchinson QC to represent you. You may think this is taking a sledgehammer to crack a nut – but in all the circumstances we cannot close our eyes to the possibility of a custodial sentence.' I very much doubt if I shall ever forget those words.

In fact John's junior had made the right decision, and certainly no one could fault his choice of counsel. Jeremy Hutchinson, who soon became a judge, was one of the most delightful men I have ever met. At our first 'consultation', instead of pointing out, as he so well might, my crass stupidity in bringing troubles on myself, he seemed to share and understand them – as if smuggling watches and telling fibs about how you got them was one of those unavoidable traps into which we are all so apt to fall. I exaggerate – but only slightly.

By the time we left his chambers, Jeremy had almost made me look forward to my court appearance. Travelling to Uxbridge by Tube six weeks later, we were accompanied by his junior – a colourful character, slightly overdressed in a red waistcoat but known to me as the son of my father's old friend, the judge 'Owly' Stable.

The moment we arrived outside the courtroom, Jeremy showed his mettle. He quickly identified the prosecutor (still a police officer in those days) and greeted him like an old friend. I strongly suspect that, with Jeremy Hutchinson QC's arm around his shoulder as they entered the robing room, the officer felt a bit like an unknown conditional or apprentice jockey accosted with a friendly greeting by Lester Piggott or A.P. McCoy!

However that may be, Jeremy's charm worked wonders. I was, of course, pleading guilty by this time – so a statement of facts by the prosecution was all the judge required. But after Jeremy and the by now cooperative prosecutor had gone through the 'statement', it contained no mention whatever of racing and very little of my regrettably untruthful 'alibi'. It came out like a simple evasion of duty – £100 fine, confiscation of watch, and that was that. Clearly I had exaggerated my own 'celebrity' value – or maybe the assembled press just were not listening. I saw one Stop Press paragraph in the *Evening News* – but that was all.

One expensive after-effect of this regrettable episode is that I don't smuggle any more. They tell me that, if convicted a second time, you really could *not* 'close your eyes to the possibility of a custodial sentence'. The trouble is that, when visiting the Middle East, especially Dubai, travelling correspondents are apt to be given all sorts of presents by generous sheikhs – carpets, for instance, and enormous Rolex watches. Grateful as you feel, paying four figures of duty to the customs on arrival at Heathrow removes quite a lot of the gilt from the gingerbread as well as nearly *all* the guilt (and profit) from the 'smuggling'.

In the days before the National Hunt season ended at Sandown Park on the day of the Whitbread Gold Cup – which I must now, through gritted teeth, call the attheraces Gold Cup – the highlight of the final phase of the season for amateur riders was the Horse and Hound Cup, initially run in 1959 during the first flush of race sponsorship: a valuably endowed hunter-chase held at Stratford-upon-Avon on the very last day of term. The race's roll of honour contains the names of most of the top hunter-chasers: Bantry Bay won twice in the early 1960s, and the wonderful Baulking Green three times, in 1962, 1963 and 1965. He might well have won it again in 1967 but for ignoring the second last fence, which left Mr J. Lawrence on Cham to fight out the finish with Royal Phoebe, ridden by Brough Scott, then an amateur and later a professional jockey before embarking on his envy-inducing career as an outstanding journalist and anchor of Channel Four Racing. The photograph of the two of us landing over the last at Stratford still – I hope – graces the wall of Brough's office, and although his seat in that picture is distinctly closer to J. Francome's than mine was, it was Cham who found more on the run-in to win by a length and a half.

But an even more memorable Horse and Hound Cup day for me came in 1971, when Credit Call – whom we met at Aintree a few pages ago – scored the first of his four victories in the race. Chris Collins was injured, and the ride on Credit Call was taken by Graham Macmillan – a substitution which caused me considerable discomfort, as Graham and I were neck and neck in the amateurs' championship (generously sponsored at the time by Bollinger), and I had arrived at Stratford that day with a lead of one!

My own ride in the Horse and Hound Cup was Jedheads, who provided an increasingly remote vantage point from which to view Graham's rear end – and my chance of winning the title outright – receding into the distance. Credit Call won easily and we were tied.

There was one meeting left – that evening at Market Rasen – and my gloom was partially lifted by a suggestion from Terry Biddlecombe. Terry himself was locked in a down-to-the-wire battle with Graham Thorner for the pros' title and, leaving no stone unturned, had hired a helicopter to fly him from Stratford to the Lincolnshire course, where he had two rides booked. Were the first to lose and Graham Thorner ride a winner Terry's cause would be lost, and in this event he would try to get me on to his second ride. With Messrs Lawrence and Macmillan tied for the amateur title and Thorner one ahead of Biddlecombe in the professionals' race, the two Grahams rushed off by car and plane, and I climbed into Terry's helicopter.

Graham Macmillan's ride was on Tiger's Breath in the seven o'clock, a handicap hurdle, and Terry and I arrived at the course just in time to witness the awful – for me – spectacle of Tiger's Breath rapidly catching the favourite Seething Lane on the run-in from the last flight. I can't remember a winning post ever taking longer to arrive, but Seething Lane held on, and Graham and I were still tied.

In the next race the other Graham survived a terrible blunder at the first fence to run out a three-length winner on Tam Kiss, with Terry on Ashgate well back in fifth.

So Terry could not now win the jockeys' title, whether his ride Arrow Trout won the eight o'clock or not, and his plan was set in motion – then almost immediately crumbled when Arrow Trout's owner, Mrs Barbara Lockhart-Smith, announced, in robustly unprintable language, that any notion of Terry Biddlecombe voluntarily jocking himself off her horse in favour of Mr J. Lawrence would be given very short shrift from her!

I was not privy to the conversation by which Terry – then as now the most amiable and affable of persuaders – managed to get her to change her mind, but not for the first or last time his irresistible charm won the day with the upshot that soon I was being given the leg-up on the joint favourite Arrow Trout. Unaware of the weight of responsibility he carried along with his new jockey Arrow Trout sauntered to a twelve-length victory and I had won my second amateur riders' title – this time with just seventeen winners.

Of course, I could not reasonably expect everyone to enter into the spirit of how I had managed to pull this championship out of the fire. A few months later I was on the panel for a horsy evening way up north, when during the question-and-answer session an indignant Scotsman demanded: 'Do you think it was very sporting to beat a fine man like Graham Macmillan by taking a professional's ride?' Taken aback, I was trying to stammer out my apologetic reply when a fair-haired lady at the back of the hall butted in. 'It wasn't exactly a spare ride on Arkle, you know,' she announced. 'It was a five-year-old having its first run over fences.'

After the session was ended I sought out my rescuer, and was introduced to Mrs Monica Dickinson, wife of trainer Tony and mother of the then jockey – and later training phenomenon – Michael.

I have been in love with her ever since.

There was life outside jump racing in the 1970s, of course, and the first two years of that decade saw three of the all-time greats of the Flat in action.

By the time of Royal Ascot in June 1970, Nijinsky was well on the way to becoming one of the legends of the Turf. He was unbeaten, had won the Two Thousand Guineas and Derby for Lester Piggott and Vincent O'Brien, and within three months would become the first Triple Crown winner for thirty-five years.

But for me June 1970 is especially memorable for my first view, before the Coventry Stakes on the opening day of the Royal Meeting, of Mill Reef, a love-at-first-sight encounter which I can adequately describe only by quoting my book *The Story of Mill Reef*, published after that great horse's enforced retirement in 1972:

Mill Reef started at 11–4 *on*. That's hardly a working man's price with betting tax to pay but the five runners had not been in the Ascot paddock long before a steady stream of determined looking punters was to be seen marching across the Royal Enclosure towards Tattersalls' rails as though a free issue of diamonds had just been announced.

They looked like people who had seen a marvel – and they had. For no lover of horses, or indeed of beauty in any form, will easily forget his first sight of Mill Reef at Ascot. With the possible exception of the 1971 Eclipse I do not believe he ever again came quite so near to physical perfection.

Though always superbly balanced and with quality etched in every line, he often tended afterwards to run up light behind the saddle in hard training. But at Ascot his middle piece was so deep and his quarters so round that no lack of scope was apparent. Under the gleaming mahogany coat the muscles of his forearms and second thighs rippled like sleepy snakes and as he danced light-footed around the tree-lined paddock, long ears cocked to the unfamiliar sights and sounds, the blend of explosive power with easy natural grace was unforgettable.

Only one of the other four runners, the Crepello colt Cromwell, had previous winning form and he was quite unable to make the Coventry Stakes anything but a triumphal progress. Clear at halfway Mill Reef drew relentlessly further and further ahead and passed the post pulling so hard that Geoff Lewis could not contrive to stop him for fully another quarter of a mile.

Mill Reef went on to win a string of big races including, as a three-year-old, the unique four-timer of Derby, Eclipse Stakes, King George VI and Queen Elizabeth Stakes and Prix de l'Arc de Triomphe; in the book I described how, at the crucial moment in the Arc, a gap appeared just when it looked as if Mill Reef would get boxed in:

It can't have been very wide and it certainly would not have stayed open very long. But for Mill Reef at this, the climax of his whole career, it was enough. One moment we were searching anxiously along the jumbled line of colours, the next they parted and, like some projectile thrown from an angry crowd, a small, dark, utterly unmistakable figure detached itself.

For what happened in the next twenty seconds or so I have had to rely on films and photographs because at the time the press box, full of supposedly hard-headed scribes, exploded into something very like hysteria. It is never easy at the best of times to analyse a finish while screaming your head off, and even harder when a large French lady is waving her parasol under your nose...

It was one of the most unforgettable moments of my racing life.

The third all-time great of that remarkable few years, and a horse whose name is inextricably linked with that of Mill Reef, is of course Brigadier Gerard, who comprehensively beat Mill Reef in the 1971 Two Thousand Guineas, the only race in which they ever met.

'The Brigadier' was bred and owned by John Hislop, but sadly a combination of Mrs Hislop and Brigadier Gerard so upset John's balance and judgement that he became, in old age, almost as unreasonable as his wife. They both turned, unforgivably against Dick Hern, whose training of the great (but by no means easy to handle) Brigadier had played a far bigger part in that horse's brilliant career than the alleged expertise of his breeder.

Peter Willett, whose knowledge of the Thoroughbred is at least as comprehensive as John Hislop's, has written a delightful biography of Dick Hern, and his account of the Hislops – and John's (perfectly justified) eulogy of the Brigadier – includes these words:

If he [Hislop] had added that they were the luckiest people alive to have bred such a horse, a champion of champions, by sending a non-winning, jady mare to a second-class stallion just because he was cheap [and stood three miles from the Hislop home], everyone would have praised their candour, rejoiced with them in their good fortune and regarded them with affectionate respect for ever. But that, sadly, was what John and Jean signally failed to do.

Instead they got themselves – and their superlative horse – involved in an undignified and disastrous row with the Thoroughbred Breeders' Association, principally over the setting up of the European Breeders' Fund. This was the European part of the scheme on which the Breeders' Cup – the nearest thing racing has to a World Championship – is based.

The Hislops' refusal to have Brigadier Gerard included in the scheme cannot, in fact, be blamed for his comparative failure as a stallion. No doubt it did not help, but the fact is that, like quite a few other 'flukes' of breeding, The Brigadier was, when you remember his practically flawless racing record, a surprisingly unsuccessful sire.

Before the 1971 Two Thousand Guineas, hearing that the Brigadier was not going to run before Newmarket, I asked Dick Hern if I could possibly come to West Ilsley to watch his final gallop. Dick's answer was: 'Yes, provided the owners don't mind.'

But next day he rang me back to say sorry but John Hislop, who of course had many friends in the racecourse press room, 'felt it might not be fair to allow just one observer'. I quite understood – and, peering out at torrential rain on the morning of the gallop, congratulated myself on being tucked up snug in bed.

Looking back now, I am still on balance thankful that I stayed there – especially when I look at the 1971 form book and hear Joe Mercer's description of what happened that morning.

He and the Brigadier were asked to go seven furlongs up the Trial Ground, a gradually uphill gallop parallel with the ancient Ridgeway. Their work companions were a four-year-old called Duration, who had won a mile handicap at Warwick the previous week, and a three-year-old called Magnate.

Brigadier Gerard, on whom Joe was told to give Duration a three-length start, was, in any case, meeting the older horse on most unfavourable terms. What no one realised that morning was that Joe's suede jacket had soaked up the downpour like a sponge. When they got back to the yard he weighed it – and found that, compared with the macintosh-clad Lindsay Davies on Duration, the Brigadier had carried a 'penalty' of at least eight pounds. Dick Hern has calculated since that he was meeting Duration (who defied a seven-pound penalty for his Warwick win thirty-five minutes before the Two Thousand Guineas) on terms some thirty-four pounds worse than weight-for-age.

So when, after giving the prescribed three-length start, Brigadier Gerard finished the seven furlongs on a tight rein upsides a hard-ridden Duration, Dick, even before he knew about Joe's eight-pound jacket, was fully entitled to enjoy his breakfast. That brand of delight is catching, and if I had been there that morning, would I have stayed loyal to Mill Reef? I just don't know – but despite the Brigadier's spreadeagling victory in the Two Thousand Guineas, am glad the temptation never arose.

Of course, in the end, invited by Ian Balding and Mr Mellon to write their great horse's biography, I fell even more deeply in love with Mill Reef – and would always have backed him to beat the Brigadier over any distance beyond ten furlongs. On soft going, of course, the only question would have been by how far. Although Brigadier Gerard's courage and huge ability did enable him to win on soft ground, such conditions demonstrably reduced him from a great horse to a very good one. Mill Reef, on the other hand, won a hotly contested Gimcrack Stakes at York as a two-year-old, by eight lengths, in ground so heavy that Ian Balding did not want to run him.

Sadly the longed-for second meeting between the two horses never happened. But let it never be forgotten that, unlike poor Mill Reef, the Brigadier, who won their only encounter strictly on merit, retired to stud sound in wind and limb. His genes, alas, did not serve him as well as Mill Reef's, but that was no fault of his. With the possible exception of Tudor Minstrel, he was the best miler I ever saw.

11

'Thrilled to mount you!'

For all the great exploits of the blue-bloods on the Flat, my first love has always been jumping, and December 1971 brought one of my most exhilarating riding experiences – on a horse named Happy Medium in the Benson and Hedges Gold Cup over two miles at Sandown Park, then one of the big races of the pre-Christmas period.

Happy Medium belonged to Colonel Bill Whitbread, who had kindly offered me the ride at the start of that season, and before getting to Sandown had run respectably when third of four at Cheltenham and then won an amateur riders' chase at Kempton Park.

Sandown had long been my absolute ideal of a jumping track – from the point of view of both spectators and participants, equine and human – and Happy Medium that day raised my love for the place to even greater heights. There is no sight in racing to compare with a two-mile chase around Sandown, but that day the best place – the *only* place – to be was on Happy Medium's back.

After jumping the first two fences in the home straight we took the plain fence on the downhill stretch, and then swung right to face that exhilarating sequence of seven down the Railway Straight.

Jeff King – the best jockey of my time not to have won the championship – was leading on the favourite Jabeg, and as Happy Medium pulled his way up to join him at the first along the back, I could tell that I was not at all popular with JSK!

Happy Medium took off in front and turned in a breathtaking display of jumping, soaring over every fence and never putting a foot wrong. Down the back we went – two plain fences, open ditch, water jump, and then the three closely positioned Railway Fences, where the first has to be met just right or you're in trouble at the next two – and on round the bend to the Pond Fence – ping! – and on to the last two. Happy Medium just glided home by ten lengths from Even Keel. The perfect ride – and one with a perfect postscript: after the race, I was reliably informed, Bob Turnell turned to his wife Betty and said, 'They can't say now that he can't ride.'

The first race that day was a handicap chase won by a horse named Tuscan Prince, who before long would take an even higher position in my affections than Happy Medium.

Tuscan Prince was out of the mare Leney Princess, and owned like her by Colonel Sir John Thomson, chairman of Barclays Bank and himself a noted horseman in his younger days: when at Oxford he had ridden in the legendary point-to-point when Frank Pakenham – later Lord Longford – fell early in the race, banged his head, groggily hauled himself back in the saddle and resumed the race in the wrong direction, meeting the other runners coming towards him!

Leney Princess had cost Sir John £200 back in 1956, and the chief reason he had bought her was loyalty to her sire Roi d'Egypte – whom he had bought not long before the war from Anthony Mildmay. Roi d'Egypte was a full brother to the 1942 Gold Cup winner Medoc II and, on the day of his brother's Cheltenham triumph, Roi d'Egypte himself won the two-mile Cathcart Chase, on what turned out to be the last jumping programme in England until January 1945.

Having missed the best years of his racing life, Roi d'Egypte was found a place as a stallion at Streamstown House near Mullingar. He sired only about a dozen winners, but one of them was the tough and brilliant Champion Hurdler Another Flash, who also won the Irish Cesarewitch. Regal Wine and Ernest were two useful chasers by Roi d'Egypte and, through his daughter

Leney Princess, he founded a dynasty that is still going today.

Leney Princess was originally owned – or at least, once trained and controlled – by the great Paddy 'Wisdom' Sleator. No man, I have always felt, more richly deserved his unforgettable nickname. I only once had the honour of riding for Mr Sleator, in an amateur riders' hurdle at Market Rasen, but that brief encounter confirmed what an accurate description 'Wisdom' was!

When first approached, I was interested – and ridiculously flattered – to find that my mount, a nine-year-old hurdler/chaser called Forgotten Dreams, had last been ridden (in a Flat race at Aintree two months earlier) by L. Piggott. On the day of the Market Rasen race – where I had two other, quite well-fancied but losing rides – I searched in vain for likely Forgotten Dreams 'connections'. But this was in the middle of that mysterious period when the Sleator horses were officially trained by Arthur Thomas, a little known and seldom seen character who looked and sounded a bit like a Midlands car salesman. The principal Thomas gallop was always said to be 'up a slag heap in the outskirts of Birmingham' – but then, I remember people saying something very like that about Martin Pipe.

However that may be, the Sleator/Thomas horses invariably turned up at the races gleaming with health and fit as fleas. When I walked, a bit nervously into the Market Rasen parade ring, Forgotten Dreams looked just as I expected – but apart from the lad leading him round, no one else seemed to be taking much interest.

At Market Rasen you walk past the bookies on your way to the paddock and I had been interested to hear evens and, in places, 5–4 being offered about Forgotten Dreams. My betting adviser John McCririck was not available (come to think of it, I had not even met him in those days), but even a cursory glance at the form book had convinced me that unless you thought I was sure to fall off, 4–1 *on* would have looked a pretty generous price. The opposition, even by Market Rasen standards, was reassuringly mediocre.

So, after being legged up by the lad – 'Good luck!' but still no orders – off I went. As we walked out, however, there were no more offers of odds against to be heard. The money was coming now – and it was no surprise afterwards to hear that Forgotten Dreams went off red hot favourite at 2–1 on.

The start for our race was across the course, and on arriving there, whom do I see, sauntering out from behind the starter's car? Why 'Wisdom' Sleator – who else? – and this is all he said: 'Just keep hold of his head till the second last. Jumps pretty good.'

How right he was. 'Led approaching two out. Comf.' was the *Chaseform* account – and 'comfortably' was an understatement.

Sadly as it happened, I never saw Paddy Sleator again. But I talked some days later to one of Forgotten Dreams' owners. The whole thing had apparently been a carefully organised – and almost completely successful – 'starting price coup'. Sadly despite the total absence of on-course support, enough of the carefully concealed off-course money 'got back', via the 'blower', to spoil the price. 'With no one there – not even Wisdom – we'd hoped for even money my informant said. But he still gave me a surprisingly generous present!

Leney Princess herself did not win under Rules. But she won a couple of point-to-points, was second in two-mile chases at Rothbury (the now defunct course in Northumberland) and Cartmel, third in a three-mile hunter-chase at Fairyhouse and fourth in a four-mile chase at Punchestown. She was due to be sold at Punchestown, too, but knocked a knee and missed the sale. So John Thomson, not long out of the army, looking for a mare by 'Nobby' (as he called Roi d'Egypte), was able to secure, for that knockdown price of £200, one of the most successful brood mares in the history of steeplechasing.

Leney Princess was first sent to Fortina – and lost no time in making him the first Cheltenham Gold Cup winner to sire a chaser good enough to follow in his hoofprints. For her first foal was Fort Leney who in 1968 made Cheltenham history as the first horse sired by a Gold Cup winner to win the Gold Cup.

The first time I saw Fort Leney he was, in every sense, a beaten horse – and, having inadvertently ruptured my spleen, I knew roughly how he felt. First time round in the 1965 NH Handicap Chase, Kapeno had just deposited me at the water and at least one of our nineteen rivals kicked me in the ribs as they went by. But, as I walked back, cursing myself (and being taken to task by Graham Macmillan, who claimed we had brought him and Union Pacific down!), it was suddenly clear that the finish of the race between Fort Leney and Rondetto might be close and exciting enough to take our minds off any such self-pitying recriminations. In those days, unless the horse I was riding was in with a chance, my interest and allegiance in any race were concentrated on whatever Bob Turnell had running. I had, of course, ridden a lot of his horses at home, and as far as I was concerned the Turnell candidates – horse, jockey trainer and stable lad – were my home team. Although I had never been allowed to ride Rondetto (who would certainly have run away with me), he had always been one of my special favourites.

He was ridden that day by Johnny Haine, and from our position fifty yards or so from the last fence it was clear, as they came down the hill, that the race lay between them and the Tom Dreaper-trained Fort Leney – whose white and orange colours meant, at that stage, nothing in particular to me. They were worn that day by Pat Taaffe, who did not spare the whip as he pushed the tired Fort Leney into the last fence – and all in vain. Up the hill, the weight he had to concede was just too much and, although this is pure wisdom after the event, it was honestly no great surprise to hear afterwards that he had strained a valve in his heart.

Like Arkle, Fort Leney had the rare good fortune to be owned by a kind-hearted lover of horses and trained by a level-headed genius. Tom Dreaper did not need to ask John Thomson for permission to give Fort Leney the time and rest he required after this effort; he knew the owner's answer would be: 'Do whatever is best for the horse.' So he did just that, and after three years – one of which the horse spent completely on the sidelines – Fort Leney and Pat Taaffe rewarded that patience by winning the 1968 Gold Cup, the high point of a long, happy often triumphant story.

For Leney Princess produced the winners of no fewer than eighty-three races, most of them trained by Tom Dreaper and Roddy Armytage – usually in that order. Many jockeys had the pleasure and privilege of riding them; my own favourite, Tuscan Prince, was ridden by twenty different men, including Fred Winter, John Francome, Stan Mellor and Pat Taaffe – and ranging from those champions down through the Duke of Alburquerque to me. I first rode Tuscy at Sandown Park in January 1972, and in all accompanied him in twenty-two races, winning five. He was a superlative jumper, and never fell at an obstacle in a race, though once, through no fault of his own, he slipped up on the flat at Taunton. In fact, in all of his seventy-two races, winning twice over hurdles and thirteen times over fences, and being placed forty-one times, I very much doubt if any of his lucky riders even *felt* like falling.

When Tuscy's racing days were over, Sir John kindly gave the horse to me, but his active life was far from at an end. He proved a marvellous, foot-perfect schoolmaster in my daughter Sara's first point-to-points, and for three years I rode him in team chases for our team The Tory Party – named not for some political purpose but after my first wife! My participation in team chasing after I had retired from race-riding was somewhat against doctor's orders, but it proved about the best fun I ever had in the saddle. Team chasing – a sort of cross-country riding against the clock in teams of four – is, when things go right, the most exciting form of riding I've ever been involved in.

Tuscy became a much-loved and highly venerated member of the family at Hill Farm – and although he once ran away with my secretary after she had asked to ride him, I'm convinced that he did it only for a joke.

When he was twenty-seven years old, a very good age for a Thoroughbred, we discovered one morning that he had got 'cast in his box' – that is, he had lain overnight in such a position that he was jammed against one wall of his box and could not get up. The poor old horse was in considerable distress, and we called the vet. When he arrived we stood there considering the prone Tuscy and deliberating what to do. In truth there was only one thing for it. 'Could you give him an injection here and now?' I glumly asked the vet, and he returned to his car to fetch the fatal dose. The moment he had left the box, Tuscy fixed me with a look which can only be described as charged with meaning, raised himself to his feet without any noticeable effort – and proceeded to live happily with us for another three years. He died in his field in the farm in 1994 at the ripe old age of thirty.

The other horses of Sir John Thomson's with whom I struck up winning relationships were Fort Leney's full brother Prince Tino – whom I rode a winner when he was fourteen and who was still winning at sixteen – and Tuscy's full brother Proud Tarquin.

Tarky was a high-class chaser when trained in his younger days by Tom Dreaper, winning the Totalisator Champion Novices' Chase at Cheltenham in 1970 and finishing second in the 1971 Irish Grand National. By the time I got to ride him he was trained at East Ilsley by Roddy Armytage, but he retained a great deal of his ability I have mentioned above the wonderful mobile grandstand with which he provided me to watch the epic Crisp/Red Rum Grand National of 1973, and in April 1974 he carved on my mind two indelible memories on two consecutive Saturdays.

The first came in the Scottish National. Three weeks earlier Red Rum had beaten L'Escargot at Aintree to win his second Grand National and join a very select group of dual winners, and despite carrying top weight he started a very warm 11–8 favourite for the big race at Ayr. Proud Tarquin, by then an eleven-year-old, had recently won a handicap chase at Doncaster and started at 16–1. Again, the *Sunday Telegraph*'s man was at the centre of events:

Three fences from home in yesterday's Scottish Grand National at Ayr, Red Rum's elegant head was not the most welcome sight in all the world. But at least in the hectic seconds that followed Proud Tarquin and I had a ringside seat as racing history was made.

We know better than anyone just how much this incredible horse had accomplished to get there at all.

And we know the dogged courage with which he came storming back when his only mistake at the second last had briefly revived our hopes.

For just a moment there it was Proud Tarquin who rallied, and between the last two fences there felt to be precious little in it. But my old friend met the last half a stride too close – and Red Rum flew like a stag.

He landed running, too, and in the first 200 yards of the run-in it was already over. A great horse had beaten a very gallant one, and I am proud and grateful to have been involved.

Until the last straight where nemesis appeared the race had been pure joy – like a long, fast hunt in the sunshine as Proud

Tarquin calmly flicked fence after fence behind him.

Pat Buckley (whom I met in rather similar circumstances eleven years ago at Aintree) had played the fox on Canharis, and to tell the truth he and Red Rum are just about the only two horses I remember seeing.

Noble Neptune held second place for one circuit but he was jumping sharply right-handed and second time round we left him behind.

The final bend at Ayr runs sharp downhill, and sliding round it like a bobsleigh on the Cresta Run I felt for the first time that even on this rock hard ground we might be difficult to catch.

And so we were, but unfortunately in Red Rum we found a horse to whom the difficult is commonplace. If he had jumped the second last as well as he did all the other fences, his third Grand National would have been as easy as the second and, giving Proud Tarquin twenty pounds, that, believe me, is some achievement...

In beating us by four lengths Red Rum became the only horse ever to have won the Grand National and its Scottish equivalent in the same season. But Proud Tarquin was not finished yet. He came out of that tough race so well that Sir John Thomson and Roddy Armytage decided on the bold course of sending him to Sandown Park the following week for the Whitbread Gold Cup, even though the weight he had been allocated meant that I would be putting up eight pounds overweight. The *Sunday Telegraph* account of that controversial race was dictated from the Sandown Park press room with very mixed emotions:

The Dikler won first prize in the Whitbread Gold Cup at Sandown yesterday but the honours, by common consent, were equally shared. And in all this great race's eventful history there has surely never been a braver 'loser' than Sir John Thomson's Proud Tarquin.

After the last fence, as Ron Barry [rider of The Dikler] fully agrees, Proud Tarquin quickened yet again and up the endless hill was always narrowly holding on. In the end he thrust his indomitable head across the line in front and for a while at least, after sixteen years, I knew again how it feels to win a Whitbread.

But the camera does not lie, and what it showed was that the Rules of Racing had been briefly broken. The Stewards found that interference did take place and their decision is final.

In the early stages of this memorable contest Credo's Daughter and Cuckolder had shared the lead, with Proud Tarquin lobbing doggedly along behind them. Every now and then The Dikler's big white face showed at my knee, but down the back straight for the second time only Credo's Daughter was left in front.

Proud Tarquin brushed her aside at the last of the Railway fences and as usual the sight of daylight clear ahead put fresh spring into his weary legs. Now, after seeing the film more times than I want to count, I know that Cuckolder, Inkslinger and The Dikler were all going well, too well for comfort but, at the time, my only thought was to get home as fast as we could manage between us.

Well, we managed it after a fashion, and no one can take that away. Nor can they spoil the memory of a second unforgettable ride in seven days – nor lessen my gratitude to Proud Tarquin, his owner and his trainer.

In the ten days preceding the Whitbread Proud Tarquin, who is eleven years old, had travelled 1,000 miles and galloped his heart out for four. Another three and a half lay behind us yesterday as he rose at the last with The Dikler snapping at his heels.

No horse could be blamed for feeling the strain of such exertions, and in the half dozen strides that followed, my old friend undoubtedly hung to his left. He has often done it before and this time I thought I was ready.

Roddy Armytage and I had discussed the danger beforehand, and coming round the last bend in front I pulled the whip through to my left hand in advance. Now, however clumsily, I used it and ten strides after the fence we were back on an even keel.

But the damage, it now turns out, was done. As we hung towards him, The Dikler had veered away in sympathy and, under his big weight, who knows, perhaps even that brief interruption was fatal.

Nor, on the other hand, should any slight feelings of self-pity detract from the achievement of The Dikler who, even with my eight pounds overweight, was giving Proud Tarquin twenty-four pounds.

As for Ron, riding with one hand heavily plastered, he did not enjoy the objection any more than I did.

He was winning the Whitbread for the third time in the last four years; for Fulke Walwyn, the greatest trainer of staying chasers in my time, this was a record fourth victory. If it contained an element of sadness, well, that is racing.

But the bitter aftermath of that great race did have its lighter moments. Fulke Walwyn, a wily old dog at the best of times, made it a practice always to have his jockey object if a Stewards' Enquiry was announced – it concentrated the Stewards' minds, he said!

– so Ron Barry duly lodged an objection. As Ron and I were waiting outside the Stewards' Room for the decision to emerge, Monty Court, then editor of the *Sporting Life*, asked Ron, 'How can you win, a poor old bogman against a barrister?' – ignoring the fact that I never made it to the Bar and Ron was neither poor nor old! And the sportsmanship of Sir John Thomson was remarkable. 'We were just thrilled to be second,' he said – and he meant it.

I soon revised that diplomatically expressed opinion that 'the Rules of Racing had been briefly broken', and the passing of time has done nothing to diminish my feeling that a great injustice was done, and that the stewards who adjudicated ought to have been tapping their way down Piccadilly with white sticks. Two of them were young enough to be my sons, and John Hislop, another steward acting on the panel that afternoon, excused himself from taking part in the enquiry on the dubious grounds that he had not seen much steeplechasing recently.

A better note on which to leave the notorious 1974 Whitbread – at least, still notorious at Hill Farm, Oaksey! – is with the words with which I described Proud Tarquin in the following week's *Horse and Hound*: 'I have never ridden a tougher or braver horse and never expect to.'

As for Tarky himself, at the end of his

racing career he was given to Colin Nash, who hunted the Old Berks hounds from his back. Once, when housed in an unfamiliar loose box, Tarky jumped out through the open top door, without bothering to undo the bottom one! I've measured the opening, and for a heavily built 16.3 hands steeplechaser it simply couldn't be done. But Proud Tarquin was that sort of horse.

Tony Richardson made – and richly deserved – a great deal of money by directing a brilliantly funny and hugely profitable film of Henry Fielding's comic masterpiece *Tom Jones* in 1963. His next effort, *The Charge of the Light Brigade*, cost more to make – and earned a good deal less at the box office when it was released in 1968.

But in 1974, Tony still had more than enough prestige – and money – to back his latest brainwave, namely that Dick Francis could be the next Ian Fleming, with an equestrian version of James Bond as his horse-riding hero. Tony had bought the screen rights to Dick's first novel *Dead Cert*, so all he needed was a few million dollars (or even pounds), a heroically versatile cross-country horse, some suitable stars, and a first-rate, imaginative script writer. That was, or should have been, my cue!

Tony tried several more or less established scribes, but somehow none of their efforts sounded quite right to him. Racing and horses, as some bright spark pointed out, have their own private jargon. Why not try someone who speaks the language?

Well, Tony thought that sounded a good idea, and that is why this promising-looking envelope – thick blue paper, elegant handwriting and a large French stamp – materialised one morning beside my breakfast egg. It contained a letter from someone called Richardson, inviting me to a drink at (would you believe it?) the Ritz. I had, to tell the truth, never heard of Tony Richardson. But then someone mentioned *Tom Jones* and a delicious vision of Susannah York waltzed across my memory's horizon. At the time, of course, Miss York was looking (in the film) at Tom Jones, alias Albert Finney so there was nothing personal about her apparent enthusiasm. But no one had ever asked me to the Ritz before, and the answer was a definite 'Yes'.

As far as I can remember, no film of any kind was mentioned in the letter, but the curtain had in fact gone up on my short and undistinguished movie-making career. It didn't last long, but at least until the early results appeared on screen it was a thrilling and almost completely enjoyable experience.

Tony Richardson sadly died in California in 2000, but his marriage to Vanessa Redgrave had already produced two elegant and talented daughters. I am pretty sure that they had small parts as children in *Dead Cert*, but so much of that precious, agonised-over celluloid wound up on the cutting-room floor that I cannot be absolutely certain.

Tony's daughters were so pretty that he would have been barmy to leave them out – but, come to think of it, quite a few of his decisions and 'directions' were, if not barmy remarkably difficult to explain. We had, for instance, filmed a genuinely beautiful early morning scene on the Downs above Findon, with a string of Josh Gifford's horses cantering out of the mist. Everyone agreed that it would make an ideal mood-setting background for the credits and titles of the film. But then, without warning or discussion, Tony cut the whole sequence, replacing it with some grotty and undistinguished graphics.

I am never quite sure exactly what 'camp' means, but in some of his limper-wristed moods Tony Richardson would probably have accepted it as a more or less accurate description of his behaviour. He could be hysterically funny – and, just occasionally, so waspish and bitchy you could hardly believe it was the same man. You sometimes felt like hitting him, but under the frills he was a kind and generous artist with a brilliant if erratic imagination, and sense of humour. To me and my then wife Tory he almost invariably showed the kinder sides of his complicated personality.

While we were making *Dead Cert* we all stayed in a hotel outside Chichester, and our party was much entertained and enlivened by a splendid Pole called Boris, picked up by Tony on some improbable-sounding Iron Curtain filming venture from which, by the sound of it, they were both quite lucky to get out unscathed. Boris had by now appointed himself the director's chauffeur. If he had other roles they were behind the scenes, and since he was six feet tall and built like a light-heavyweight I suppose bodyguard may have been among them.

Like many Poles of my acquaintance, Boris had a splendid store of jokes, anecdotes and songs – in several languages. Considering their repeatedly invaded and victimised history, God knows what the Poles have to laugh about, but provided you keep off certain subjects (with Boris, for instance, politics and recent history were not advisable topics), laugh they do.

Looking like a younger but slightly part-worn version of Rod Steiger, Boris had a magnetic effect on women and was not afraid to use it. Tony always let him drive his car – a Jaguar, I think – and one afternoon, coming back from some errand in Portsmouth, the Pole picked up a remarkably pretty hitchhiker, not as risky a practice in those days as it has regrettably since become. She turned out to be a South African undergraduate 'doing' Europe, and, finding himself within easy distance of our hotel, Boris lost no time in asking her in for a drink. Dinner followed and, by this time, the old Polish charm had begun to work...

Elena was the lady's name, and a few drinks later she found Boris's advances impossible to resist. He, of course, was not in the resisting business, and, since they were alone, no one knows how long, or how often, they made love. All we do know is that, at some *moment critique*, Boris suffered a massive heart attack and died.

It is hard, impossible perhaps, to imagine Elena's feelings. Alone in a strange country in bed with a dead stranger. What would you do? Get up, dress and get the hell out. Surely that would have been the first answer to come into the head of any normal 21-year-old? But not Elena. I never met the lady – but I wholeheartedly admire her. She did get dressed; but then she rang for the hotel manager and told him exactly what had happened. I don't know the South African equivalent of the Victoria Cross, but in my opinion Elena deserved it, or perhaps, since she was definitely not in uniform, the George Cross.

Of course, she got no medal of any kind, but to his eternal credit the manager realised that silence was the best reward he could give her. 'Death by natural causes' was the coroner's verdict on Boris, and Tony Richardson sensibly said nothing. I have always wondered about Boris's story. Who knows what the first forty years of it may have contained? At least it must be long odds-on that he died happy.

The English are thoroughly mixed up about their attitude to animals, but then of course we always were a mixture and are now, in the twenty-first century a positive cocktail of differing bloods, breeds, traditions, upbringings, educations, histories and, in sadly diminishing proportions, religions and moral codes. Put all those into a human cocktail shaker, like London, Liverpool, or the Shires, and what do you get? I certainly do not claim to know the answer – but no one in his or her senses denies that we are, in all sorts of different ways, an extremely maybe even excessively mixed-up lot.

Anyone setting out to entertain this potentially explosive mixture with a film should acknowledge, to start with, the old rule about eggs. The harder you try to avoid breaking them, the bigger the omelette is apt to be.

You are long odds-on to offend someone.

And that in the British Isles applies especially to any film involving animals – especially dogs and, to an only slightly lesser degree, horses. Size, beauty, courage and intelligence (real or apparent) are crucial links between you and the audience, and the Thoroughbred racehorse, big, beautiful and brave, might have been designed specifically to wring the hearts of sentimental filmgoers.

Perhaps luckily for us, they hardly talk at all – at least, not when they are running; and we probably wouldn't understand them if they did. But just imagine half a dozen exhausted jumpers being 'encouraged' up the Cheltenham hill at the end of a three-mile steeplechase in heavy going. If their response to the whip was a scream of pain – or, as it might well be, a roar of anger – how long do you think the National Hunt Festival would continue?

Even after making *The Charge of the Light Brigade* – not one of his masterpieces, but definitely a film in which horses suffered and were seen to suffer pain – Tony Richardson could not really understand their comparative lack of vocal expression. On the first 'rushes' (early experimental shots) of *Dead Cert*, the horses were neighing to each other as they galloped towards the first fence in the Grand National!

But our first and biggest difficulty in filming was the crime on which the whole plot was based. The hot favourite for a steeplechase at somewhere like Windsor (the racecourse was not identified) was 'nobbled' (prevented from winning) in an original and singularly unpleasant way. It was, as quite often happens beside the Thames, a foggy day. Out in the country one of the baddies stretches a wire across a fence – and pulls it tight just as the hero horse (presumably a known front-runner) is approaching. The base-over-apex somersault which almost inevitably follows, could, I suppose, have been dismissed in real life as carelessness or over-confidence. With the wire removed, what other explanation could there be?

But just a moment. How in the name of Dick Turpin, never mind Dick Francis, are you going to 'create' this crucial and central disaster on film? All films which involve animals – especially horses – are fraught with peril for a director. Tony Richardson had been able to use the Turkish cavalry in *The Charge of the Light Brigade* – and found the Ottoman version of the RSPCA surprisingly permissive! But he knew the home team would be watching his every move.

Despite all our precautions, we did in fact have one fatal casualty making *Dead Cert* – a riderless horse slipping up on a bend. But that, I'm afraid, can and does happen wherever Thoroughbreds are asked to gallop anything like flat out.

To follow Dick's original idea was, we decided, downright impossible. Whatever tool or contraption you used, tripping a horse in mid-jump was just not on. Equity (the actors' union) provided us with plenty of trick riders able and willing to bail out at full gallop, but none of them looked in the least like jockeys. In any case 'UR', the *Chaseform* code for 'unseated rider', was no part of the original Dick Francis plot.

The problem about filming racing action, as we found with our supposedly climactic Grand National scene at Aintree, is that if you film two or more jockeys carving one another up in a studio, that is precisely what they look like on the film – dummies assaulting each other in a studio. There just is no realistic ersatz substitute for men behaving badly on horses, especially when the horses are supposed to be moving at upwards of thirty miles an hour.

So in the end we compromised, by having our hero-horse doped at the start with a drug which partially blinded him. That, of course, involved at least one more 'baddie' – in this case the starter's assistant, who according to our admittedly improbable script had time and opportunity to administer the drug as he adjusted the hero's girths before the start.

That in turn involved getting the right

horse, in the right colours, to fall, as if blinded, at the right fence! You would be surprised how difficult it is to achieve that sequence of 'rights'. In the end, needing a fearless cross between a jockey and a stunt man, we were lucky enough to have the late and much-missed Paul Kelleway among our team of jockey 'extras'. 'Piece of cake' was Paul's immediate reaction, 'but only if I can do it at the water jump'.

Well, in real life the water is never the first fence in a steeplechase, so that required another slight stretch of imagination. But by then who cared? Precise realism had long ago gone beyond recall.

We had, by this time, collected a team of 'extra' horses and more or less unemployed 'extra' jockeys. In those days there was still a midsummer off season in which quite a few jump jockeys were delighted to be earning – daily and for jumping two or three fences at a time – more than they would in a week for ten or more much longer and less predictable rides.

One of the 'extra' horses, we had been assured by its owner, 'has never got beyond the fourth fence in five point-to-points', so it was aboard this guaranteed faller that Paul Kelleway set off, in the right colours, determined – by a combination of intentional pilot error, going too slow and/or taking off too early – to land in the middle of the water.

He needed four attempts – at the first three of which, needless to say the unfortunate horse developed a hitherto unheard-of degree of surefooted agility. Finally Paul persuaded him *not* to clear the ditch: they made a sufficient splash to satisfy Tony and as for Paul, he took off as if jet-propelled, and cleared the ditch with ease.

With a bit of judicious speeding-up, the whole scene looked on film like a disaster. You needed a fairly vivid imagination to put it down to dope-induced blindness, but by this time our determination to stay as close as possible to reality was showing signs of fatigue.

I doubt if there are many copies of *Dead Cert* about these days – and my personal video, emphatically not for sale, can only be seen at *very* private parties. My own appearances are limited, and mostly unrecognisable. As a riding extra, taking the place of the non-riding star Scott Anthony I had to wear a wig – and resembled a geriatric Beatle.

From my point of view, the best thing by far about the film was that Mary Gordon-Watson very kindly lent me her gold-medal-winning eventer Cornishman V (hereafter 'Corny' for short). Eighteen by then, this marvellous horse had won two gold medals for Mary and Richard Meade in two consecutive Olympic Games. Now, in less than a week, he gave me more pleasure and excitement than I have had on horseback ever since.

Let me give you a respectful account of Corny's activities in the first week of August that year. *Dead Cert* includes a chase across country in which the hero and his horse are pursued from a racecourse (where they have just won a race) by a murderous firm of radio-taxi drivers. In order to escape, Corny has to jump the following obstacles: into and out of a crowded yard full of cows, over several rollers, harrows and other agricultural implements, into and out of a level crossing (easy for him but pretty spectacular on film) with an express train apparently missing us by inches, and finally – most nervous of all for me – over the bonnet of a taxi.

Corny in fact, made the taxi look insignificant. But what if he had 'spooked' and, for instance, put one (or even two) of his forefeet through the windscreen? That was what spoiled my sleep for several nights. But all was well. Fear did not travel down the reins and my nightmare turned into a commonplace.

Throughout the cross-country chase, of course, Corny had to be ridden bareback. He had, don't forget, just won a race and been unsaddled. Well, to be honest, I did not fancy even on this superlative jumper, negotiating that variety of obstacles without stirrups. A Red Indian would no doubt have found it a piece of cake – but not an amateur well into his thirties. So we faked it – with a three-pound saddle under Corny's sweat sheet, and holes cut in the sheet for stirrups. You could only see them if you knew what you were looking for...

After a short rest, Corny boarded his horsebox and was driven to Aintree, where five of the Grand National fences had been built and faced especially for him to jump next day. A supporting cast of 'extra' jockeys and horses had also been enlisted – fifteen of them: enough, we thought, to make at least the background to a 'real' National.

So there we were – an admittedly sketchy crowd of spectators, perhaps, but enough to fill the background. We jumped (four times) the fence before Becher's, then Becher's Brook itself, Foinavon's fence, the Canal Turn and Valentine's.

Corny of course, had never been to Aintree before; but, not at all surprisingly he much preferred it to the agricultural antics he had been asked to perform two days earlier! As for me, what a joy and privilege to have a chance of jumping the world's most famous fences on one of the world's best cross-country performers.

When Tony asked us, rather hesitantly. Would we mind doing it again?, I don't think there was a single 'No'. In fact, we jumped the five fences I've named four times. There were three fallers, but I honestly believe that our make-believe Grand National looked at least as real as any of the other 'imitations' I have seen.

But back to Corny's Odyssey. Aintree was Friday. On Saturday with not a mark on him, he was driven down to Finmere, and there, on Sunday, Mary won a dressage competition, out-pointing several much younger Badminton performers. I have known faster horses, but for intelligence and all-round ability Cornishman V stands alone.

Sad to relate, despite Corny's expert assistance, *Dead Cert* was a bad and deservedly unsuccessful film. The plot just did not hang together and the mixture of racehorses and taxis simply did not work. I have always felt that we robbed poor Dick Francis of millions. He has never complained, but when you think of the money the James Bond saga (admittedly with Ian Fleming's stories distorted beyond recognition) has made for Messrs Broccoli and Saltzman, Dick might well feel hard done by. Luckily he is far too nice a man to bear a grudge...

Corny of course, was not the only star we had. Judi Dench (now Dame Judi) and her husband Michael Williams (now sadly dead) were also there, neither especially well cast. Judi, who dislikes horses, was a trainer's wife and Michael a villainous jockey – who would, by his waistline, have had a job to do thirteen stone! Perhaps, all in all, it was no surprise that *Dead Cert* was never in the running for an Oscar.

Oh, yes: my only line. An extra, supposed to be a vet, did not turn up one afternoon at Findon. 'Here, John, you take his place,' said Tony rather reluctantly: 'You've only got one line.'

So, always willing to help, I sprang forward, ready to put all my thespian expertise at the director's disposal. Was it tested? Well, to be honest, no. My line ran as follows: 'Sorry Guv'nor, the urine sample's no good.'

To tell the truth, neither was the film.

But *Dead Cert* did enjoy one triumphant night. We took over the London Pavilion in Piccadilly Circus for the premiere, in aid of the Injured Jockeys' Fund. No expense was spared. Princess Anne was there – and an almost entirely racing audience.

That, of course, was the secret of the evening's success. Scarcely a frame went by without a delighted roar of recognition. Even my 'urine sample' got a laugh, and Tory's 'Bring another bottle' – yes, she was roped in too – brought the house down. What was supposed to be a thriller became a blackish comedy. I don't suppose poor Tony or the real actors got many professional brownie points – but the racing world was grateful.

On 30 December 1974 I rode Miller Boy to win the Pytchley Novices' Hurdle at Leicester and register my 200th winner under Rules, a feat which Jeff King greeted with a characteristic turn of phrase: 'You took a ****ing long time about it!'

Miller Boy's owner generously marked the event by giving me a framed photograph of horse and jockey sweeping stylishly over the last flight, with Lord Oaksey doing one of his better impressions of J. Francome. This photo, which has pride of place on my bathroom wall at Hill Farm, is inscribed:

> Thrilled to mount you!
> Camilla Parker Bowles

I have always loved Camilla, and have very much admired the stoicism with which she has coped with the sensational coverage of her friendship with the Prince of Wales. That photo is now one of my most treasured possessions, and if the inscription has a slightly familiar ring, it's probably because you've read those words before – in Jilly Cooper's book *Riders*. Jilly lifted them from my bathroom wall!

Miller Boy turned out to be one of the last winners I rode. In March 1975 I turned forty-six years old, and the following month took a crashing fall from Clover Prince when leading four fences out at Folkestone. One of our pursuers trod on my face and fractured my jaw. I eventually made a reasonable recovery but the doctors advised me with due gravity that one more fall might result in permanent paralysis. The inevitable announcement of retirement from the saddle was made in November 1975, not far short of twenty years after I had ridden Pyrene at Newbury. Audax wrote these words in *Horse and Hound*:

One day maybe I will have space and time to thank them all – the men, the women and the horses. But for the moment, all I can say is that, without them, the future looks a little bleak.

And if, by chance, I ever find myself owner of a horse with Taxidermist's final speed, Proud Tarquin's stamina and the agility of Carrickbeg or Happy Medium – well, then you may see the quickest comeback there has ever been.

12

'We don't want any of that emotional claptrap'

The Chair fence at Aintree is an open ditch – that is to say, a fence preceded (unlike the 'plain' ones), by a timber guard rail and ditch, which in the Chair's case is six feet wide. The fifteenth of thirty fences in a Grand National and deriving its name from the wrought-iron seat above it on which the 'distance judge' used to sit during steeple-chases over the big fences, it is jumped just once in the great race. The fence itself stands five feet two inches high, and at only fifteen yards wide is much the narrowest obstacle on the Grand National course.

The narrower a fence, the higher it looks from the ground and, approached for the first time on foot, the Chair is a genuinely terrifying sight. If you are unwise enough to climb down into the ditch, the fence towers above you, and whoever compared it unfavourably to 'a bloody great green stone wall' was not exaggerating much.

Not surprisingly, the Chair has been the scene of many disasters, tragedies and more or less serious injuries, but if the shade of the late Paddy Farrell will forgive me, his headlong fall here on Edward Courage's Border Flight in the Grand National of 1964 could now, in one special, slightly ironic sense, be seen as a blessing in disguise.

Four months earlier, at one of Aintree's minor meetings in December 1963, a six-year-old mare called Lucky Dora had taken it into her head to run out at the fifth flight of a two-mile hurdle race. The resulting fall, which broke poor Lucky Dora's neck, also ended the career of her rider Tim Brookshaw. But that fall, and Tim's injury, combined with Paddy Farrell's in the Grand National three months later to inspire the creation of the Farrell–Brookshaw Fund. The name of the fund changed several times – but not its purpose. For injured jockeys, nothing was ever going to be quite the same.

Champion jockey in 1958-9, Tim Brookshaw was one of the toughest, most cheerful and most resilient men ever to enter a jump jockeys' changing room. He was, among many other things, a dairy farmer and 'How now, brown cow?' used always, for some unknown reason, to be his chosen greeting to me. The fact that my father had what Tim considered a somewhat 'upmarket' herd of pedigree Guernseys may have had something to do with it! But whatever their origin, I had only to hear those four words to know that T. Brookshaw was in the vicinity. If we were riding together in a race, it almost certainly meant that Tim would shortly be trying to poke up along the inside rail!

Even in a Grand National he was always full of chat, and Michael Scudamore never forgot the immortal remark when one of his stirrups broke on Wyndburgh at Becher's Brook second time round in the 1959 race. 'Look, no feet!' he called across to his old friend as they landed over the fence; and, kicking his other foot out of the stirrup, Tim rode home virtually bareback. There is a picture of him and Wyndburgh landing over the last fence which could easily be used as a blueprint for a perfectly balanced cross-country seat, and they were only beaten a length and a half, by Michael on Oxo.

Calling at Tim's farm at crack of dawn next morning, a friend found the proprietor busy milking one of his cows. 'A bit stiff in the crotch' was his only reference to the eight fences he and Wyndburgh had crossed so unconventionally!

The spinal injuries Tim incurred on that dreadful December day in 1963 were not quite as severe as Paddy's in the 1964 National, but they still left him to a large degree paralysed, and there was, at that time, little or no official compensation for such injuries. The recently formed Levy

Board had a scheme under which a jockey unable to ride was paid £12 8s a week – but only for a maximum of two years – plus the woefully inadequate lump sum of £4,000. What on earth they supposed that was going to pay for, we shall never know.

It was these two crippling falls which inspired Paddy's employer Clifford Nicholson and Border Flight's owner Edward Courage to set up what they soon decided to call the Farrell-Brookshaw Fund. Mr Nicholson was a millionaire landowner, while Mr Courage, a member of the brewing family, bred and trained his own jumpers from the wheelchair to which a serious attack of polio had confined him. His wonderfully consistent Aintree mare Tiberetta ran second, third and fourth in the Grand National, her son Spanish Steps won him a Hennessy, and although I managed to fall off Royal Relief at the first fence of the 1974 Grand National, he had already won the Two Mile Champion Chase at Cheltenham twice when professionally handled.

Soon after the 1964 Grand National these two sporting philanthropists decided to launch an appeal on behalf of the two stricken jockeys. They found that although Paddy Farrell, a married man with four children, had done his level best to save while riding, he had, not surprisingly precious little cash to spare for emergencies like paraplegia.

Tim Brookshaw, who had his own farm and had been doing quite well with his dairy herd, was slightly better off – but had to employ at least one man, or do the milking himself, before going to the races. Following his accident Tim was typically from the first, determined to conquer or at least make nothing of his disability He rigged up a pulley and tackle to lower himself on to a horse's back, and, although grateful for everything done on his behalf, did his level best to lead as near as possible a normal life.

He still insisted on riding most days – including in one unforgettable charity race in Ireland, run on behalf of his own fund. Fred Winter and I were also involved, and I wonder what the Charity Commissioners would have made of two trustees going hell for leather into the first bend of a mile-and-three-quarters Flat race, with one of the Fund's two principal beneficiaries riding knee to knee between them! Needless to say Fred won the race, but the fact that Tim got round – with neither leg under full control – was, I suspect, just about as heroic an achievement as any in his adventurous career as a professional jump jockey.

In the end Tim died as I suspect he might have wished – from yet another fall, which may well have been caused by a stroke or heart attack. It was, anyway, quick, and no one else was involved. That great heart just stopped beating.

From the very beginning, Clifford Nicholson's appeal had been a runaway success. The world of National Hunt racing, indeed the racing world as a whole, had been shocked – and, in some cases, let's face it, deeply ashamed – to hear how inadequate the official compensation was for such desperate injuries, even when they involved paralysis.

Protective equipment was primitive compared with today's mandatory helmets and back protectors, and most jockeys wore little to withstand the impact of a fall apart from a simple cork skull-cap. And such improvements in safety measures as did take place did not necessarily meet with the approval of all followers of the sport. Soon after the 1963 Grand National the *Sporting Life* printed a letter signed by 'B.L.' of Dublin:

Watching the Grand National on Saturday last I was surprised to see the strange headgear worn by some of the jockeys. So far as I could see they were wearing crash helmets under their caps.

This is weak-kneed and ridiculous. It takes ninety per cent of the thrill from the sport when the jockeys cease to take a risk in such cases. Why hold a steeplechase if there is no element of danger in the business?

It makes things too easy for the cowardly

rider who in ordinary circumstances would never ride with a bit of dash and courage...

I don't want any man to risk his neck in a reckless fashion, but there must be a limit to the protection which they use.

What use would it be to watch a bullfighter tackling an animal while wearing a suit of armour?

Luckily for the new fund, not everyone shared the uncompromising views of 'B.L.', and the money started to come in without any elaborate publicity In fact, it immediately became clear – and has, thank Heaven, been becoming clearer ever since – that for jockeys in general and jump jockeys in particular there was and still is a huge, enthusiastic band of admirers out there, many of whom had, until 1964, been searching in vain for a way to express their admiration. They were delighted to be offered one.

I had been proud to be invited by Clifford Nicholson and Edward Courage to be a trustee of the original Farrell–Brookshaw Fund. Fred Winter, already four times champion jockey and soon to head the trainers' list for the first of eight triumphant seasons, had already accepted the same invitation.

There were all sorts of legal hurdles to be crossed in the complex business of setting up a charitable trust, and Edward Courage agreed to ask my cousin John Barstow, an experienced solicitor and a senior partner of Lincoln's Inn solicitors Trower, Still and Keeling, to become the Fund's first secretary.

It was a choice neither Edward nor anyone else connected with the fund ever regretted. John, who had fought throughout the Second World War in the Horse Artillery winning a DSO, threw himself wholeheartedly into the organisation of the new charity and – a few years later – it was largely through his energetic initiative that we managed to secure the patronage of Queen Elizabeth the Queen Mother.

Queen Elizabeth had, of course, begun owning steeplechasers herself in 1950, and suffered the dreadful blow of Devon Loch's still unexplained collapse fifty yards from victory in the 1956 Grand National. From the start, you might say she knew both sides of the jumping game – and never forgot that there are two of them.

The *Daily Telegraph* was from the first unfailingly helpful, and I shudder to think of the burdens I so carelessly unloaded on to my unbelievably long-suffering friends in the sports room. Frank Coles, Kingsley Wright, Bob Glendinning and Tony Stafford, among many others, had of course been pretty keen on racing in the first place

– the punting side of it anyway though they soon learned to avoid my tips, especially if I was riding them. But however regularly the tips went west, they like many others, genuinely liked the idea of doing a bit to help the men who had so often carried their money and even, just occasionally made it pay a dividend.

The first meeting of the trustees was held rather grandly at Claridge's – Clifford Nicholson was staying there – on 21 April 1964. In addition to Messrs Courage, Nicholson and Lawrence, the other founding trustees were Wing Commander Peter Vaux and Fred Winter, and I'm sorry to notice in the minutes that Fred was 'unavoidably' absent: he was in hospital following a fall. As it turned out, Fred was to become not only a trustee but also, alas, a beneficiary.

Ironically, it was a non-racing fall – down his own stairs in September 1987 – which rendered Fred a virtual cripple. The only very slight, consolation is that the Fund which he did so much to found and launch has been able to help him ever since that terrible accident.

To describe the nature of the acorn from which the oak of the Injured Jockeys' Fund grew, the minutes of that initial meeting are worth quoting:

Mr Nicholson said that he had been to Southport and seen Farrell. He was in fairly good spirits. He disclosed very frankly his financial position. When he started to ride he had nothing. He has been careful and saved a little but not a great deal. Since his accident he has received direct some presents and he disclosed these fully. He is not in immediate need at the moment... The whole of his ideas and feelings were of gratitude and he wished to leave everything to the Trustees.

Mr Nicholson then went to see Tim Brookshaw. He owns his own farm of approximately 157 acres: a good dairy farm. He has been doing well. He employs a man or two. He used to do the milking and then go racing and cover long distances. Mr Nicholson thinks Tim Brookshaw financially is alright in a small way but will be very grateful for anything that is done for him.

But both Paddy and Tim were more than just grateful, as the key paragraph in those first minutes declares:

Mr Lawrence said he had been approached by various people regarding other jockeys who had suffered injury... Mr Nicholson said that both Farrell and Brookshaw had expressed the hope that other injured jockeys as well as themselves might be considered for help.

Widening the remit of the fund from the initial pair to all jockeys involved some adjusting of the legal niceties, and at the second meeting – on 5 June 1964 – John Barstow was able to report that the Charity Commission had provisionally agreed to our setting up a new charity which we called the Injured National Hunt Jockeys' Fund. Furthermore:

It was agreed that injuries should not be restricted to injuries sustained whilst actually riding a horse but that the wording [of the Trust deed] should be extended to cover any injuries sustained by an object of the Fund (e.g. motor accidents) in the course of their employment or profession. It was also agreed that all employees of Race Horse Trainers licensed by the National Hunt Committee should also be included in the objects.

It remained the Injured National Hunt Jockeys' Fund until 1971. We had become conscious that by restricting our help to jump jockeys we had been unable to help the odd injured Flat jockey. The Charity Commissioners would not allow us to change our objects clause, so John Barstow came up with the idea that we start a new charity called the Injured Jockeys' Fund, to which all future donations would be paid, and gradually wind down the old injured National Hunt Jockeys' Fund. I well remember John Barstow venting spleen on civil servants when he reported these difficulties to the Trustees!

The early donations that came in when we first started the charity were extraordinary and heart-warming, and many had a humorous side. I remember a £10 note attached to a postcard which explained that this sum was 'the carcass value of my old hunter. As I gather he was the cause of injury to a number of jockeys in his earlier life, it seems only appropriate that the money should come to your new fund!'

The minutes of another of those very early meetings ended with these words:

Mr Lawrence suggested that the Fund might make some money by selling a Christmas card. He had been told that we might expect to make one – or even two – thousand pounds.

Well, that turned out to be one of my very few winning tips, and from that tentative suggestion blossomed the core of the Fund's annual money-raising schemes. The very first Christmas card in 1964 was a wonderful painting by Peter Biegel, and subsequent images were contributed by a succession of notable equine artists – including John Skeaping, Susan Crawford, Lisa Sandys Lumsdaine, Roy Miller, Joy Hawken, Peter Curling, Neil Cawthorne and (from a rather different artistic tradition) Giles and Norman Thelwell. The Christmas card now sells in quantities of over half a million every year, and when we last added up in June 2003 we calculated that in all the Fund had raised over £3 million from its Christmas sales.

Needless to say no one foresaw that kind of success; but from the first, great – sometimes quite heated – arguments raged among us trustees about the choice of card (and later calendar) each Christmas. How 'Christmassy' should it be? How many Father Christmases? (I think we have avoided him most years.) How much holly, mistletoe, etc.? How much racing should you have? And hardest of all, perhaps, which artist?

It isn't easy. Just get the best painting you can, some expert said. So we chose a Stubbs – one of our few failures so far! Never mind, I thought, let's go for humour. So the great *Daily Express* cartoonist Giles drew us what I considered a screamingly funny sketch – a horse's head, with a mournful, apologetic expression and a bunch of flowers in his mouth, poking through the door of a hospital ward to say sorry to his heavily bandaged jockey who lay with his leg in a plaster cast suspended from the ceiling.

The jockeys all loved it, and the cartoon was pasted up in several changing rooms over Christmas and Boxing Day – but with our sentimental public it went down like a lead balloon. 'How *could* you?' they wrote: 'How *could* you make a joke of a poor injured jockey with his leg in a plaster cast?' The sales were even sparser than those of the Stubbs, and I honestly think it took a year for us to live it down.

The Injured Jockeys' Fund calendar was first produced in 1980 and now sells 30,000 copies every year, while other popular lines include diaries, playing cards, handkerchiefs, notebooks, keyrings and all manner of other merchandise – which gets its most public airing during the weeks leading up to Christmas, when our gallant almoners and other volunteers brave all sorts of inclement weather to set up stall on racecourses all over the country.

Nowadays all our merchandise is sent out from a well-appointed warehouse under the administrative offices in Newmarket, but in the early days distribution was less sophisticated. A splendid lady named Barbara Bateson – wife of one of the partners at Trower, Still and Keeling – commandeered her garden shed and turned it into the warehouse from which were dispatched the

Christmas cards and, as the range of material grew, everything else – and the Herculean efforts of Barbara and her trusty helpers were, to their very great delight, quite properly recognised when Queen Elizabeth the Queen Mother, in her role as Patron of the Fund, paid a royal visit to that very garden shed!

The IJF has long been blessed in its voluntary workforce – as indeed it has in the calibre of the trustees, which over the years have included Lester Piggott's wife Susan, Lord Porchester (later Lord Carnarvon, the Queen's racing manager), my old friend Bob McCreery, Dick Saunders, John Winter (Fred's trainer brother) and former royal jockey Bill Smith; among the current trustees are Brough Scott (who has now 'done' over thirty years), Peter Scudamore and Jack Berry.

Recently I have been pleased to take a back seat, and the Chairmanship of the Fund has been ably taken over by my old and dear friend Edward Cazalet, himself a Trustee for over fifteen years.

It may not have been financially responsible, but our attitude always was to provide money for an injured jockey wherever or whenever it was needed. This meant that we grew rather slowly. The capital of the charity after five years amounted to a miserable £40,000. However, somehow word of our work got around, and our supporters have proved loyal, supportive and generous. Because of them, we have now been able to build up our assets to some £15 million – a glowing testament to the generosity of racegoers. During our life we have received well over £7.7 million in donations alone, and £7.3 million has been paid out directly to injured jockeys. Add this to the £3 million we have outstanding on interest-free (but index-linked) loans, and you can see that all the money sent in by our supporters in the form of donations has been paid out. We have built up our reserves through the generosity of legacies and the money we have ourselves made from our Christmas sales.

Raising the money is one thing, but how is it spent? On such things as the provision of seven flats in Newmarket, all occupied by injured jockeys; medical advice, including the provision of 'flying physios' who treat jockeys at race meetings (making the point that the IJF is not only for those with serious or career-ending injuries, but also for jockeys still in action but in need of running repairs); annual holidays for beneficiaries; help with the cost of education of special-needs children; transport, including specially adjusted cars; television rental; and cash support to dependants when death or sudden injury strikes. In addition, the Fund was instrumental in setting up, and continues (with the Jockeys' Association) to support, JETS – the Jockeys' Employment and Training Scheme, which exists to retrain in other pursuits jockeys whose injuries prevent their continuing to ride. JETS has led to a complete change of culture with regard to a jockey reaching – for whatever reason – the end of his or her career, and at last the great majority of jockeys are anticipating the shock of that change and preparing for employment out of the saddle. Dana Mellor – daughter of Stan and Elain, who have themselves been tireless workers for the cause – has been hugely influential in making JETS such a success. (Dana is now an IJF almoner.)

All that assistance is dispensed in a variety of forms – pastoral as well as financial and practical – and to a variety of beneficiaries, from well-known names like Tim Sprake (who suffered terrible injuries in a car crash in 1999) and Scott Taylor (who suffered serious head injuries in a fall at Perth in August the same year) to stable staff whose withdrawal from active service was accelerated by riding injuries.

The case of David Harrison, the popular Flat jockey who had a horrific fall at Sha Tin in Hong Kong in 2001, illustrates the range of IJF assistance: we have been funding a neurophysiotherapist to help David recover movement in his limbs; we have helped him and his wife move into a bigger house which can accommodate ramps for his wheelchair; and we have converted the double garage at this new house to provide a gym, an essential aid to his recovery.

The day-to-day operation is run from our Newmarket base by Jeremy Richardson, who has been with the Fund for over thirty years, having first become involved when a young assistant solicitor working for John Barstow at Trowers, and our work in the field is spearheaded by our six wonderful almoners. Jeremy now the Fund's chief executive, has played a vital part in its work very nearly from the beginning. No one knows more of its history and if any new problems appear it is invaluable to have a chief executive with such a long and comprehensive experience of the Fund and its operation. It is literally true we could not do without him.

In the early years of the Fund the trustees used to do their own visiting, but it soon became clear that this would become impossible as the number of potential beneficiaries increased. John Barstow introduced his niece-by-marriage Sue Mills, and suggested that she should undertake the visiting and report to the trustees. No one suggested at that stage that she should be paid, and with two young children Sue must, in the early days, have worked unacceptably hard. It was soon obvious that we needed at least two almoners – as someone decided to call them – and a wonderful stroke of luck was that Hilary Kerr, a trained social worker, happened to come into contact with one of our beneficiaries. She then rang the Fund asking if she could help and, scarcely able to believe our good fortune, we enrolled her on the spot. She became one of our best, most sympathetic and knowledgeable almoners and remained such for at least twenty-five years. Married to a doctor, she had nearly the ideal set of qualifications; she was also fearless, and took the first party of beneficiaries on the Tenerife holiday (of which more in a moment) all on her own. Then, when Newmarket trainer John Oxley died he left a widow, Serena, who immediately took over the obviously hectic post of Newmarket almoner. Sadly all these three 'originals' have now retired, but they have left a pretty clear definition of a IJF almoner's job. The current almoners are Elaine Wiles, Sarah York, Barbara Hancock, Dana Mellor, Liz Carroll and – last but not least – my wife Chicky to whom you will be properly introduced in due course.

Put simply the almoner's job is to provide an active link between the beneficiaries and the trustees, so that when the trustees meet, which they do ten times a year, they can receive up-to-date reports on the condition of the beneficiaries. The almoners are in constant and regular contact with beneficiaries, and if an immediate need arises they can ask either the chief executive or a trustee for emergency help.

The almoner must be ready for anything and to go anywhere. Sue Mills once had to stand by one of her beneficiaries when he was charged for murder (and acquitted, I hasten to add!) at the Old Bailey and Hilary had to step over a number of drunks in the back streets of Glasgow to get to one of her beneficiaries. Elaine Wiles was once called out on Christmas Eve when a beneficiary was rushed to hospital, unconscious from a kick on the head. All over Christmas she sat by his bedside comforting the parents, but very sadly he died. Almoners (who are now paid a small salary, though at first they insisted on working for nothing) have been known to mow lawns, cook meals, have beneficiaries to stay with them, and take cover when they get angry! They are the infinitely reliable rock on which the whole health and effect of the IJF depends.

But of course the Injured Jockeys' Fund is not concerned only with the day-to-day and each spring brings our trip to Tenerife.

Sending a party of para- and tetraplegics with their carers and other supporters to the Canary Islands costs around £50,000 – and never is our money better spent. The trip – now a permanent part of the IJF year, thanks to the extraordinary generosity of racehorse owner Robert Hitchins, who donated £1 million to the IJF in memory of his late wife Elizabeth and who himself sadly died in 2001 – is the brainchild of the former trainer Jack Berry a trustee since 1999 and an utterly fatigue-proof toiler for the IJF. Jack's son Sam was a jump jockey whose career was brought to an untimely end by a fall in 1985 which left him disabled. Sam took an apartment in Tenerife, where he discovered the climate exceptionally beneficial to his condition. It was after visiting him there that Jack had the idea of an annual holiday for IJF beneficiaries – and, with characteristic determination, raised the finance to fund it.

In the spring of 2002 Alan Lee of *The Times* came on the Tenerife trip, and in an article describing the experience so perfectly caught the essence of the work of the Injured Jockeys' Fund – which, I suppose, has given me more pride than any of my other activities within horse racing – that I take the liberty of quoting it here:

It is the laughter that is so striking, laughter where there must have been tears. Well past midnight, it cascaded from the palm-fringed terrace, where a circle of chairs surrounded a figure prostrate on a sunbed. The group was diverse in age, gender and familiarity but the unbreakable bond was that all had been damaged by the sport they loved.

For ten days each spring, the pains and injustices of dreadful racing injuries are temporarily eased. Sufferers cast together, sometimes in trepidation, bloom in the sunshine and comradeship of Tenerife. The annual holiday organised by the assorted heroes of the Injured Jockeys' Fund (IJF), is into its tenth anniversary and, to any observer with a pulse of humanity it belongs to the theatre of life-enhancement.

Mawkishness, however, is strictly forbidden. The throng share their stories happily – and there are some profoundly sad cases here in the Canary Islands – but sympathy is the last thing they seek. Rebecca Hewitt, wheelchair-bound by a fall in a Hereford hunter-chase, stridently summarised the spirit when she warned me: 'We don't want any of that emotional claptrap.'

Shane Broderick lay at the centre of the late-night laughter, smiling contentedly at the anecdotes and wisecracks. Five years ago, only days after finishing third in the Cheltenham Gold Cup on Dorans Pride, he was paralysed from the neck down by a fall at Fairyhouse.

Career over, life in limbo, all at the age of twenty-two.

Sharron Murgatroyd sat in her wheelchair

facing him. She has had six years longer to adjust to immobility and, being a feisty Yorkshire lass, she has done so inspirationally. Apart from planning her fifth book, all typed with stabilising pegs on her traumatised fingers, she is learning to play the piano.

Alongside her was the mischievous face of Lee Davies. His promising riding career on the Flat ended in a car accident. He is a tetraplegic, but sporting life goes on and his aim is a place in the Great Britain wheelchair rugby team for the Paralympics in Athens in 2004. 'Apart from a rule that you can't pull anyone out of their chair, it's full contact,' he said with a grin. 'It gets rid of all my frustrations.'

Des Cullen and Ronnie Singer, elfin epitomes of the caricatured Flat jockey sat close by. Movement is not their problem. Memory and coherence are the elusive assets for riders with brain damage. The irrepressible Singer, constantly flat-capped, reminisces vividly about waking from three months of unconsciousness after a fall at Aintree more than forty years ago. What he cannot remember is that he told you the same story five minutes earlier.

Then there is Sam Berry just twenty when disabled by a fall at Sedgefield in 1985. Unwittingly Berry was the instigator of all this when he bought an apartment at the

Mar y Sol resort, designed for the disabled. His father Jack, the former trainer, came out to visit him one Christmas. 'I could see the good it was doing him and I remember sitting on the poolside and thinking of my old riding mate, Paddy Farrell, who was in a wheelchair. Then I counted the other ex-jockeys I knew who would benefit from it. By the time I went home, I was determined to bring them out here,' Berry said.

Berry a saint-like figure in this story raised more than £40,000 to fund the first holiday and repeated the miracle even as costs rose in the next six years.

'We couldn't get people to come at first. They were frightened by the idea of going abroad in wheelchairs,' he said. 'Now, they are scared that they won't be asked.'

The financial burden was lifted by an unexpected cheque for £1 million from the late racehorse owner, Robert Hitchins, but Berry still attends each year, more talismanic for the cause than the resident black cat that slinks symbolically around the sunbeds. For the luckless in life, coming here is truly a ray of good fortune.

The resort lies in that area of Tenerife where half-finished apartments hustle for space with tacky bars called Desperate Dan's and Big Ben. There are holiday-makers from hell in the vicinity but Mar y Sol is a haven of peace and dignity. There are hot and cold pools, a fitness centre, physios and doctors on site.

In past years, Fred Winter, his speech virtually gone since an accident at home in 1987, was a silent, smiling presence. Lord Oaksey the indefatigable chairman of the IJF, said: 'It wasn't so much what he got from the holiday as what he gave to it. He was just about the best at riding and training jumpers and being around him was inspiring to many who would never otherwise have known him.' Too ill to travel this time, he is much missed.

Constantly present are the IJF almoners, among them Elaine Wiles and Lady 'Chicky' Oaksey. Murgatroyd calls them Baby Spice and Posh Spice, but the affection for them is evident as they fuss florally around the site, nothing too much trouble.

The able-bodied may make an excursion to the seafront bar, where racing from Britain is shown and bets surreptitiously taken, or to the Sunday market by the harbourside. Mostly though, the group – 53-strong this year – make their base near, or in, the pool.

There is a chairlift to ease entry but Murgatroyd disdains this.

Each sunlit afternoon, when she gives the word, her two carers will tip or even throw her into the water, one more expression of a free spirit that has even extended to deep-sea diving on a previous holiday here. Wiles said: 'We had to lay her out on the stones to get her diving suit on. People were staring and I was worried. But she came back and said it was fantastic.'

Murgatroyd, 41, has written movingly of her frustrations and deprivations since her life changed for ever on the opening day of the National Hunt season in 1991. 'The simplicity of running a hand through my hair or snuggling between crisp fresh sheets and being enveloped by a hugging duvet is a distant dream – as is the feeling of ground beneath bare feet,' she said. Here, though, she feels almost liberated.

The release is not immediate for all. Hewitt, 39, describes her first visit here, soon after her accident. 'I was completely unapproachable and it freaked me out a bit,' she said. 'I felt like an outsider looking in and I didn't want to be part of it. But I've learnt it's what you want it to be – you can do everything or nothing.'

Murgatroyd, showing that she can now raise her left hand high enough to drink wine, looks back without rancour. 'I've never been bitter, but I have seen people here still too angry about their injuries to appreciate it,' she said. 'When I first came, although I was mentally OK, I couldn't handle the pain and it showed in my face.'

The hollow face of Dennis Wicketts shows

little as he is lowered into the pool and his voice can say nothing. Behind the emptiness, though, lies an intensely moving tale, demonstrating that the IJF and its holiday cares as much for the grass roots of racing as for its glamorous upper level.

Wicketts met his fate in a remote Cornish point-to-point eighteen years ago. His remarkable wife, Jane, said: 'We were both riding in the Hunt race at Crimp and Dennis was in front when he fell. I actually went on to win the race before I realised how badly he was hurt.'

Jane, who was pregnant at the time, has continued to run the family farm, until recently milking seventy cows a day single-handedly while raising a son and caring for her deteriorating husband. No one can ever have deserved a holiday more.

Another point-to-point rider, Jenny Litson, is wheeled around the site by her devoted parents. She rode more than seventy winners before a fall at Larkhill deprived her of so much – mobility, speech and even the ability to cry. At least here, among so many friends and fellow sufferers, she does not feel the need of that.

Jonathan Haynes is not here this year, but his spirit lingers on. He was twenty when his back was broken at Southwell in 1980 and his first holiday since was to Tenerife, where he raced his wheelchair down the hill to the seafront, then literally crawled across the beach to demand a try at paragliding.

Haynes, by awful irony was attached to the Midlands stable of Jimmy Harris, himself confined to a wheelchair in 1971. Harris, who trained with dignity and diligence, was a veteran of Tenerife holidays until his death last June. His widow, Ann, was persuaded to come this year.

Last night, as music rang out and Berry twirled wheelchairs on the dance floor, she reached into her bag and produced a photograph of Jimmy tanned and smiling at Mar y Sol. 'This is how he would want me to remember him,' she said. It was a simple, significant testimony to an extraordinary venture.

13

'Dear Bastard'

In the *Horse and Hound* article in 1975 announcing that I was giving up race-riding I'd admitted that 'the future looks a little bleak'. Indeed it did, but at least retirement from the saddle provided the opportunity to do more work for television.

That helicopter ride round Aintree before Carrickbeg's Grand National in 1963 was my first assignment for the BBC. Whether they were struck my by innate broadcasting skills or (rather more likely) were simply impressed by the prophetic nature of the piece, they used me again for the occasional feature over the next couple of years – notably a programme during the run-up to the 1965 National which, if nothing else, underlined my remarkable powers of clairvoyance.

The BBC had decided to film the Aintree preparation of two horses likely to run prominently in the National, and eventually latched on to Freddie, the great Scottish hunter-chaser trained by Reg Tweedie, and Jay Trump, who would be a first Grand

National runner for first-season trainer Fred Winter. As you'll have already read in Chapter 9, Jay Trump beat Freddie by three-quarters of a length in one of the most exciting Grand National finishes of all – and my reputation at the BBC was done no harm.

BBC assignments gave me opportunities to work with two of my all-time racing heroes: the late Clive Graham and his *Daily Express* comrade Peter – now, of course, Sir Peter – O'Sullevan.

Clive – whose writings as 'The Scout' in the *Express* were followed almost as avidly as Peter's, and who as paddock commentator was an essential part of the BBC racing coverage – died of cancer in 1974. I had the privilege of giving the address at his memorial service in St Martin-in-the-Fields in Trafalgar Square:

'Never Forget' is the Graham family motto, but a foolproof, almost photographic memory was only one of the tools young Clive Graham took with him to that first job at the Daily Express – the paper to which he was to give devoted and conscientious service throughout the forty-three years of his working life. Among the other tools were a first-class brain, a clear, uncluttered mind, and sentences which flew to the heart of their meaning like arrows to the gold.

On this foundation Clive built over the years a highly developed nose, both for winners and for news. And he stored away in his capacious memory an encyclopaedic knowledge of racing in all its branches of form, of breeding, and most of all of the infinitely varied actors – human as well as equine, villains as well as heroes – who make up the daily sporting drama to which he devoted his life.

Peter O'Sullevan, a very old friend, is someone I love and admire almost more than anybody in racing, and I am well aware that most of his good works are quietly carried on behind the scenes. That there are horses and animals literally all over the world who owe Peter their comfort, and in some cases their lives, is attested by the list of charities that are the prime beneficiaries of the Sir Peter O'Sullevan Trust: the Brooke Hospital for Animals, Compassion in World Farming, the International League for the Protection of Horses, Racing Welfare and the Thoroughbred Rehabilitation Centre. The last-named was founded in 1991 by the indefatigable Carrie Humble, who has worked tirelessly for the welfare of former racehorses, and Peter has been highly influential in getting Carrie started and in directing donations her way ever since. I am proud to be a patron of the TRC.

My regard for 'The Voice' – as the greatest of all racing commentators has long been affectionately known – was summed up in a piece I wrote for the *Racing Post* (which I had joined as a columnist in 1988) in 1989, soon after the publication of Peter's superb autobiography *Calling the Horses*:

The chief blessing, of course, for his readers, viewers and listeners – indeed, for the racing world as a whole – is that, almost ever since the war, Peter has been actively, often hectically involved, closer to the professional summit and centre of that world than any other single human being I can think of. To say that he has a 'talent for friendship' is a serious understatement. I cannot think of anyone who has been liked, respected and trusted by a wider variety of racing professionals, and amateurs as well. Who placed bets for Vincent O'Brien, Aly Khan and, often unwisely, for that eternal optimist Paddy Prendergast? Who shared the confidence (well, sometimes, anyway) of remote Gallic geniuses like François Mathet and Etienne Pollet? Who refused an offer of £5 from the young Lester Piggott and proposed Michael Stoute as a BBC racing correspondent? The list goes on and on, and, looking down it, you can easily understand how regularly those 'scoops' used to appear in 'Off the Record' and

Peter's other *Express* columns.

Mind you, Peter benefited pretty handsomely from me as well. *Calling the Horses* recalls the time in the 1970s when he and I both served as directors of Lingfield Park racecourse, and Peter writes of board meetings 'before which I showed a fair profit betting on the late arrival of Lord Oaksey. John only let me down once when, obviously due to an oversight, he arrived three minutes before the "off".'

Late in 1965 I was approached by Pay TV, a revolutionary new pay-as-you-view (sixpence in the slot!) television service which had done a deal with Kempton Park racecourse to cover all races at all its meetings. (Pay TV did not last very long, but it did survive long enough to deprive terrestrial viewers of the sight of Arkle's 1965 King George VI Chase and, the following year, the great horse's sad, hobbling defeat in the same race.) My duties covered paddock commentary and general interviewing, and I was joined in this role by my old friend Colin Ingleby-Mackenzie who, as an animated talker, was ideal for the Kempton job. Unfortunately we found it difficult keeping up a regular supply of people to interview, so we often ended up having to interview each other!

The King George duly returned to the

BBC for the 1967 running – but then frost intervened and the race was abandoned. With commendable expedition the BBC arranged for a computerised version of the race to be run a few days later – remember, in these primitive days computers were a far cry from the streamlined little machines we use today and tended to take up a large room! – and kindly invited all the jockeys who had been engaged to ride in 'the real thing' to a well-lubricated lunch before the computer tapes were set whirring into action. I had been booked to ride Master Mascus in the Kempton race and duly presented myself for the lunch – where BBC presenter Julian Wilson generously laid me 100–1 against my horse. Rules forbidding jockeys betting could not be considered applicable in a computerised race, I reasoned, and I happily availed myself of ten shillings (fifty pence in today's money) on the nose.

Buttons were pressed, and the computer, which had been programmed with what was considered all the appropriate information (including the relative abilities of the jockeys), started to spew out the positions of the runners at the first fence, then the second, and so on. On the second circuit of the computer-generated Kempton Park the prospects of Master Mascus – and of my ten shillings – became progressively less forlorn as more fancied horses fell by the wayside, and to the delight of J. Lawrence and the utter horror of J. Wilson, we crossed the electronic line in front (with Mill House, no less, back in third!).

Julian, to his eternal credit, paid up the £50 like a man and without demur.

To my eternal *dis*credit – but no doubt flushed with the success of my one and only King George VI Chase winner – I wrote a lyrical account of how I had won the race through superlative jockeyship and despite the moderate abilities of my horse. One person left distinctly unamused by this *jeu d'esprit* was Master Mascus's owner, who sent me an indignant letter and never let me up on his horse again. It just goes to prove the old saying that you may insult a man's wife, but *never* his horse.

It was in 1969 that I was asked by ITV to join their racing team as paddock commentator and interviewer, a wonderful opportunity but one which could involve the most hectic schedules if I happened to be riding at the meeting we were covering. Saturday afternoons became a whirl of rushing from jockeys' changing room to commentary position to paddock and unsaddling enclosure – and at the end of the day's racing I still had to knock out copy for the *Telegraph*. But ITV viewers seemed to like the idea of having someone on the commentary team who was actually taking part in the afternoon's action.

For me this was a mixed blessing. On one occasion at Market Rasen I managed to win a steeplechase on an admirable chaser of Jakie Astor's called Harper's Ferry, despite making what felt to me a catastrophic blunder at the second last fence. As was our rather vainglorious habit at that time, our fresh-faced and ever-youthful young interviewer Brough Scott debriefed me afterwards – and my description of the second last was, to say the least, dramatic.

'Let's have a look,' said Brough, turning to the monitor – and there followed a deeply embarrassing sequence. Because although we could see, all too clearly, the exaggerated 'recovery' which so nearly caused me to fall off, Harper's Ferry himself had jumped the fence perfectly without touching the proverbial twig – and could certainly have sued me for libel! (Sadly Harper's Ferry broke down in winning the race – but enjoyed a happy and active retirement carrying Dick Hern out hunting.)

On Saturday afternoons featuring the 'ITV Seven' – seven races from two meetings, with viewers encouraged to go for a seven-race accumulator – the commentary and presenting team had to be especially on the ball through a relentless two-hour programme showing a live race every fifteen minutes, but ITV were very good about allowing me to fulfil my riding commitments.

For me, the greatest difficulty when broadcasting was always managing to speak while a babble of other voices is coming through the headphones or, if you're on camera, the earpiece discreetly inserted before you go on air. There is a distinct knack to speaking in a measured and intelligent manner while somebody is talking in your ear.

The other lesson to be learned without undue delay is not to assume that your microphone is turned off when you think it should be – or at the very least to express yourself in language which takes into account the possibility that it just might be live.

Forgetting this can land you in hot water. In 1971, during a transmission from Warwick on London Weekend Television, I tipped a horse named Myritus to win the race, and after a photo finish was confident that he had just prevailed – only for the judge to declare that the winner was Hard Nut by a short head. '*BUGGER! ... DAMMIT!*' assaulted the sensitive ears of the nation, and the following morning some of the newspapers carried accounts of this scandalous episode under headlines such as 'HIS LORDSHIP TURNS THE AIR BLUE'. But there was only one soul so affronted by such blue language as to complain to LWT, whose spokesman put the affair in due perspective: 'Lord Oaksey obviously did not realise that his mike was up, but I do not think it was too extreme.'

In 1984 midweek coverage of racing moved from ITV to Channel Four (which had started transmitting in 1981), and in 1985 all racing on the independent network was transferred to Four – and so was born Channel Four Racing. The transition was seamlessly masterminded by the producer Andrew Franklin, and you couldn't want to work with a nicer or more able man. In all the years I worked with him I practically never saw him angry – and God knows he's had plenty to be angry about, with a team like the Channel Four Racing presenters!

Not that things have always gone smoothly of course – at least through the Oaksey microphone. One of my earliest gaffes came at York, where the racecourse was then under the stewardship of clerk of the course Major Leslie Petch. New steppings had recently been put around the paddock, and having described this feature I suggested to viewers: 'Let's go down to the parade ring now and see Major Petch's marvellous erection.' The cameraman started to fall about laughing, but for me it was too late to call those words back.

I seem to have been more accident-prone than some of my Channel Four Racing colleagues. John Francome, for example, hardly ever makes a gaffe – or, if he does, he turns it into a joke so instantly and so adroitly that no one is quite sure he did not intend it in the first place.

John – the second-best jump jockey I ever saw ride (no one will ever dislodge Fred Winter from the top of my list) – is the most natural broadcaster I've ever worked with, a man who seems to have been born to the role (a quality which he shares, incidentally with Clare Balding on the BBC). He's a natural at telling a tale and deploying the one-liner – for years he's been telling me that I've reached the age where I cannot take 'yes' for an answer! (Francome's ability to excel at anything he turns his hand to is a source of admiration and envy not just with me. A few years ago I was phoned by a highly excited Brough Scott. 'Great news!' Brough exclaimed. 'He can't play golf!' Typically, within a few months Francome had rectified that situation, and is now a familiar – and highly competent – player at charity golf tournaments.)

But the question I'm most often asked about my Channel Four Racing colleagues is the predictable one: 'What is John McCririck really like?' I wish I could give a confident answer, but to tell the truth I simply don't know. As far as I've ever seen, off screen he can be exactly as he is on screen. What cannot be disputed is that he's immensely hard-working, puts a huge amount of preparation into each programme (notably on 'the stats') and is not shy of voicing his opinions – however ill-thought-through they might be. Sometimes he says things that make the bile rise in your throat, but he always has the good of racing at heart, and is immensely well informed and knowledgeable about the sport.

Which is not to say that he cannot be irksome. The first time he referred to me on air as 'My Noble Lord' many years ago I swore to Brough he'd never do that again – but had I backed this opinion with a spread bet, I'd have been proved the biggest loser of all time!

Robustly held opinions, of course, are not confined to broadcasting pundits, and it is an occupational hazard of appearing on television – even in the comparatively low-profile role of paddock commentator for Channel Four Racing – that you end up on the receiving end of some briskly expressed views. I once received a note which read:

Dear Bastard
I am writing to tell you that you could not tip more rubbish if Channel Four bought you a forklift truck.

And what makes it worse is that your awful toffee-nosed voice makes it sound as if all the losers went to Eton.

I would have written back to thank the correspondent for these kind observations, but the letter was not signed.

Derek Thompson gets his fair share of abusive mail, but it's all water off a duck's back to him, and as a broadcaster he's the answer to every producer's dream. If you ever want a presenter to intercept the Queen at a race meeting and ask what colour knickers she's wearing, Tommo's your man. If you want a presenter to speak for eleven seconds to fill a gap, Tommo will talk for eleven seconds – not ten or twelve, but exactly eleven.

Nobody in sports broadcasting is more professional than Derek – which may explain his role in one of the oddest episodes of my time at Channel Four Racing.

The abduction of the Aga Khan's stallion Shergar – a wonderful racehorse who had won the 1981 Derby by ten lengths – from the Ballymany Stud in County Kildare in February 1983 stunned the racing world and reverberated well beyond. Three nights after it happened, I was having dinner in London at Boodles (one of those 'gentlemen's clubs' which we have in England and which the rest of the world probably regards with a mixture of amazement, disbelief and sometimes even contempt). Almost all of the dozen people present were either professionally or personally interested in racing, and the conversation inevitably turned to Shergar. No one had any worthwhile up-to-the-minute news, except that the late and much lamented Charles Benson, a long-time friend of the Aga Khan, was able to provide a more or less first-hand account of the actual abduction.

Charles also told us that should a ransom be demanded the Aga was in the highest degree unlikely to cooperate. In his opinion, to pay anything would be to open the floodgates to racehorse kidnappers of every kind – and poor Shergar had, in any case, been syndicated for breeding purposes among upwards of thirty shareholders.

As we were discussing what might be done to recover the horse, or at the very least to discover his fate, a waiter came in with an urgent message for me from the Press Association.

The message purported to come from the kidnappers themselves, and it was simple. If Derek Thompson (then my colleague on ITV), Paul Campling (a veteran football correspondent on the *Sun*) and I would go to the Europa Hotel in Belfast, we might hear news of interest about Shergar.

Neither Derek nor Paul was at the Boodles dinner, but with the help of the Press Association it did not take long to locate them – nor, after only a brief discussion, to book all three of us on the next morning's Belfast plane. We all realised that a wild goose chase was an odds-on favourite, but beggars cannot be choosers, and with not a smidgen of news on Shergar since he disappeared, faced with a message claiming to have come from his abductors we had to go and see what happened. More important, our various employers declared themselves ready to stump up the fares.

The general air of mystery which surrounded this venture can be detected if we pick up the story – such as it was – from the report I phoned through to the *Daily Telegraph* for the morning edition of Friday 11 February:

The last thing we heard on Thursday night from a mystery voice which may or may not represent the kidnappers was a statement that no further instructions would be given until the whole syndicate had agreed to a £40,000 'reward'.

But there is still no proof that the voice (codenamed Arkle) is not a hoax. Danger was very much in my mind yesterday morning [Thursday] when the news first broke that a telephone call to the *Belfast Newsletter* and BBC had asked for negotiations to be started through Derek Thompson of ITV, Peter Campling of the *Sun* or myself.

We were invited to be in the Europa-Forum Hotel by yesterday evening. Since this seemed to be something of a no-stone-unturned situation, all three of us caught the 12.30 shuttle, complete with toothbrushes, pencils and misgivings.

There followed a series of those hectic and ridiculous airport scenes with convoys of cameramen trying to break the Olympic record for walkbacks while you take pictures.

To Miss Sophia Loren it would no doubt have been old hat, just another day – but to Messrs Thompson, Campling and Oaksey it was something entirely new.

Before we boarded the almost virginal Boeing 757 one significant piece of news had fallen into my lap. Mrs Judy Maxwell, whose husband Jeremy trains near Downpatrick racecourse south of Belfast, called to say that a man using the codename Arkle had rung her at 1 a.m.

His message – the first of several – was the same as that received by the *Newsletter* and BBC. But by 9 a.m. the Arkle voice (Irish according to Mrs Maxwell, but neither deep south nor far north) had become a great deal angrier, infuriated by the publicity given to his original request.

By 2 p.m., when Arkle made his third call to Mrs Maxwell, our ill-assorted three-man embassy had run two more media gauntlets at Belfast airport and in the lobby of the Europa-Forum.

Here, with recording machines and cameras snapping like piranhas, Derek Thompson himself took a call from Arkle. 'Ring the Maxwells', the voice said, and rang off.

But when we obeyed a brand-new voice replied – that of an RUC Detective Inspector. Mrs Maxwell had told them of her early calls and now, following Arkle's instructions, had gone with her husband to a nearby hotel.

The telephone was ringing as they arrived – Arkle again – but before they could get to it there 'the voice' had rung off.

Back in Belfast, our problem was to leave the Europa-Forum without a trail of media bloodhounds. With kindly guidance from the management we crept out James Bond-like through the back door.

We finally arrived at the Maxwells thirty frightening miles later (driven by a freelance cameraman with a Fangio fixation) with two press cars still on our tail.

Out in the chilly Northern Irish countryside the presence of several large policemen was frankly reassuring. But patiently though we waited by the telephone, Arkle made only one more call – the somewhat optimistic hope that we three would in ten minutes or so contact the 34 syndicate members.

As I write, therefore, the £40,000 is the voice's last demand and there is still no news of where the £10 million worth of Shergar is concealed.

So as we swigged Irish whiskey and waited hopefully for the telephone to ring, it seemed about time to spare a thought for the handsome and courageous horse all the fuss is about.

In his all-too-short career Shergar never did the human race anything but good. He made money for some, gave pleasure to many and only ever disappointed once.

The only truly important thing about this whole extraordinary story is that he should be restored to his home and owners healthy and in one piece.

We now know, of course, that that last hope proved tragically ill-founded. Although there has never been a definitive account of what really did happen to Shergar, the accepted view is that the great horse was killed by his abductors a few days after his kidnap.

Our own 'trail', such as it was, had gone rapidly cold. We had a call from a man purporting to be the Aga Khan, but the game was given away somewhat by his Irish inflexion becoming more difficult to suppress as the conversation went on, to such an extent that one listener-in claimed that 'He sounds more like Aga O'Khan to me!'

Nothing else happened. Our whole journey was probably all just a hoax – though we'll never know for sure – and the three of us flew disconsolately back to England, all thoughts of 'How We Rescued Shergar' stories left in the dustbin along with the whiskey bottles.

14

'One more bang on the head won't make much difference'

Do you play Trivial Pursuit? If so, I can give you the answer to one question which you may be faced with if you're playing an edition produced in the late 1980s: 'Which racing Lord galloped off with his neighbour's wife?' Answer: 'John Oaksey'.

My first wife, Tory Dennistoun, was an enthusiastic and highly capable rider – I have written elsewhere in these pages about her prowess team-chasing with The Tory Party – but by 1987 she had given up riding completely owing to injuries to her back. A very fine painter, she decided to concentrate her attention on that side of life, which led her to spend more and more time away from home, in London.

Our marriage had not been going too well, and since we were in effect leading separate lives we both decided that it would be better to divorce. I hated the thought of this because of what my mother and father, married for fifty years, would have felt. But they were no longer alive (my father had died in 1971 and my mother in 1984), and in the end divorce did seem the right course to take. My three sisters supported me all the way.

The 'neighbour's wife' in that Trivial Pursuit question was Rachel Crocker – known as 'Chicky' – who with her husband Frank had moved to the cottage at the end of the Hill Farm drive, Frank having recently retired from farming. I had known Chicky long before they moved to live so close, and over the years we seemed to do more and more together. Perhaps it was inevitable that, as we eventually realised, we were falling in love – at which point, of course, her situation became impossible.

Needless to say the press soon got in on the act. No doubt it was a mistake to break the news in August, the so-called 'Silly Season'. To be fair to my fellow journalists, I have to admit that there were some fairly humorous headlines along the lines of 'LUSTY LORD RUNS OFF WITH FARMER'S WIFE'. Chicky and I did our best to keep out of sight of the paparazzi and more or less succeeded, though at one stage we were reduced to hiding under the dining-room table at Sara and Mark's to shield ourselves from the prying lenses. Meanwhile other members of the press were camped outside Hill Farm, and in the village pub free drinks were available for anyone who wanted to talk. No one chose to – with the regrettable exception of the then vicar of Oaksey, Canon Brian Phillips. With true Christian charity the canon pronounced, 'I will not marry them in the church.' He had not been asked to do so, never has been and never will be.

Two people in particular resisted all pressure to spill any available beans. Marjorie Boulton has been with us for well over twenty years, finding everything I lose and doing her best to tidy in my disorderly wake. Although she has passed the time when she qualified for her OAP's bus pass, neither Chicky nor I could do without her: she is truly part of the family So is Geoff Boulton, a relation of Marjorie's by marriage and maddeningly referred to on television by John McCririck as 'Boulton the Butler'. Geoff has just retired after more than fifty years at the Hill Farm. When he first came my mother was told that he was 'uneducatable'. Nothing could be further from the truth: you should see him searching the lists of runners each morning in the *Racing Post*. His memory of horses we have had here at the farm is comprehensive.

Chicky and I were married in March 1988 at Chippenham Register Office. She is adamant that on the morning of the wedding she asked whether I had the ring, and received the reply. 'What do I want a ring for?' I suggested we leave for Chippenham half an hour early and drop in at Ratner's! The wedding, she says, was nearly called off there and then. Luckily Chicky knew me well enough: she had her grandmother's wedding ring handy.

Over the years since that wobbly start to our married life, Chicky has become not only the *châtelaine* of Hill Farm, but also a true linchpin of the Injured Jockeys' Fund. As chief almoner, she coordinates the pastoral and practical contact with our beneficiaries and, as the weather gets ever colder from October to December, is a familiar sight on racecourses, selling the IJF Christmas cards and exhorting customers to double, if not treble, the quantity they first thought of. The IJF would simply not be the same without her, and if I ever manage to finish this book I am looking forward to joining her on the road.

Of course, the IJF is not the only charity for which racing people dig deep into their pockets, and in 1989 the programme for the annual charity day on the Friday of the Ascot September meeting included the Shadwell Estates Private Stakes, generously sponsored by Sheikh Hamdan al Maktoum (who also supplied all the horses) and pitching the BBC racing team – Jimmy Lindley, Richard Pitman and Bill Smith – against Channel Four Racing: Brough Scott,

John Francome and myself. Admittedly I was the oldest member of our team, but providing a wheelchair to transport me from the weighing room to the parade ring seemed to me to be labouring the point! Jimmy Lindley on Wabil won the race by a short head from Bill Smith on Polemos, with myself and Hateel a somewhat remote third, ten lengths behind the runner-up. At least I beat my two Channel Four colleagues, and I must have made some contribution to Hateel's racing education, as the following year he won three races, including the Old Newton Cup at Haydock Park and the Bessborough Handicap at Royal Ascot. On the other hand, if Hateel was that good, surely I should have won the Ascot race...

Hateel was trained by Peter Walwyn (whose first ever winner, Don Verde, I had ridden some twenty-nine years earlier), and Peter supplied my ride for the same race the following year in the shape of Gharah (who finished fifth). In 1991 I came last on Mutarjjam, but finished close enough to witness high jinks at the front of the field. That good commentator Robin Gray riding Magic Secret, was doing his best Lester Piggott impression when leading inside the last furlong – at which point John Francome cruised up from behind on Shaleel and, as he passed, reached over towards the elegant Gray posterior and 'goosed' his rival.

'Irresponsible riding' surely if ever there was a clear-cut case. To their eternal credit, the Ascot stewards saw the joke.

In the 1992 Ascot charity race I came fourth on Kabayil (another P.T. Walwyn charge), with Brough – who admittedly could ride a bit on his day – beating Joe Mercer, the most stylish, graceful and effective Flat race jockey I have ever seen, to win on Kitaab. The video of the finish was not, for some unknown reason, available afterwards. I have no proof, but I strongly suspect that Brough pinched it to play to himself in private: it *was* his first winner for twenty-one years!

The 1992 Shadwell Estates race has another claim to a minor footnote in racing history. Kabayil was shoulder-charged by Robin Gray on Rajai on coming out of the stalls, and after that we were always struggling. By the final turn I was pushing along like mad, head down, and as we straightened for home I looked up: the winning post seemed to be about four miles away. There and then I decided that at the age of sixty-three the time had come to hang up my geriatric race-riding boots. It was a decision that I have never (much) regretted.

I always hankered after being 'a Lord on the Board' and for a while enjoyed such a role, in an extremely non-executive mode, for

Harlech Television (HTV). But that fizzled out, and in 1992 I was offered an even more interesting position as President of the Elite Racing Club.

Elite was the brainchild of Tony Hill, an extraordinary businessman who, luckily for racing, was small in stature and therefore often asked, 'Are you a jockey?' He very much wanted to be one but was turned down by various trainers and never managed to reach even the first rung on that precarious ladder. Then he spotted and acquired the car registration number-plate HTV 1, and wrote off to Harlech Television asking if they would like to buy it. Rather surprisingly they refused (I was not yet on the board), but that gave Tony an idea, and when he advertised the number in the press it turned out to be amazingly popular.

From that start Tony built up a hugely profitable business which he called Elite Registration Numbers. As each set of new numbers came out he bought (and sold) those which seemed to him the most attractive ones. He had always been keen on racing, and with the profits from Elite Registration Numbers he set up Elite Racing – arguably (though I appreciate that I am biased) the most successful of all current racing clubs.

Elite Racing sets out to bring ownership of racehorses within the reach of the so-called ‘ordinary’ man or woman, and the club has grown amazingly. At its start in 1992 it had fifty members. By 1994 there were five thousand, and by 1996 that number had doubled. In June 2003, helped by the wonderful success of our homebred filly Soviet Song (who won the Fillies’ Mile at Ascot as a two-year-old and at three finished fourth in the One Thousand Guineas and runner-up in the Coronation Stakes; as I write, there is surely more to come!), membership has risen to sixteen thousand. Soviet Song’s record is no mean achievement, particularly for Maurice Camacho, who runs the Elite breeding enterprise and was responsible for sending Soviet Song’s dam Kalinka to her sire Marju.

Our best jumping horse was Mysilv, purchased from another racing club – the Million In Mind Partnership (in which I had a share) after she had won the 1994 Triumph Hurdle at Cheltenham. A wonderfully tough and determined mare, Mysilv brought Elite members a massive amount of enjoyment, winning many hurdle races and going down only narrowly to Cyborgo in the 1996 Stayers’ Hurdle at Cheltenham. She finished second in the Grande Course de Haies at Auteuil the same year, but cruelly was unable to provide any more magic moments for Elite members, as she fractured her pelvis on the gallops in January 1997 and had to be put down – a terrible loss not only to Elite but to racing in general.

Membership in Elite currently costs only £169 a year, which buys you an interest in the twenty horses Elite has in training: not every one is a Mysilv or a Soviet Song, but having that number of horses in training means a regular stream of Elite runners. There is a weekly newsletter, stable visits are arranged, and when we have a runner you can go and watch it – even going into the paddock if you have been successful when applying for one of the limited number of tickets. In many other ways Elite keeps its members informed and makes them feel as close as possible to being an actual paid-up racehorse owner.

For Chicky and me I can honestly say that Elite, which operates all the year round, jumping and Flat, is a constant and unfailing source of interest, and I know many people for whom it is, and has been, infinitely well worth the small amount of money it costs. Watch racing on television, and before long you will see the easily recognisable 'white, large black spots, black cap' which are our racing colours and our trademark.

Late in March 1993 I could be found suspended upside-down on an elastic band twenty lengths or so above Uttoxeter racecourse – where since Stan Clarke, Gordon Brown and David McAllister had taken over control at the track, entertainment had become the first priority – good going to attract competitive fields and plenty to look at or listen to between races. In search of a brand-new attraction for Midlands Grand National day they had engaged a bungee-jumping team, complete with 194-foot crane and a crew of muscular men, expert at persuading people to take leave of their senses.

It is not altogether clear who first suggested how nice it would be for one of the Channel Four Racing team to have a go – and even less clear why after some ill-informed discussion, the oldest member was elected. Comments like 'One more bang on the head won't make much difference' and 'What a splendid present for Chicky' did little for morale.

But my last attempt at a deterrent – 'Only if you find £1,000 for the Injured Jockeys' Fund' – was generously swept aside by Stan and Hilda Clarke and my son-in-law Mark Bradstock, who insisted on being the first to go, was so thrilled he wanted to go again. His boldness was rewarded when Montagnard, whom he trains, won the 4.40 race at 25–1!

'Just fall backwards when I blow the

whistle,' the captain said. 'Don't worry it's just like lying on cotton wool.' The amazing thing is, not counting half a second of pure terror, he was absolutely right – though my initial suggestion, that I would make the jump provided McCririck went down first, met with singularly short shrift from the bewhiskered betting expert!

A less hazardous broadcasting assignment at this time came with an invitation to appear on *Desert Island Discs*. For a start, I fell in love with the presenter Sue Lawley, who conducted the interview brilliantly: she had done a great deal of research into my past and present, and we got on well throughout.

In fact there were two interviews rather than the customary one, because we talked at some length about the Grand National, which was about to take place when we recorded the programme – and then, since this was 1993, we had to record a second interview taking account of the fiasco of the false starts and void race.

Before the second interview Chicky arranged lunch for the new date at my favourite London restaurant, L'Etoile – where, somewhat to my surprise, Sue Lawley advised that we should not have a drink with our meal: apparently you sound quite different with even the smallest drink inside you. You won't be surprised to hear that this good resolution lasted until the first course!

As for the programme itself, the most original of my discs was certainly 'The Borgia Orgy', a song which John Julius Norwich used to sing at Oxford. We could not find a recording, but the BBC very kindly entered into the spirit of the programme and invited John Julius to one of their studios, where my old friend was delighted to take up his guitar and give a spirited rendition:

The Borgias are giving an orgy,
There's a Borgia orgy tonight.
But isn't it sick'nin', we've run out of strychnine,
The gravy will have to have ground glass for thick'nin'.
The poisoned chianti is terribly scanty,
But everything else is all right.
I've hidden an asp in the iced cantaloupe,
There's arsenic mixed in the mock-turtle soup,
And straight benzedrine in the apricot coupe
At the Borgia orgy tonight.

I think it may well have been the only Desert Island Disc recorded for its own sake.

I was a bit worried about my other choices on account of being tone deaf and almost completely ignorant of classical music. But another old friend came to my rescue: Gay Kindersley with his great favourite from the

Irish Ballads, 'Slattery's Mounted Foot'. (In our younger days Gay used himself to deliver 'Slattery' so energetically that he almost always dislocated his shoulder. I remember driving him to London late one night and summoning Bill Tucker to 71 Park Street in order to put the shoulder back. The great surgeon appeared at eleven o'clock in his dinner jacket, and seemed not a jot put out by having his dinner disturbed.)

The piece of music I chose to take above all others went to a photo finish between 'These Foolish Things', sung by Bing Crosby and 'Jerusalem', with the latter getting the verdict because, I explained, it would make me feel 'sloppily patriotic' at low moments. My chosen book was an omnibus edition of P.G. Wodehouse's Mr Mulliner stories, and for the luxury Sue Lawley allowed me to cheat by pretending that a ship had been wrecked on my island with a cargo of champagne. Without a bottle a day I would certainly never have survived, let alone built myself any kind of shelter, since I am one of the least handy DIY workers there has ever been.

I mentioned earlier that when my father died in 1971 I succeeded to his titles Oaksey and Trevethin in the House of Lords – and was proud to do so. He had earned and richly deserved his own peerage by presiding over the Nuremberg trials. His other title, inherited from his father, was of course hereditary and I quite see that a Labour government would be bound by all its political traditions to oppose and abolish the hereditary principle. In fact Mr Blair and his merry men have made an extraordinary mess of reforming the House of Lords, and when in 2000 the 'cull' of hereditary peers was put into action I was not inclined to justify my existence in the House of Lords by writing the required seventy-five words stating my case. Accordingly I have not been entitled to enter the chamber ever since!

But before that half-hearted and bungled attempt at reform I did make the occasional appearance. Indeed, I actually voted in the Lords before I had been sworn in – a misdemeanour, as it turned out, very much frowned upon.

As I was wandering through the magnificent chambers of the House, Lord Margadale (whose son I had known at Eton, and who is sadly now dead) hailed me and said, 'Come and vote.' 'I can't vote,' I replied. 'I don't even know what they are voting about.' 'Good God!' said Margadale cheerfully, 'If you let that stop you, you'll never get far!' He was an enormous man, a former leader of the House of Commons and, I thought, one whose advice you could rely on.

So off I went through the complicated division routine, and duly registered my vote. Next day it came out that a new Lord had voted before being sworn in, and all hell broke loose: I was compelled to apologise in the chamber to the Lord Chancellor Lord Hailsham, who was in fact a relation by marriage of mine. 'You have got me into all sorts of trouble,' he said – but smiled as he said it. I went through the formalities of taking the oath there and then, in front of a mere handful of peers in the chamber.

Since then I have heard some wonderful speeches in the House of Lords, notably one by George Thomas, the former Speaker of the Commons, who then became Lord Tonypandy. I went into the House determined to vote against a measure (I can't now remember what it was), and ended up so convinced, or rather converted to his point of view so eloquently expressed, that I voted in favour of it.

I am therefore wholeheartedly against the Blair Government's makeshift 'reform' of the House of Lords. I understand their opposition to the hereditary principle, but believe that the House of Lords does have a valuable revisionary role, especially in times when one political party has a overwhelming majority in the House of Commons.

Personally I would not any longer want to be part of the new House of Lords in any case if, as seems likely, it is a more or less full-time job. At seventy-four I certainly wouldn't want to become a 'professional politician' – and if I want to get involved in racing politics I can always do so through the Jockey Club, of which I was proud to be elected an honorary member in 2002.

Mind you, I have seen one 'sharp end' of politics at first hand. Richard Needham, our local Conservative MP until his retirement from the House of Commons in 1997, worked for some years in Northern Ireland, becoming something of a legend for his outspokenness and skill in negotiation with Northern Irish businessmen on both sides of the communal divide.

As part of his work as Parliamentary Private Secretary to Jim Prior, Richard was allowed – indeed, encouraged – to take Members of Parliament on tours of Northern Ireland to make them familiar with its problems, and taking the view that my seat in the House of Lords made me a 'Member of Parliament', he was kind enough to invite me on one of these tours.

We flew over to Belfast and travelled on by road to Londonderry during which journey Richard – who is not only very bright but also both funny and indiscreet – kept up a flood of information and gossip about his political colleagues and adversaries.

Our first stop was Londonderry where the City Council's chief executive Colm Geary showed us over some splendid new civic buildings. He was particularly proud of an enormous gymnasium and swimming pool, and we were looking down from the first floor at a crowded pool in which a tall good-looking man with reddish hair was playing with three small children when our guide said, 'There's Martin McGuinness with his kids. I wonder what he'd think if he knew you were here.' Richard did not reply but we left the building without delay.

I was still appearing regularly on television at that time, and throughout our visit Northern Irish punters kept recognising and accosting me. One blind man even recognised my voice; no doubt from the 'toffee-nosed' accent. (Actually we had with us Nick Budgen MP, who had an even posher accent – but was clever enough to keep his mouth shut.)

Back in Belfast that evening, Richard and I were taken on patrol in an RUC Land Rover. The first thing we saw was a number of people gathered on the side of the road around a prostrate figure. Our driver, a female constable, pulled up and enquired what was happening. When told that someone had just shot himself, she got back into the Land Rover and advised us not to get out.

Next we arrived at what I now realise was the famous, or infamous, Divis flats. I shall never know what persuaded our driver to enter the courtyard, but she did – to find groups of people, including children, lighting bonfires around the perimeter. They were only small fires, but the scene was reminiscent of a painting of Hell by Hieronymus Bosch. As she started to drive out somebody shouted 'SLAM!', and a protective visor crashed down to cover our windscreen. It was followed immediately afterwards by an even louder bang as a heavy object landed on the now-armoured Venetian blind covering the windscreen. Our gallant chauffeuse drove on, and one of her uniformed colleagues said, 'Never mind – it was only a fridge. They must think we're collecting for a jumble sale.' They did not say what would have happened if the fridge had hit our unprotected windscreen and left us helpless.

After this eventful visit I thought the least I could do was invite Richard to help me open Oaksey's new golf course. I regret to say the opening ceremony was marred by an air shot and two four-letter words...

A great joy nowadays is the number of 'family' relations who are clustered in Oaksey village. Freddy Burnaby-Atkins (my brother-in-law, whom we last met confronting an armed German soldier beside a haystack) bought his house from me thirty years ago, and his daughter Charlotte with her husband Patrick and four children bought Oaksey House in 2001. Until Charlotte arrived in the village Chicky and I would entertain the whole family at Hill Farm on Christmas Day, but Charlotte now very kindly spreads the load. The gathering always includes my five grandchildren. Patrick and his wife Lucinda have three offspring: two daughters, Calypso and Cleo, and their son Oliver, who has just got into Eton, which means that his grandfather, 'that greatest of posts, Mr Lawrence', is looking forward to watching plenty of Wall Games. Sara and Mark have two: Alfie, who a few years ago rode his pony in the parade on an IJF day at Wincanton, accompanied by none other than Lester Piggott riding Desert Orchid, and Lily. Also at the farm every Christmas are Chicky's children Clare (whose husband Nigel, a fluent Russian speaker, is now in the British Embassy in Moscow) and Mark.

On Boxing Day we have a fine all-aged and both-sexes family football match: all the cousins come from far and wide, and in 2002 the number of players was over sixty with ages ranging from zero (though that infant did not have an influential role in the football match) to eighty-four. After the game we all sit down to a cottage-pie lunch in the village hall – with no pressure on parents to make their children behave, and a great deal of pressure on grown-ups not to sneak away and watch the King George VI Chase at Kempton Park.

Another great joy over the last few years has been a mare named Plaid Maid – 'Rosie' to her friends – who was trained by my son-in-law Mark Bradstock to win five races, including four steeplechases at Exeter, in the Oaksey colours (white, black diamond, red sleeves, red cap). Tony McCoy who won on her three times, paid her the ultimate compliment of saying that 'She tries as hard as I do.'

On her retirement from racing we pondered long and hard about which stallion she should visit – the aim, of course, being that she would produce a champion – and finally opted for Kayf Tara, a brilliant stayer on the Flat (dual winner of both the Ascot Gold Cup and the Irish St Leger) and a magnificent-looking racehorse.

Rosie was covered by Kayf Tara in 2002, and on 1 April 2003 gave birth to a fine bay colt foal, with a distinct 'C' marking on his forehead. This mark led us to think in terms of C-words when naming the colt, and eventually we registered him as Carruthers, in homage to one of my favourite (and briefer!) after-dinner stories. Two retired cavalry officers are reminiscing about former comrades-in-arms:

'Whatever became of old Carruthers?'
'Don't you know? He's out in Malaya, living with a chimpanzee.'
'What?! Not a *male* chimpanzee?'
'Oh Lord, no – there's nothing queer about Carruthers.'

My friend Sean Magee, who has written several books for Channel Four Racing and has assisted me with the research for this volume, has struck a bet of £10 at 1,000–1 (thanks to the good offices of William Hill's Graham Sharpe) that the equine Carruthers will during his lifetime win a Gold Cup – either the Ascot or the Cheltenham version – with proceeds going to the Injured Jockeys' Fund. The IJF may have to wait a few years, but the money is as good as in the bank.

Rosie and her son Carruthers, to say nothing of Dick Hern's former hunter Badger, who has been with us for many years, owe a huge debt to the tender loving care of Vicky, the girl who has expertly looked after them for the last three years.

As I write these words on a sunny June afternoon, Rosie, now in foal to Alflora, has sought the shade of a large chestnut tree in the very field I used to charge round on Mince Pie. Not far from her, Carruthers, three months old, is stretched out on the ground taking his afternoon nap – and dreaming, I trust, of glory to come at Ascot or Cheltenham, or both.

The publishers hope that this book has given you enjoyable reading. Large Print Books are especially designed to be as easy to see and hold as possible. If you wish a complete list of our books please ask at your local library or write directly to: